MANPOWER PROBLEMS
AND ECONOMIC DEVELOPMENT
IN NIGERIA

MANPOWER PROBLEMS AND ECONOMIC DEVELOPMENT IN NIGERIA

Report of the International Seminar on
'Manpower Problems in Economic Developme~~~~
held in Lagos, 2–11 March, 1964

Edited by

T. M. Yesufu, PH. D.(LONDON)

Professor of Applied Economics, University of Lagos

PUBLISHED FOR THE NIGERIAN INSTITUTE OF
SOCIAL AND ECONOMIC RESEARCH

IBADAN · OXFORD UNIVERSITY PRESS · 1969

Oxford University Press, Ely House, London W.1

GLASGOW NEW YORK TORONTO MELBOURNE WELLINGTON
CAPE TOWN SALISBURY IBADAN NAIROBI LUSAKA ADDIS ABABA
BOMBAY CALCUTTA MADRAS KARACHI LAHORE DACCA
KUALA LUMPUR SINGAPORE HONG KONG TOKYO

Oxford House, Iddo Gate PMB 5095, Ibadan, Nigeria

PRINTED AND BOUND IN ENGLAND BY
HAZELL WATSON AND VINEY LTD
AYLESBURY, BUCKS

Preface

This book is the outcome of the deliberations of an international seminar which met in Lagos in March 1964 to consider the nature of Nigeria's manpower problems with special reference to the needs of economic development. The general nature of these problems had been sensed for some time, as a result of which the Nigerian Government, in 1959, appointed the Ashby Commission to conduct an investigation into Nigeria's needs in the field of Post-School Certificate and Higher Education over the next twenty years. One of the major recommendations of the Commission, which was accepted by Government, was the necessity to establish an inter-regional manpower board which would concern itself continuously with manpower development and planning throughout the country.

At its first meeting in December 1962, however, the newly created National Manpower Board found itself faced with the difficulty of attempting to formulate effective manpower policies in the absence of reliable data. Accordingly, the Manpower Secretariat undertook as its first major task a survey to assess the current stock of, and future needs for, high-level manpower, both in private and public employment. The survey, which was carried out between April and August 1963, also made an assessment of the existing and projected out-turn of trainees for prospective high-level employments. It was decided that a report on the survey should be submitted to a seminar, with international participation, to examine and make recommendations on the main manpower problems indicated by the survey and on any other allied questions.

It is against this background that the Seminar was organized, and representatives attended from the following countries and organizations:

India	United Arab Republic
Kenya	United Kingdom
Liberia	United States of America
Nigeria	U.S.S.R.
Poland	The Economic Commission for Africa
Sierra Leone	The Ford Foundation of America
Tanzania	

v

The Seminar met from 2–11 March 1964, under the chairmanship of Chief S. O. Awokoya, the Federal Chief Adviser and Permanent Secretary, Federal Ministry of Education. A list of the other officers and participants is annexed. The work of the Seminar was carried out partly in plenary sessions and partly in specialist study groups.

In December 1964, the National Manpower Board received a report on the Seminar and a summary of its recommendations, and it was approved that the proceedings of the Seminar should be published. The following chapters are accordingly based on the working papers submitted by selected experts and the discussions and recommendations of the Seminar. The authors alone are responsible for the statements and opinions expressed in the papers bearing their name.

Special thanks are due to the Ford Foundation of America which rendered the generous financial assistance that made the convening of the Seminar possible. This book is also being published with financial assistance from the same source. The deepest appreciation goes to all those who participated at the Seminar for their valuable contributions.

The Board wishes also to express its gratitude to Professor T. M. Yesufu, Dean of the Faculty of Business & Social Studies of the University of Lagos, who, as Secretary to the National Manpower Board at the time of the Seminar, was largely responsible for organizing it and ensuring its smooth working as well as editing the papers included in this report.

Contents

vii

PART FOUR

The Unemployment Problem

PART FIVE

Productivity

Appendix

Foreword

This publication is the result of the most comprehensive study of Nigeria's manpower problems ever made by a group of international experts. The importance of manpower for economic development cannot be overemphasized. There was an early realization in Nigeria of the need for a rapid Nigerianization of the civil service and establishments in the public and private sectors. The great success achieved in this respect is a reflection of the high priority which the country has attached to educational development since 1952.

The pattern of educational development has, however, tended to create an imbalance in the supply of various categories of manpower. Thus, at a time when Nigeria is turning out between 300,000 to 400,000 persons per annum from all levels of education and training, the country still suffers from an acute shortage of the professional and skilled manpower which are vital to sustain a growing modern economy. Concurrently, the problems of unemployment and under-employment are increasing when the need is for total and effective mobilization of all the human and other resources of the nation. The imbalance in our human resources is not only vertical (in terms of desirable ratios of manpower categories) but horizontal, in terms of regional and geographical distribution of trained manpower. It is gratifying to see from the chapters that follow how these and other manpower problems have been seriously tackled by eminent experts from various parts of the world.

The synthesis of the Seminar's discussions and the relative ease with which it reached agreed conclusions and recommendations—as recorded at the end of each Part of the book—confirm that wisdom is not limited to any particular nation and that Nigeria, from the point of view of economic development at least, stands to benefit from the experience of other countries irrespective of their social or political systems.

The findings and conclusions of the Seminar as herein recorded serve also to confirm the wisdom of some of the steps which the authorities in Nigeria have taken in regard to some of our most pressing manpower problems. The greatest value of the Seminar, however, lies in pointing

out how much more needs to be done and how it should be done.
More particularly, it is worthy to note that the recommendations are
directed not only to the Governments, but also to private industry,
educational and training institutions, and workers. The richness and
variety of the learned papers and the breadth and depth of the discussions and recommendations are such that I have no hesitation in com-
mending this book to the attention of the general public and to the
academics and other experts who are interested in Nigeria's economic
future. Manpower remains one of Nigeria's greatest assets and public
policy must be directed to the maximum utilization of this often
untapped source of national economic development.

A. A. Ayida
Permanent Secretary, FEDERAL MINISTRY OF ECONOMIC DEVELOPMENT;
Chairman, NATIONAL MANPOWER BOARD.

11 April 1967.

Introduction
T. M. Yesufu

The critical appraisal and analysis of the manpower problem in developing countries remains the purview of a small but growing body of dedicated experts. Indeed, it appears that if there be still a 'mystery' in the all-comers game of economic development, it is that of the human factor. This is not due merely to what is often conveniently referred to as the peculiarity of human nature, which is suggestive of man's unpredictability. Economic analysts took care of that long ago in their presumption of the rationality of the consumer— and, one might add, of the entrepreneur also.

There is, of course, no mystery at all. The problem is that economists, in discussing economic progress or stagnation, have for too long been concerned almost exclusively with questions of the money market, capital goods, and natural (again material) resources. The human element, when it was considered, received recognition under the title of 'entrepreneurship', or 'labour' as a factor of production. In the latter case the analyst talked of units of labour just as he talked of units of capital—with the implication that one man was as good as, and therefore a perfect substitute for another. If in reality, as highly populated but underdeveloped countries soon found, labour was far from being homogeneous, the implications for the economist were too great. It was more convenient to side-track them.

The fact that in depression years mass unemployment was (and is still) generally regarded as merely a consequence of imperfections in the interplay of other economic variables, lent still further justification to the lower priority traditionally accorded to the manpower factor. Even when the Soviet Union, at the end of its first Plan had apparently wiped out unemployment, at the very time when other economic systems were being overwhelmed by the same problem, the methods used by that country were such as could only inspire condemnation, not emulation. Accordingly, what might have served as an economic lesson only resulted in a further confusion of ends and means. On the other hand, President Roosevelt's Civilian Conservation Corps, designed to achieve the same ends under a more liberal political and social system, apparently failed to yield the same spectacular results and so the outside world took but little notice.

It was, therefore, not until the Second World War and its aftermath that the prevailing conditions compelled the rethinking that led to the current awareness of the central importance of manpower not only in the economics of war, but of peace also. As the writer put it on another occasion, 'the experience of Germany and other countries and their phenomenal economic recovery after the devastations of much of their capital during the war, and also the amazing development of Israel which is not particularly well endowed with natural resources, had the salutary effect of drawing attention to the importance of brain power and manual skills in the processes of economic growth.'[1] The success of the Soviet Union in competition with the United States in the arms and space races, the continued shortage of scientists and engineers even in developed economies such as that of the United Kingdom, again serve to emphasize the point.

Perhaps as important, if not as spectacular, recent advances in micro-economic theory vis-à-vis developmental models seem to confirm beyond doubt that observable increases in production and economic growth cannot now be fully explained by the traditional analysis of the cooperating factors of production, per se. Nor equally is it adequate (as is sometimes attempted) to attribute such increases to 'technological change'. For this characteristically begs the question. Fundamentally, technological change presumes innovation, and innovation means the application of new knowledge to meet practical problems—both attributes of man. To say this is to repeat the obvious —but, if it does nothing else, it emphasizes once more the importance of the manpower factor in economic development.

Throughout the following chapters the theme recurs that man is the raison d'être as well as the means of economic development. The former is perhaps self-evident, but a constant reminder to this fundamental fact is important for two reasons. In the first place, economists have often tended to consider man in this respect only in terms of how much he consumes from the proceeds of economic activity and, con-

---

[1] T. M. Yesufu: *Development and Productive Utilization of Human Resources* (Paper delivered to the Conference on Management Development and Productivity, Enugu, 8 October 1964).

sequently, how much can be saved for further investment. Secondly, the politician, as frequently, seems to be lost in the admiration of the outward and superficial signs of development—what Galbraith refers to as 'symbolic modernization'[2]; for example, tall state buildings, an ultra-modern if economically wholly unjustified airport, etc. Both types of emphasis tend to minimize the welfare of the individual and to regard economic development as an end in itself.

On the other hand, the point of view of man as a means of production, involves both the questions of quantity (i.e. the relative as well as the absolute size of the employed labour force) and also its quality, in terms of skill, efficiency, brain power, experience, etc. These are some of the factors which underlie any consideration of the manpower problem in economic development.

The problem, therefore, is evidently multi-dimensional. So, within the time-limit of the week-long Seminar of which this book is a record, it is clear that only limited aspects of the problem could be adequately dealt with. As already indicated, the Seminar was called at the instance of the National Manpower Board, whose primary aim was to seek to benefit from the experiences of other countries in its task of formulating 'realistic policies to be adopted to meet our manpower problems'. Attention was accordingly limited to selected major problems as seen from the point of view of Nigeria. These problems were succinctly set out in a study circulated to the participants at the Seminar.[3] They were identified and discussed by the Seminar in plenary sessions and in special study groups under the following main headings:

> Economic Planning and Human Resources
> Machinery and Methodology of Manpower Planning
> Education and Training
> Unemployment and Under-employment
> Productivity

The Seminar's proceedings were facilitated by working papers submitted in advance by some of the participants and the chapters that follow are based upon those working papers[4] and the subsequent

[2] *John Kenneth Galbraith*: Economic Development (Harvard University Press, 1964), p. 4.
[3] *Manpower Situation in Nigeria* (National Manpower Board) Manpower Studies, No. 1, 1963. See also, T. M. Yesufu: 'Nigeria's Manpower Problems', in *Nigerian Journal of Economic and Social Studies*, November 1962.
[4] It is regretted that limitation of space does not permit the publication of all the papers submitted to the Seminar. But a full list is annexed at the end of the book.

discussions and conclusions. They are arranged in five Parts as indicated above. In Part One, a group of four contributors discuss the problems of manpower planning and policy within the context of overall economic development planning. Mr. Okuboyejo provides the setting and narrates the experience of Nigeria in the field of economic planning since 1945. The growing complexity of planning and the difficulty of achieving a rationally integrated economic policy are clearly revealed, and appear to stem predominantly from the transition which Nigeria has made from a unitary to a highly decentralized federal system of government.

Nevertheless the need for close co-operation between the Federal and Regional Governments is increasingly realized and resulted in the formulation of a national Six-Year Development Plan, 1962–8. It is this plan which sets the pace, as well as the limits, to all economic policy including manpower policy. As Ayo Ogunsheye points out, however, the Plan is significantly deficient in regard to manpower goals. The need to remedy this deficiency is clearly stressed. But as John Hilliard comments, there is an equal danger in equating manpower development too narrowly with the requirements for economic growth since there are 'several important aspects of national development (which) in no concrete way contribute to economic development: some actually make heavy claims upon the economy. Yet they require manpower and important human skills which must be taken into account by intelligent national manpower policy.' Among these are the manpower requirements for the development of political institutions, government administration, participation in international affairs, cultural affairs, etc.

Part Two deals with the machinery and methods of manpower planning within the context of economic development. While economic planning has become rather general since the Second World War, it was often considered that adequate employment opportunities, for example, would materialize as a by-product of development. And there was an apparent belief that since the more advanced nations had no special machinery for manpower planning in their early stages of growth, it followed that developing countries today could do without one. Not only is the argument falsely based, but the situation now is that machinery for manpower planning and development has been found to be a desideratum not only for the under-developed nations, but also for the most economically advanced countries such as the

U.S.A. and Great Britain. On these grounds, the soundness of establishing a National Manpower Board in Nigeria cannot but be appreciated, and Yesufu's account of the manpower planning machinery gives room for hope, but emphasizes the urgency of removing the bottle-necks which appear to make the machinery less effective than it should be. For as Harbison points out, the key to successful manpower plan-ning and development is the competence of the staff of the Manpower Secretariat, 'because deliberations of busy and powerful political leaders on human resource or general planning boards can only be as sophisticated as the quality of their secretarial services'.

The usual methods of manpower forecasting, projections, or target setting are also analyzed by Harbison and Yesufu. This aspect of man-power planning has received more than its fair share of criticism on the ground that the methods savour too much of crystal-gazing to warrant the acceptance of the results for rational planning. This attitude, how-ever, is only indicative of the general and obsessive fear of planners in developing countries to avoid the possibility of a mistake which is likely to generate criticism in the future. No progress, however, can be achieved without mistakes—indeed, in human affairs, the cost of avoiding mistakes is often stagnation, if not outright retrogression. In so far as manpower forecasting or target setting is concerned, no method is foolproof. What matters is to set goals, provided these are based on reasonable assumptions so as to indicate an approximately correct direction for action.

In Part Three the relationship between educational policy and economic development receives exhaustive treatment. No aspect of manpower or, indeed, of economic and social policy, is as topical today as that of education in developing countries. From the concept of education as a human right there has, as it were, suddenly dawned the realization that educational expenditure is as much an investment in economic progress as expenditure in material capital. This realization, however, has only exacerbated and, to a large extent, transformed the associated debate. Above all the problem remains of how to reconcile education for cultural and social development with education and training for economic growth. It is not a question of choice, for it cannot be too strongly emphasized that the choice is not the one or the other, but both. The mere fact that the Governments of Nigeria spend between 25 and 50 per cent of their annual revenues on education, is sufficient to demand the attention of economic planners and policy makers. For if, as is sometimes argued, education were purely consumptive, then such high public expenditure on it would clearly be untenable at the prevailing standards of living and available investment resources for economic development.

This fundamental cleavage of thought on the purpose and goals of education, and the various methods by which educational planning and administration can be most efficiently carried out, will for long remain a basis of controversy—the nature and magnitude of which are clearly demonstrated in the contributions of Awokoya, Fafunwa, Shaffer, and Dike. No *précis* can do justice to the dynamic views expressed by these authors. Throughout, the need to adapt inherited educational forms to local conditions is forcefully emphasized. In dealing with specific issues, however, many points are raised which have for long cried aloud to be said. In a number of cases the immediate effect would probably be to sharpen existing controversy. For example, Fafunwa's call to gear educational policy and curricula realistically to the needs and aspirations of the people, is sound commonsense. But it may raise the questions, who determines the need and how to rationalize the aspirations. Awokoya's prescription for a Defence Education Law will naturally raise many an eyebrow. But it indicates the urgency with which those directly concerned with the subject now view the challenge of education. Similarly, when Dike wades into the dispute between 'education for its own sake', and 'education for economic development'. He apparently takes no sides. But he feels that since economists and statisticians are likely to be wrong in 'forecasting' manpower requirements anyway, it is better in educational development to err on the side of producing a 'surplus' of high-level manpower. Once more this is a large issue demanding exhaustive discussion, involving as it does the associated problem of the possibility of generating what one might call 'high-level unemployment'.

The general question of unemployment and the traditional underemployment in developing economies are considered at length in Part Four. The causes of growing unemployment in Nigeria have become almost obvious and have been chronicled many times. The high rate of population growth, the general poverty which limits effective consumer demand, the consequent inadequacy also of investment savings and capital resources which are essential for generating employment opportunities, as well as the social attitudes often related to the educational process (attitudes which discount agricultural employment, for example)—these are some of the vital factors. Against this background the cumulative nature of the problem might seem inevitable and there is evidence that in some urban areas in Nigeria, unemployment has risen to as high as 15 per cent of the labour force.

If the magnitude of the problem is clear, however, there is far from being agreement on how to tackle it. Yet tackled it must be, and urgently. For in Nigeria, as in other developing African countries, mere economic growth, however rapid, as the consequence of development is no longer sufficient. More than any other criterion, economic plans in Nigeria will, for the foreseeable future be judged by the general public (for whom after all the economic bell tolls!), by the impact which such plans make upon the employment (or rather unemployment) situation.

The sharpness of the controversy of how to deal with the problem is illustrated from the remedies proposed by Sachs and Callaway. While the former suggests (on what might appear irrefutable arguments) that an initial solution be sought in traditional agricultural development, Callaway stresses the need for emphasis on small-scale industries, although he does not wholly discount the role of agriculture. The urgency of the problem, however, is such that this controversy is rapidly taking on the character of a luxury which can ill be afforded. What is required, is action—prompt action on all fronts. This is one field where there should be no dogma but that which works; and if theory conflicts with reasonably successful practical action then so much the worse for the theory.

Finally, the problem of efficient utilization of the employed labour force is discussed under the heading of Productivity in Part Five. S. K. Wolf examines the concept and the difficulties in measuring productivity. His treatment suggests that the subject is far from achieving finality and leaves much scope for further research. Patrick Chukwumah summarizes the results of the research which has been undertaken in this field in some African countries. This indicates clearly how unscientific but nevertheless tenaciously-held notions of the African's incapacity have been blasted by empirical research. Much, however, remains to be done. At a time when the gap in personal welfare is widening between the advanced countries on the one hand, and the developing countries on the other, the research findings, though important in restoring personal dignity to the African worker, have really not solved the fundamental problem. That problem which must be continuously emphasized at all levels is the need for the African to be more productivity-conscious than hitherto—conscious, indeed, that the worker in developing countries needs to be more productive and to work harder than his counterpart in the more advanced countries. These considerations and the conclusions of the Seminar indicate clearly that no developing country can afford to do without an effective productivity agency.

The contrast in background, research and experiences of the contributors to this book will be obvious to the reader. No attempt has been made by the editor to reconcile the expressed views, even where they have seemed to be diametrically opposed. The dynamism of the subject makes this inevitable and has, as such, immensely enriched the debate. The significant thing is that the Seminar, in spite of the various viewpoints of the participants, was able to come to broadly agreed conclusions as recorded at the end of each Part. While no one need agree with all of them (indeed, there is much for the dogmatic to quarrel about), the conclusions and recommendations provide a practical working guide to the National Manpower Board. And this, after all, was the Seminar's objective. Nevertheless, the theoretician and the student of economic development will find much that is useful if only in clarifying concepts and putting this vast and obviously complicated problem of manpower planning and development in a somewhat clearer perspective.

Part One

Economic Planning
and Human Resources

I

Economic Development and Planning in Nigeria 1945–1968

N. A. A. Okuboyejo

FEDERAL MINISTRY OF ECONOMIC DEVELOPMENT, LAGOS

Three periods of economic development planning in Nigeria can easily be identified: (i) 1945–55; (ii) 1955–62; (iii) 1962–8. This paper will give a factual account of Government planning efforts during these periods and will go on to examine the prospects of future development.

1945–1955

At the end of the Second World War, the United Kingdom Parliament authorized the appropriation of a sum of £200 million for the promotion of economic and social advancement of British colonies and other dependent territories. In order to determine how the amount was to be allocated and for what schemes, the United Kingdom Colonial Office instructed each Colonial Government to draw up a plan of development and welfare for its territory covering a period of ten years. In response to this call, the Nigerian Government prepared 'A Ten-Year Plan of Development and Welfare for Nigeria'.[1] This Plan made provision for the capital expenditure of a total of £55 million out of which the United Kingdom Government was to provide £23 million.

To be able to assess its worth as an 'Economic Plan', it is necessary to examine its mode of preparation. The Nigerian Government requested each Head of Department to submit proposals for the expansion of his departmental activities over the ten-year period, and these proposals were subsequently collated and embodied in the 'Plan'. The departmental schemes were not related to any national objectives of economic growth, nor was there any overall co-ordination of the projects in order to achieve consistency or coherence. The ends of

[1] Sessional Paper No. 24 of 1945.

3

the Plan were directed towards building up the social services because, according to the Plan, 'no properly balanced plan of development and welfare for a country in the present condition of Nigeria could possibly be successful until . . . plans had first been made to ensure that the people were, at least simultaneously, put in a position where they could participate and take full advantage of such activities'.[2] Emphasis was therefore placed on providing adequate and pure water supply and reducing the prevalence of endemic and epidemic diseases. In pursuit of this aim 25 per cent of the total resources for the implementation of the Plan was earmarked for the improvement of water supply and medical services. Only 6 per cent of the resources were provided for primary production (agriculture, veterinary, fisheries and forestry) and 0·4 per cent was earmarked for industrial development.

One may appreciate in retrospect that due to the highly undeveloped state of the economy, very little could have been done in the way of preparing a conventional economic Plan. There was as yet no Department of Statistics and accordingly no organized statistics of national accounts or other important data was available. The first comprehensive national population census was not organized until six years later in 1951. The inadequacies existing in this direction were recognized when provision for the establishment of a Department of Statistics was made in the Plan. Attention was also focused on the great role to be played by export produce in building the Nigerian economy when money was provided for the establishment of a Department of Commerce and Industries, for, inter alia, 'the development and improvement of marketing or products for export'.

Five years later, a Revised Plan[3] covering the period 1951–6 was issued. It suffered from the same weaknesses of preparation and lack of data as the original Plan and new and unrelated projects were substituted for earlier ones. This was justified on the ground of flexibility, but the result bore very little resemblance to the original Plan.

It is true to say, however, that the Ten-Year Plan together with its revised edition made possible the expansion of public health and education services and of such public facilities as roads, ports and water supplies. The private sector of the economy also participated in and benefited from the expansion, and the productive capacity of the economy rose to a higher level.

2 Ibid., p. 3.
3 Sessional Paper No. 6 of 1951.

1955–1962

In 1954, the Nigerian Government in association with the United Kingdom Government invited the International Bank for Reconstruction and Development to send a Mission to the country 'to assess the resources available for future development, to study the possibilities for development in the major sectors of the economy, and make recommendations for practical steps to be taken, including the timing and co-ordination of departmental activities'.[4] In its report,[5] the Mission recommended that much of the effort of the following five years must be directed towards strengthening Government services which would support an expansion in production. In agriculture, the Mission suggested that priority should be given to research, surveys, extension and demonstration. For industrial expansion it urged Government to give technical and management assistance to small business, provide credit facilities and offer more and better technical education. The publication of this report coincided with the constitutional and political changes which gave the Regions a large measure of autonomy and responsibility in economic matters. Consequent on the new status, five separate development programmes (including one for the Southern Cameroons which was then part of the Federation of Nigeria) were published in place of one national Plan.

In the Economic Programme[4] of the Federal Government which made provision for the capital expenditure of an amount of £91 million over the next five years, more systematic planning than hitherto was discernible. Emphasis was shifted from expansion of social services to gearing the economy towards modern industrialization. Priority was given to the building of the infrastructure, with communications getting the largest slice of 60·5 per cent of the total resources committed. The Federal Government justified such a large allocation by reference to the statement of Professor Arthur Lewis that: 'a cheap and extensive system of communications is the greatest blessing which any country can have from the economic point of view'.[6] The wisdom of such a generous provision is probably debatable in view of other equally pressing demands on scarce resources; but in addition to the possible economic advantages, the over-riding responsibility

[4] *The Economic Programme of the Government of the Federation of Nigeria 1955–60.* (Sessional Paper No. 2 of 1956.)
[5] The Economic Development of Nigeria, Lagos 1954.
[6] Arthur Lewis: *The Theory of Economic Growth.*

for providing communications services in a federal set-up presented the Federal Government with an opportunity to knit together the far-flung and invariably centrifugal units of the Federation, and it seized the chance according to its own light.

An appreciation of the need to build up the security services to meet the needs of a growing nation was shown by the allocation of 5 per cent of total commitments. Industrial expansion got more attention than in earlier plans accounting for 2 per cent of the cost of the Plan. An interesting departure from the old plans was the loan provision made for Government's statutory corporations to assist them in their own development programmes. Just under 30 per cent of the whole programme was committed for this purpose, and demonstrated the great importance which was attached to the role of the Corporations in economic development.

Although the programmes in the Plan showed a greater degree of integration than hitherto, and greater emphasis was now placed on economic considerations, they all fell short of the standards of true perspective planning. No conscious attempt appears to have been made to accelerate economic growth by laying down certain national goals and objectives, as the five governments of the Federation were virtually working in water-tight compartments. The lack of central direction thus inevitably resulted in duplication, competition and, possibly, waste. On occasion there were *ad hoc* consultations between Ministries of the various Governments dealing with similar subjects, but such consultations seem to have been rather ineffective in changing the views of the Governments. The National Economic Council[7] had its first meeting in October 1955, but, by then, the development programmes had either been prepared or were in the last phase of completion and the Council could then scarcely exert any influence on the development policies of the Governments.

1962–1968

The first serious attempt at comprehensive economic planning was initiated in 1959 when the National Economic Council decided that

[7] The National Economic Council was established in 1955 following a recommendation of the World Bank Mission to Nigeria. Membership consists of the Prime Minister who is the Chairman, the regional Premiers and four Ministers from each Government of the Federation. The Economic Adviser to the Federal Government is the only official member. The Council's main function is to coordinate the economic and development activities of the Governments.

a National Development Plan should be prepared. It enunciated a clear economic policy for the guidance of the planning committees of the Governments, and stated the fundamental objectives of the integrated Plan in the following terms:

'The achievement and maintenance of the highest possible rate of increase in the standard of living and the creation of the necessary condition to this end, including public support and awareness of both the potentialities that exist and the sacrifices that will be required.'[8]

This policy directive was further spelt out to include the attainment of a growth rate at least as high and preferably higher than that achieved in the previous decade. Since this was really the first national planning exercise undertaken in Nigeria, it would be as well to look a bit more closely at the processes adopted, and the assumptions upon which projections were based.

The first task to which attention was directed was a study of the aggregate economic structure and an analysis of existing and past trends and implications in order to find a basis for evaluating the estimates for the future. A set of national accounts[9] had then just been prepared by Dr. Okigbo in current and constant prices, covering the period 1950–7 and was brought up to date (1960) by the Federal Ministry of Economic Development. Other detailed studies were undertaken of foreign and domestic financing of the public and private sectors of the economy, including an analysis of foreign trade and payments. Four significant features of the economy over the previous ten years (1950–60) came to light. Firstly, the Gross Domestic Product (G.D.P.) rose at an average annual rate of 4 per cent. Secondly, Gross Fixed Investment (G.F.I.) rose from 7 per cent in 1950 to 15 per cent in 1960. This implied a trend of decreasing productivity in the pattern of Gross Fixed Investment. Thirdly, consumption was relatively constant at 90 per cent of G.D.P. but Government consumption increased from 3·4 per cent to 7·5 per cent whilst private consumption declined from 87 per cent to 85 per cent of Gross Domestic Product. Fourthly, Gross Domestic Saving was relatively constant at 10 per cent. This meant a net export surplus in the early years up to 1953 and an import surplus for the rest of the decade. In other words, in the later years, the

[8] National Development Plan, 1962–8, Chapter 6, p. 1.
[9] Pius Okigbo: *Nigerian National Accounts, 1950–57.*

increased Government consumption and increased Gross Fixed Investment were financed by drawing on past savings. The picture presented
by the studies is shown in Table 1.

In considering aggregate projections for the Plan period, 1962–8,
it was assumed that the 4 per cent annual average rate of growth of
Gross Domestic Product in the previous decade could be maintained if
Gross Fixed Investment was levelled up at 15 per cent of G.D.P. and
the composition of the G.F.I. was shifted sharply to highly growth-
inducing investment, such as industral and agricultural projects. This
assumption was necessary since there was no guarantee, in future, of
the favourable terms of trade that had prevailed in the past. Private
consumption was to be allowed to rise by 1 per cent as an incentive as
against an estimated population growth rate of between 2 and $2\frac{1}{2}$ per
cent per annum. One might in passing, point out that the 15 per cent
G.F.I. is to include both Government and private sector investments, and specific Government policies have been formulated
to stimulate the inflow of private foreign investment into the
country.

The programmes presented for consideration for inclusion in the
Government plans, were prepared by each Ministry and the Statutory
Corporation independently of the proposals and projects in the
programmes of other Ministries and Corporations. The programmes
were trimmed and co-ordinated by Ministries responsible for economic
planning in the light of the assumptions and the policies indicated
above. At every stage of the planning process, discussion and consultation about the procedure, assumptions, priorities and size of the programmes (Federal and Regional) went on in the Joint Planning Committee.[10]

To ensure that the total investment programme remained within the
limits of feasibility, an estimate of total recurrent expenditure over the
Plan period was calculated. This was important because at any given
moment, recurrent and capital expenditures, so far as funds were concerned, were competitive. For political reasons, the Governments had
decided that they should find enough resources to meet the full cost
of recurrent expenses from their own resources; but half of the cost
of the total capital programmes, should be met from foreign sources.

[10] The joint Planning Committee is a Committee of Officials and Planners of the
Governments of the Federation. It makes its recommendations to the National Economic Council.

TABLE 1   *Gross Domestic Product by Category of Expenditure at 1957 Prices**

	1950	1951	1952	1953	1954	1955	1956	1957	1958	1959	1960
Consumer's expenditure	609·4	650·2	695·9	717·3	774·6	805·5	798·9	815·5	830·0	830·0	870·0
Government expenditure on goods and services	24·0	26·8	33·5	29·9	31·2	45·5	43·8	47·6	56·7	70·7	77·0
Gross Fixed Investment in Nigeria	48·4	59·7	75·0	79·9	92·9	102·6	108·0	113·0	122·3	136·7	158·0
Increase in Marketing Boards stocks	−7·3	6·3	1·5	−0·1	−6·2	4·6	−4·8	9·1	−0·3	n.a.	n.a.
Plus Exports (f.o.b.)	99·9	93·6	111·7	114·8	131·9	126·9	138·5	129·1	144·0	163·0	171·0
Final Expenditure	774·4	836·6	917·6	941·8	1,024·4	1,085·1	1,084·4	1,114·3	1,163·2	1,208·2	1,276·0
Less Imports (c.i.f.)	75·1	82·6	108·3	114·1	131·6	163·3	180·9	175·6	182·0	212·0	253·0
Gross Domestic Product at market price	699·3	754·0	809·3	827·7	892·8	921·8	903·5	938·7	970·7	987·7	1,023·0
	%	%	%	%	%	%	%	%	%	%	%
Consumer's expenditure as percentage of G.D.P.	87·1	86·2	86·0	86·7	86·8	87·4	88·4	86·9	85·5	84·0	85·0
Government expenditure on goods and services as percentage of G.D.P.	3·4	3·6	4·1	3·6	3·5	4·9	4·8	5·1	5·8	7·1	7·7
Gross Fixed Investment in Nigeria	6·9	7·9	9·3	9·7	10·4	11·1	12·0	12·0	12·6	13·8	15·4

* National Development Plan, 1962–68, p. 13.

Thus a pound saved in recurrent cost would serve as a basis to generate two pounds for capital development expenditure. The exercise on recurrent costs would also affect Government's ability to execute the capital investment programme since it had been established that for every pound invested in economic, social and administrative sector projects generated respectively two, four and six shillings of recurrent expenditure annually. In other words, investment in the administrative sector, for example, was not only less directly productive in purely economic terms, but it tended to generate recurrent expenditure (and reduce budget surpluses which could be diverted towards development projects) by a factor of three compared to investment in projects in the economic sector. Other feasibility tests of the investment programme included calculations of prudent levels of foreign debt repayment. As already indicated, 50 per cent of the programme was intended to be financed from foreign sources and estimates of the share of loans and grants, the possible terms and build-up of the debt repayments were made. An important consistency and feasibility test involved the analysis of specific investment projects. High priority was attached to industry, primary production and technical education. If estimated rates of return in these projects easily equalled or exceeded 4 per cent per annum, on the average, and granting the predominant share of agriculture in G.D.P. and higher rates of growth in other sectors, then the pattern and size of G.F.I. would most probably result in the required increase in the G.D.P.

A point not yet discussed related to the degree of interrelationships and linkages in the Plan. The detailed foreign trade estimates were made consistent with aggregate economic projections and with the detailed calculations of projects in the agricultural and industrial sectors. Estimates of the traffic effect on the transport system were also linked with the rest, and any change in the above variable would accordingly require adjustment in all the others in order to ensure a consistent and feasible pattern.

What finally emerged as the National Development Plan (incorporating the three Regional and the Federal programmes) was adopted by the National Economic Council just before the March Session of Parliament in 1962. It made provision for the capital development expenditure of £676·8 million over the 6-year period (1962–8) with a sectoral breakdown as follows:

	Percentages
Development Sector	71·4
Social Sector	20·3
Administrative Sector	7·7
Financial obligations	0·6
	100·0

Development Sector projects include primary production, trade and industry, electricity, transport systems and communications.

The realizability of the estimates and projections indicated above depends on many factors, among which are the pursuit of a prudent financial policy (avoiding inflation and maintaining the international value of the Nigerian pound), the adequate inflow of external finance and the availability of skilled manpower. Apart from political considerations, the general scarcity and the high cost of recruiting highly skilled manpower from abroad makes it undesirable to rely on a regular supply of foreign manpower. The Governments of the Federation have accordingly accepted those aspects of the recommendations of the Ashby Commission [11] that would facilitate the supply of trained manpower, and the Plan provided for the appointment of a Manpower Board to deal with question of manpower training and generally to co-ordinate the education programmes in order to meet the needs of the rapidly developing economy.

The prospects and conditions for development

The National Development Plan is seen as the first in a series (some people suggest three) which will bring Nigeria to the 'take-off stage'; i.e. the stage where Nigeria will be able to generate enough income and savings to enable her, on her own, to finance a steady rate of economic growth without the need to depend on overseas sources for capital and technical skills. What prospect does the future hold for achieving this goal? Nigeria depends to a considerable extent for her future growth and development capital upon the resources which are generated from the sales of her agricultural produce. The peculiar feature of the Nigerian economy is that each Region depends on the building of its economy on one principal agricultural product, or at most two—thus the Western Region has cocoa, the Eastern Region, palm produce, and the Northern Region, cotton and groundnuts.

[11] *Investment in Education* (Federal Ministry of Information, Lagos), 1959.

Petroleum oil is a significant new discovery but it is not yet possible to assess its full impact on the economy. The disturbing aspect of this phenomenon is that prices of the primary produce are subject to wide fluctuations in the world market and weather vagaries, thus making planning for steady growth difficult. The planners made some estimates of the likely fall in world prices of these commodities. It is thus clear that if prices fall more rapidly than was estimated, it would result in a worsening of the terms of trade and possibly of the rate of growth.

With a view to reducing such heavy reliance on primary produce the Government have embarked on projects for greater diversification of the economy, and for a start, have made provision in the Plan for building a solid infrastructure to sustain a buoyant economic super-structure. Thus the £80 million Niger Dam at Kainji would, by 1968–9 be able to supply hydro-electricity to virtually the whole country through a network of transmission lines and possibly facilitate an all-the-year-round navigability of the River Niger. The Nigerian Ports Authority has planned for a £24 million expansion of port facilities. The Railways, the Ministries of Communications and of Works all have extensive proposals for improvement of their services. Apart from the attention given to the infrastructure, 13·4 per cent of total resources available for the implementation of the Plan has been earmarked for the development of the Trade and Industry Sector. Proposals are in hand to erect at least one £30 million iron and steel complex. The Nigerian Industrial Development Bank with a capital of £5 million has been set up to give medium-and long-term industrial loans on purely commercial considerations. Policies have also been evolved to stimulate the investment climate in the private sector.

These are all significant steps in the right direction. But economic development does not consist only of projects and budgets. It consists also of motivations of the population and the incentives to which they respond, all of which are conditioned by the social and economic environment. The people's attitudes to work, to accumulation of capital, and taking of risks in Nigeria (and this is common to the areas now known as developing countries) differ from those in the developed countries. The 'captains of industry' who promoted industrial develop-ment in Europe in the nineteenth century were not men whose motive in going into business was a desire to make a mere living but those who wanted to make a fortune. Their chief interest in life was in risk-taking and profit-making. There must be change in the attitudes and motivations of a large number of people in Nigeria, in order to bring about the emergence of an entrepreneurial class. Their present number is ridiculously low and it is politically undesirable and economically unwise to leave the field in the hands of foreigners. In this context the social environment is also very significant. The extended family system, for example, is not conducive to the development of saving habits. It is therefore important to note that the system may be dying down.

The development of an entrepreneurial class presupposes the existence of investment opportunities. With an internal market catering for a population of over 55 million, and the effort of the governments to promote import substitution by protective tariffs etc. in favour of local manufactures, investment opportunities present no serious problem. Our psychological attitudes do not relate to entrepreneurship alone. They pervade the entire gamut of our life. The average Nigerian's attitude to work may be summed up in the phrase 'a little bit of work and plenty of money'. Yet, without a sustained rise in productivity and the shedding of this relic of colonial mentality, economic growth will be slow.

An economic plan is only a statement of intentions. Its successful implementation requires a bold effort to stick to the priorities of the plan. If easy and prestige projects are first executed whilst projects with high pay-off calculations are relegated to the last years of the plan, enough resources will not be generated to implement the plan. If unrelated projects, howbeit with high political significance, are substituted for others in the name of flexibility, then the goals set will be hard to reach. Within the limits of available resources, this need to reconcile immediate political expediency with long-term economic objectives, presents one of the greatest problems confronting not only Nigeria, but virtually all developing countries.

2

Manpower Problems in the Context of Economic Planning

Ayo Ogunsheye

DIRECTOR, DEPARTMENT OF ADULT EDUCATION AND EXTRA
MURAL STUDIES, UNIVERSITY OF IBADAN

For the purpose of this paper, planning will be taken to mean a way of arriving at policy decisions designed to achieve desired objectives. In the context of economic development, it generally denotes a deliberate effort on the part of a government to accelerate the rate, and influence the shape, of economic growth. But it is not every action of a government that affects economic growth which qualifies as planning. For this reason, Hagen has listed the elements which make up development Planning.[1] In his view, planning involves the screening of individual proposals, ensuring that the facilities and services planned are complementary, evaluating the relative desirability of all components, proving measures to increase or reduce the prospective level of aggregate demand for goods and services if it promises to be too high, and determining the shares of the country's production to be devoted to investment and consumption. By spelling out the content of development planning in this way, Hagen has emphasized the point that planning is a method.

As the head of the three-man economic advisory team involved with preparing the National Development Plan, 1962–8, has testified,[2] 'in no country in the world is economic and social development free from some deliberate effort to speed up the process. Governments everywhere play a vigorous role in shaping the design of a nation's economic development. The basic objective of planning in Nigeria is not merely

[1] Hagen, Everette E. (Ed.): *Planning Economic Development* (Homewood, Illinois, 1963), pp. 11–16.
[2] Stolper, W. F. 'The Main Features of the 1962–68 National Plan', in *The Nigerian Journal of Economic and Social Studies*, Vol. 4, No. 2, July 1962.

to accelerate the rate of economic growth and the rate at which the level of living of the population can be raised; it is also to give her an increasing control over her own destiny. The Plan envisages the harnessing of all resources for economic growth.'[3]

Among the resources which the governments of the Federation have decided to harness are manpower resources. It was partly out of recognition of the need to develop high-level manpower that the Ashby Commission was set up and a leading authority, Professor Fredrick H. Harbison, invited to prepare for the Commission, a special report on 'High-Level Manpower for Nigeria's Future'. Harbison's main recommendation, that an inter-regional Manpower Board should be set up for the purpose of forecasting the manpower needs of the country and advising Governments on how these needs can be met, has been implemented. So has the recommendation of the Commission on the establishment of new universities. Mention should also be made of other recent investigations into school systems and problems of staffing in the civil services conducted at the request of the Regional Governments. Among them are the Dike Committee on Education in Eastern Nigeria, the Banjo Committee appointed to review the education system of Western Nigeria, and special reports on matters connected with the civil service prepared by Dr. D. Kingsley for some of the Regional Governments. It is clear, therefore, that manpower planning is one of the features of Nigeria's drive towards more rapid development.

Planning as a subject has its theories as well as prescriptions on how the theories should be applied, and case studies of planning in practice are growing day by day. Viewed in this light, planning can usefully be regarded as part of that science, based on technology and invention, which Kuznets considers to be the necessary condition of modern economic growth. In his words, 'science is the base of modern technology, and . . . modern technology is in turn the base of modern economic growth.'[4] In discussing the relationship of science to economic growth, Kuznets distinguishes three important stages, namely,

(a) a scientific discovery—an addition to knowledge;
(b) an invention—a tested combination of already existing knowledge to a useful end; and,

[3] *National Development Plan*, 1962–8, (Lagos, 1962), pp. 2–3.
[4] Kusznets, Simon: *Six Lectures on Economic Growth* (London, 1959), pp. 29–41.

(c) an innovation—an initial and significant application of an invention, whether technological or social, to economic production.

I suggest that planning as a body of knowledge can be conceived as
consisting of theories (based on the findings of economics, social
psychology, mathematics, statistics, engineering, etc.), planning
techniques, and the application of the techniques to economic programming and other types of planning. In considering the problem of
integrating manpower planning with general planning in Nigeria,
these three aspects should be borne in mind.

Analytically, one should distinguish between the demand for
manpower from the supply of manpower. Not only are they not
necessarily governed by the same factors but it will also be found on
examination that the definition of manpower usually employed in
discussing the demand for manpower in Nigeria is not always the
definition used in relation to supply. For example, while Harbison
dealt with 'high-level manpower'[5] and the National Manpower Board
with 'high-level and skilled manpower'[6] (both from the point of view
of demand needs and supply), the National Development Plan specifies
as one of its targets increasing employment opportunities for all
citizens.[7] The Plan appears to have been based on a Domar-type model
in which a minimum rate of growth of 4 per cent per annum is postulated on a minimum investment rate of 15 per cent of the Gross
Domestic Product and which is buttressed with a number of tests for
technical consistency, administrative feasibility and financial realism
in relation to projects contained in the Plan. Although we are assured
that employment requirements were taken into account in evaluating
individual projects,[8] no employment targets have been built into the
model. The assumption seems to be that more jobs would come as a
by-product of the increase in G.N.P. Only one regional plan, that of
Western Nigeria, went further to set a target for the amount of new
employment which was likely to be created between 1962 and 1968;
however, the target was limited to the public sector.

[5] Harbison, Frederick H.: 'High-Level Manpower for Nigeria's Future' in, *Investment in Education* (Lagos, 1960), pp. 50–72.
[6] National Manpower Board: *Nigeria's High-Level and Skilled Manpower 1963–8*.
Report submitted to the Seminar. (This report has since been revised and published
as 'Nigeria's High-Level Manpower, 1963–70'.)
[7] *National Development Plan*, 1962–8, p. 23.
[8] Peter Clark: 'Economic Planning for a Country in Transition: 'Nigeria', in
Planning Economic Development, op. cit., pp. 277–8.

In fairness to the authors of the Plan, it should be granted that in the time at their disposal, and considering the paucity of reliable data they could not be expected to operate with anything more than a crude model. All the same, a model can only be judged by its results. The fact remains that the National Development Plan, 1962–8, has little to say on the problem of employment, which is one of the thorniest the Nigerian economy has to face at this time. As Komiya observed in his critique of the model underlying the Indian Second Five-Year Plan, 'any model which pays no explicit attention to the major objectives which have to be achieved by the plan cannot form a working theoretical basis for economic Planning.'[9] The question arises of what should be done in the circumstances.

One possible answer might be to put a premium in the Plan on agricultural schemes, new manufacturing industry and investment projects using labour-intensive methods. As far as agriculture is concerned, there is little cause for concern because we know that it is possible to achieve remarkable increases in yield by using better seeds and fertilizer. Japanese agriculture did wonders with such simple methods between 1885 and 1910. In Nigeria also, striking gains in output have resulted from using better strains of seeds and insecticides in cocoa, cotton and groundnut production. But the imbalance in the allocation of resources of research and extension as between staple food production and agricultural products for export needs to be corrected. Greater resources will have to be diverted to the former. It is the largest single sector of our economy and yet it is the one with the slowest rate of growth. In short, provided the farmer can be shown new agricultural techniques which promise good returns, there is scope for labour-intensive methods especially in food production.

With regard to labour-intensive manufacturing industry, matters are not so simple, for two reasons. In the first place, there may be conflict between employment on the one hand and output and growth on the other. Labour-intensive industry provides more employment but it may do so at the expense of output and the rate of growth. Nigeria which has witnessed a slackening in the rate of growth of the economy since 1955 should thus be cautious in accepting the suggestion to put a premium on labour intensive manufacturing industry.

In this connection, the experience of India is illuminating. In her

[9] Komiya, Rynt: 'A note on Professor Mahalanobis' Model of Indian Economic Planning', in, *The Review of Economics and Statistics*, Vol. XLI, No. 1, February 1959.

Second Five-Year Plan she had two objectives. In order of importance they were, first, to maximize the growth in real income and, secondly, to create enough jobs to match the increase in the labour force so that the numbers unemployed, while not curtailed, would not be allowed to rise. This modest objective was not achieved. In a recent study, John P. Lewis has explained why. 'The principle means that the second plan chosen for implementing the employment objective was the promotion of cottage industries. This was an unpromising choice. For the most part, the traditional handicrafts could be promoted only at the expense of more efficient factory production. As it turned out, they did not expand rapidly enough—despite elaborate promotional schemes—to keep the residual unemployment problem from growing during the second plan years.'[10]

This leads to the second complication. A policy of using labour-intensive methods in manufacturing may defeat its own purpose with regard to increased employment because it may slow down the rate of output. In a recent study of economic development and employment in a number of countries including Nigeria, Galenson[11] points out that it is not in the manufacturing sector of newly developing countries, but in the tertiary sector that the bulk of the new employment is to be located. His most important finding, however, is that, in most developing economies, it is the growth of the manufacturing sector which is apt to be the dynamic force in generating new employment. The more rapid the rise of manufacturing output, the more employment can be afforded by the tertiary sectors.

As Harbison had emphasized, the objective of a manpower or human resource development strategy is to arrive at an effective balance in choices of policy objectives.[12] A strategy for achieving maximum increase in employment must strike a balance between the rival claims of output and employment, between capital-intensive and labour-intensive techniques of production and between the rival claims of different sectors of the economy for new investment. All this has to be worked out within certain limitations such as total investment during the plan period and the target volume of employment. Properly formulated, this is a linear programming problem in which a given objective has to be attained subject to certain constraints. Komiya has

[10] Lewis, John P.: 'India', in *Planning Development*, pp. 86–90.
[11] Galenson, Walter: 'Economic Development and the Sectional Expansion of Employment', in *International Labour Review*, Vol. LXXXVII, No. 6, June 1963.
[12] cf. Chapter 6 herein.

shown in the study cited above that, if the author of the model underlying the Indian Second Five-Year Plan had used simple linear programming, the allocation of resources would have been more efficient. But
it could also be argued that the National Development Plan, 1962–8,
as it stands, was not fundamentally deficient because, in the long run,
there is no conflict between the goals of maximum growth in output
and employment. Since, however, it is not specified how long the long
run is, the employment situation in the short run may deteriorate in a
way as to make the long run solution more difficult. Moreover, the
preliminary report on the Census of 1963, if correct, throws serious
doubt on the adequacy of the Plan. An apparent population growth
rate of about 5 or 6 per cent per annum makes nonsense of a Plan which
is geared to a growth rate of 4 per cent.

By taking account explicitly only of the income-generating effect of
new investment, the authors of the National Development Plan seem
to have assumed implicitly that the employment-generating effect is the
same. Although it has been argued that the income multiplier would
tend to be identical with the employment multiplier under certain
conditions,[13] in the final analysis, it is a matter for empirical verification. It does not appear that any such verification was ever carried out
for the purpose of the Nigerian Plan but in the case of India's Second
Five-Year Plan where this was done, it was found that the two multipliers differed not only within sectors but also between sectors.[14] The
four sectors into which the Indian economy was divided for the purpose
of the plan model were: Capital goods, consumption goods produced
by modern factories, Consumption goods produced by small-scale
household industries, and service. The fact that the Nigerian Plan does
not break the economy into sectors, makes it less easy to accept, on its
face value, any assumption of identical income and employment
multipliers.

To summarize the burden of the argument so far, it is submitted
that, although the model on which the National Development Plan is
based represents a considerable improvement on earlier efforts, it does
not take explicit account of or specify any employment objective. Yet
the employment problem looms larger now than it did three years ago.
In the circumstances, the best thing would be to revise the Plan so as

[13] Keynes, J. M., *The General Theory of Employment, Interest and Money* (London, 1937),
pp. 115–16.
[14] Tsuru, Shigeto, 'The Applicability and Limitations of Economic Development
Theory', *The Indian Economic Journal*, Vol. IX, No. 4, April 1962.

to maximize the growth in income and employment, making judicious use of the best techniques available in the field of economic programming. It is easy to be sceptical of this suggestion on the grounds that:

(a) the economic data available in the country are fragmentary, of uneven quality, and do not lend themselves to sophisticated methods; and

(b) the so-called sophisticated methods sometimes lead to nonsensical results.

But as emphasized earlier, planning theory and techniques are essential to modern economic growth, and a developing country should exploit them to the full. Used intelligently, they make clearer the implications of choices which politicians and other policy-makers are called upon to make. The mathematics and statistics employed in most of the advanced programming methods are not too advanced by the mathematician's standards;[15] it is the assumption behind the methods and the economic interpretation of the results which are so crucial. It is important, however, that undue reliance should not be placed on any single method and that different methods should be used to crosscheck each other.

As far as data is concerned, it pays to endeavour to use some of the more refined methods. In the process, gaps in available data are seen in sharper focus and the need for collecting data specifically for planning purposes, and not as a by-product of administrative functions, becomes more obvious. For example, if as suggested here it is intended to devise a planning model which takes account of income and employment, it will be necessary to compute coefficients of the productivity of investment and coefficients of the amount of new capital needed to employ an additional worker in as many sectors as it is considered advisable to disaggregate the economy. This would call for an intensive study of small-scale industry of the kind conducted by the U.S.A.I.D. in Eastern Nigeria, in order to supplement the Federal Department of Statistics' annual survey of manufacturing which covers only firms with at least ten employees. Forms and questionnaires sent out would also have to be tailored to suit the level of statistical awareness of the people concerned.

---

[15] Some of the finest examples of mathematical reasoning in economic planning do not use a single equation. The section on forecasting methods in Professor Harbison's paper (chapter 6) is a case in point.

It has been said that in preparing the National Development Plan, the Joint Planning Committee 'never presented the National Economic Council with a set of alternative future planning targets for choice and endorsement at the political level'.[16] The writer cannot urge too strongly that in revising the Plan or formulating future Plans, every effort should be made to present alternative planning targets on income and employment for the politicians' choice. With the uncertainties surrounding the export trade and the availability of foreign capital, for example, alternative planning targets based on different assumptions would have some educative value for those whose responsibility it is to make a choice; it would also make for greater flexibility when the revised plan gets to the implementation stage.

So far the employment problem has been treated as if it were homogeneous. But at this stage it would be useful to examine one or two special cases. The first is how to make fuller use of labour which is subject to what is usually termed disguised unemployment. That there is substantial disguised unemployment in Nigeria, especially in the agricultural sector, cannot be doubted, although the precise magnitude has yet to be determined. Such an exercise should rank high on the Manpower Board's study of unemployment. At this stage, all that needs to be stressed, perhaps, is that any attempt to solve the problem of disguised unemployment through a wider use of labour-intensive methods in the manufacture of consumption goods would be self-defeating for the reasons given earlier. Greater employment will for a time be bought at the expense of greater output. But lower output will eventually lead to lower savings and lower capital formation; the economy will end up with less employment. It would be far better for the most efficient methods to be used in the manufacture of consumption goods so as to ensure that the marketable surplus should be as large as possible. Labour which is not fully occupied should be put to work in the construction of irrigation projects, factories, road-making etc.[17] This is a lesson India seems to have taken to heart in her Third Five-Year Plan.[18] The focus now is away from cottage industries and on a greatly expanding rural public works programme. To be effective, however, steps have to be taken to fit in such constructional works with the seasonal pattern of disguised unemployment, as far

16 Peter Clark, op. cit., p. 273.
17 Vakil, C. N. and Brahmanand, P. R., *Planning for an Expanding Economy* (Bombay, 1956), pp. 159–66.
18 Lewis, John P., op. cit., pp. 89–90.

as possible. In addition, to protect the balance of payments, the programme must go hand in hand with measures to increase food production.

The problem of unemployment among school-leavers is the subject of a separate paper by Dr. A. C. Callaway.[19] The usual definition of the unemployed as those who are able and willing to work but cannot find jobs, leads one to ask to what extent primary school-leavers are in fact employable. Two reasons would seem to cast doubt on the assumption that they are employable. In the first place, an increasing range of jobs which used to be open to them now require better educational preparation. Examples are teaching and nursing. In the second place, even long before the problem of unemployment among primary school-leavers assumed the existing dimensions, many of them were apprenticed out by their parents in order to train as carpenters, masons, mechanics, etc. This would seem to suggest that parents recognized that children needed additional preparation before entering the labour market. Except in the case of primary school-leavers going on for further education the Nigerian educational system does not seem to recognize this need.

In order to make the bulk of primary school-leavers employable, it is suggested that no adolescent should be sent into the world until he has had at least a year or two of some basic vocational training on top of his normal primary school course. This suggestion assumes that primary education is basic education and that there is a limit to which it can be made vocational without destroying its purpose. The extra expense of increasing the school leaving age should be regarded as part of the social cost of avoiding unemployment. In fact, it is more than that. It is an investment in human resources which should pay off in the future. The proposal put forward here provides a link between educational and manpower planning.

On the question of manpower training in general, which falls within the scope of supply, the writer will confine himself largely to raising a number of questions. The first concerns the word 'manpower'. As used by Professor Harbison and the National Manpower Board it is usually qualified with the adjective 'high-level'. The assumption seems to be that high-level manpower is one of the limiting factors of Nigeria's economic growth.

The word 'manpower' has come to stay and it is to the credit of

19 cf. Chapter 16.

those who have developed it into a respectable field of study that they have made governments, including the Nigerian Governments, more keenly aware of its importance to economic growth. But by confining the use of the word operationally to high-level manpower, there seems to be a real danger that the importance of other types of manpower may be obscured. High-level manpower may be a limiting factor to Nigeria's economic growth but there is a common-sense view that the quality of that other manpower which forms the bulk of the country's labour force, is also essential to rapid growth. It is true this other manpower is not left completely out of account; but it seems to be regarded merely as something like a chorus in a play in which high-level manpower are the real characters. Yet farmers, for example, enter into the manpower problem when the ratio of extension workers to farmers is being computed.

It is significant that since the Second World War, public policy in Nigeria has gone through bouts of enthusiasm for universities, primary schools, teacher training colleges, training for the civil service, trade centres, high-level manpower. The only exception so far is education for those who have not had any formal schooling. It is true that community development gets more attention in the present plan but it has not yet achieved the status of a major instrument of rural uplift as understood in Mexico and India. For functional literacy as part of a programme of social and economic development very little provision has been made. The writer is far from suggesting that high-level manpower is not important. His plea is that the harnessing of our human resources should be conceived in much broader terms than hitherto.

Another assumption behind the tendency to glorify high-level manpower appears to be that if only it can be developed, all else would be well. In planning which is concerned mainly with the public sector, such a way of looking at high-level manpower is understandable. And yet we are told that 'unless the people of Nigeria as a whole are enthusiastically behind and directly involved in the National Plan . . . the Plan objectives will be difficult to achieve'.[20] If facts must be faced, it should be admitted that probably a major part of the people who constitute the senior category of high-level manpower are incapable of arousing enthusiasm for the Plan on the part of the ordinary Nigerian. Although they speak their mother tongues for conversational purposes, they have great difficulty in using them to convey ideas in a

[20] *National Development Plan*, 1962–8, pp. 2–3.

way to touch and move the man in the street. They frame their ideas first in English and then translate them mentally into the mother tongue. The result is that you have a set of words which are Ibo, Yoruba and Efik, but the idioms, the thoughts behind the words, are foreign. In short, to use an American saying, there seems to be a communication barrier between a key section of our high-level manpower and the ordinary man.

This gap does not appear to have been recognized in the Plan. Unless it is bridged, it will slow down the development of the country. Hitherto it has been assumed that the way to bridge the gap is to raise the educational level from below. But there is need to work downwards from the top as well. Nigeria's high-level manpower must be brought nearer the ordinary man.

The least that can be done is to make the mother tongue a compulsory subject throughout the educational system. For high-level manpower whose education was virtually conducted in English there should be remedial courses designed to enable them to express ideas in speech and writing in at least one Nigerian language. But it would be a mistake to think that the problem is one of language only. In the days when the bulk of Nigeria's senior service personnel was made up of people from the British Isles, they were given special university courses, often extending over a year, in Nigerian anthropology, law, economics, history, etc. before coming to take up appointments. Now with a predominantly Nigerian senior personnel, it seems to be that such a preparation is no longer necessary. The point to bear in mind is that every member of the senior category of the public services is or ought to be an extension worker, whose job is to communicate ideas to the people at large, with a view to adopting better practices in health, production, etc. The people who are being persuaded to adopt new ideas are likely to react in terms of their culture and their aspirations. In short, there is need to understand them as social beings before they can be effectively helped, and in the process of trying to understand them, they in turn assist to sharpen the administrator's insight into the complexities of what it involves to bring about social change.

Happily, some Nigerian universities are making courses in African history and culture an integral part of their undergraduate programmes. But the bulk of the existing senior category high-level manpower received their higher education abroad or had hitherto no opportunity of studying African history and culture in Nigerian universities. It is

suggested that every department of the public services should arrange
to have prepared for its senior staff, a manual on Nigerian sociology
oriented towards the tasks they have to perform and the sections of the
society with which they have to deal. Such a manual on Nigerian rural
sociology has been prepared for extension workers by Mr. Tunde
Oloko in connection with the annual seminar on methods of agricultural extension organized by the Department of Adult Education and
Extra-Mural Studies of the University of Ibadan. The warm reception
which the manual has received locally and overseas suggests that it is
meeting a felt need which may not be confined to agricultural officers.
Such manuals should be used in intensive training courses for senior
staff before embarking on their careers. Communication techniques
should also be included in the courses.

Earlier in this paper, it was emphasized that new knowledge, the
application of new knowledge and the embodiment of applied knowledge in production is a necessary condition for economic growth. In
any country where planning is adopted as an instrument for accelerating
development, the public services have a key role to play, especially
in ensuring that the economy takes advantage of the latest knowledge
and technology. For them to fulfil this function effectively the members
of the senior category of high-level manpower, in particular, must
remain intellectually alert and abreast of developments in their field.
The impression formed by some observers who are in a position to
judge, is that too many of Nigeria's senior personnel consider their
education to have come to an end when they get their degree or professional diploma. If this is true, it means that people who are expected
to be innovators in the public sector are not likely to be equal to the
task. It may be useful to speculate on how such an attitude came about.
Firstly, it is possibly connected with the generalist tradition inherited
from the British civil service in which specialization is not held in high
regard and the gifted amateur was the pride of the administrative
service. Secondly, the practice of frequently changing the postings of
members of the administrative service gives little time or incentive to
develop any specialization. Thirdly, and this list does not pretend to
be exhaustive, it may be a reflection of the fact that the modern intellectual tradition in this country is relatively new. Be that as it may,
Britain herself has found that to adapt quickly to changing conditions
and to hold her own against energetic competitors, calls for a different
kind of upper civil service, whose members must, increasingly, be

specialists. It is clear, therefore, that in order to achieve the goal of rapid economic growth in Nigeria and to enable her to play an effective part on the world scene, the intellectual level of the members of the public services must be raised. Lastly, recent experience shows that scholarship programmes now need to be more closely related to national manpower requirements. It is heartbreaking to see university students being sent down for being unable to pay fees while forecasts reveal substantial vacancies in posts requiring the degrees for which they are studying. The reasons for this state of affairs needs to be constantly looked into by the National Manpower Board.

In one respect the present Plan falls short of the Ten-Year Development Plan launched in 1946. While the Ten-Year Plan specified the manpower requirements of each department, only the current Plan for the Eastern Region embodies any estimates of manpower needs—albeit, in agriculture, education and public works. It would be an important step forward if in preparing the financial side and physical targets of projects, manpower budgets would, as far as possible, be concurrently prepared. Fortunately, the methodology of how to set about doing this in Nigerian conditions has received the attention of economists.[21]

[21] In this connection, the writing of Professor Harbison comes to mind. See also the chapter on 'Manpower Planning' by C. Davis Fogg in the book, *Managing Economic Development in Africa*, Ed. Warren H. Hausman (Cambridge, Mass., 1963).

3

Toward an Integrated Manpower Policy for Accelerated National Development

John F. Hilliard

AGENCY FOR INTERNATIONAL DEVELOPMENT, UNITED STATES
DEPARTMENT OF STATE, WASHINGTON

Introduction

It should be noted at the outset that while the subject of the seminar
and of this book is 'Manpower Problems in Economic Development',
the subject of this paper is 'Manpower Policy for Accelerated National
Development'. There is a rather widespread tendency to equate
economic development and *national* development, but this is, I believe, a
misconception. Economic development focuses its attention upon
the development and use of resources to increase the supply and improve
the distribution of economic goods. While this is obviously one of the
more important goals of national development, there are several others.
For example, all the affairs of political and cultural life, institutions
for modernization of the society, participation in international political
and cultural affairs—all these are essential parts of national development.

For purposes of this paper, therefore, national development is
defined to include economic development, but also encompasses the
overall process of creating the concepts, symbols and institutions which
give a philosophy, structure and identity to a modern nation-state. As
will be mentioned later, in connection with specific manpower policy
problems, several important aspects of national development in no
concrete way contribute to economic development; some actually
make heavy claims upon the economy. Yet they require manpower and

important human skills which must be taken into account by intelligent national manpower policy.

Every industrially advanced country today has a complex of manpower policies, expressed in legislation, fiscal budgets, labour-management agreements and traditional practice. Few such countries have anything approaching an integrated national policy relating to the development and utilization of their human resources to meet national goals. Now there is no special magic in an integrated national manpower policy. Indeed, if national development is to be allowed to take its normal course, a pragmatic, piece-by-piece policy development has much to recommend it. However, for countries which have adopted a definite programme for *accelerating* national development, requiring co-ordinated effort in many different sectors, usually with the primary leadership and financing provided by the Government, there is no reasonable substitute for integrated national manpower policy. Moreover, that policy must be derived from and continuously related to the various major objectives of national development.

Manpower policies may be expressed in many different ways. Allocation of funds for technical education is an expression of manpower policy; so is a determination of the size and composition of the armed forces, or decision to establish a new university. The problem is that unless all these questions are examined in the context of an overall view of the national objectives, they are frequently resolved by fragmentary or conflicting answers. The unique function of a national manpower policy, therefore, lies in its requirement that all individual or specialized manpower proposals be examined, not only in terms of the particular problem, but in the light of the overall problem of manpower resources to meet national goals. There are accordingly many facets to this question.

And since it is impossible to deal comprehensively with manpower policy problems in this short paper, four important ones have been selected, which will, I believe, suggest the importance of the subject and illustrate the need for integrated manpower policy planning. These are:

(a) Investment in education
(b) Development of the present labour force
(c) Full employment, and
(d) Employment of women

Some long-term manpower policy problems

Some economists have attempted to persuade us that the true course to maximizing so-called 'human capital formation' is best charted by the compass of economics alone.

They calculate present manpower resources and future requirements and not infrequently adduce these data as the basic guide to educational investment by levels and types of training to meet manpower requirements of the next five to twenty-five years. As one who has participated in such studies in many countries, I have no particular quarrel with this process, as long as it is recognized, firstly, to be, at best, only approximately correct and, secondly, to be related to *economic* development. If this is then equated with *national* development, answers may not only be incorrect but seriously misleading. Let us take an illustration. In recognition of the fact that modern economies, both industrial and agricultural, are built on technology, technical education has become a world-wide and popular activity of educational systems. Many economists feel that wide-spread elementary education must be sternly limited in order to make available adequate funds for education in the 'critical fields'. It is at this juncture that economic development and national development must be differentiated, not to the detriment of technical education, but in order that the policy makers may be clear on what policy it is that they are deciding.

One of the great problems of leaders of developing countries is to stir the hopes and aspirations of a population, mainly rural, who have for centuries had little reason for belief in a better future. An increase in income, important as it is, starts from such a low base that it does not seem likely to average men and women to promise any extraordinary improvement in their lifetime. The thing that *development* means to most adults in a developing country is a better life for their children. That better life, they feel, can proceed from no other source nearly so important as education. It is the availability of education for their children that above all else motivates them to have hope for the future and faith in the new order. And unless faith and hope can be widely diffused throughout the population, development is not likely to succeed. Thus a decision regarding the investment of scarce resources in education becomes not simply an equation in 'human capital formation'. It is intimately bound up with the whole strategy of national development.

This problem takes a variety of forms. Not long ago, I heard an educational leader say: 'In education we have to stick to our basic needs, which are for people to do practical jobs. These other things like literature, history and even the social sciences just have to wait.' Yet one of the over-riding problems of his country is to establish its identity and culture—to create a respect for its own arts, crafts, music and literature. In the strict sense, these add little to the gross national product in economic terms, but they add enormously to the national product in terms of a nation finding its own personality, reasons for development and confidence in its own talent. I was very much interested to see a few days later a project for the training of museum technicians for the rapid expansion of the national museum. This museum has already made a notable start in bringing together the authentic civilization of that country, extending over a period of 2,000 years. Viewed from a strictly economic standpoint, this may be regarded as a misuse of resources. From the standpoint of national development it may in the end be worth more than a steel plant.

It should be reiterated that I am in no way down-grading technical education. It is perfectly obvious that technically trained manpower is the indispensable ingredient of economic development and one of the indispensable ingredients of national development. Normally technical training is thought of in terms of the physical sciences and the applications which stem from these sciences. Yet almost all experience of the past fifteen or twenty years would seem to indicate that national development is impeded at least as much by problems of social technology as by lack of scientific technology. The creation or re-establishment of concepts and social habit patterns essential to a free, democratic nation-state is at least as difficult to achieve as scientific technology, and far more difficult to import. It is sometimes forgotten that industrializing societies require a constantly rising level of both technical and social skill.

What then are the guides to long-term manpower policy as expressed in educational investment? Certainly the technical skills must occupy a central role—the practical job of economic development demands this. But the arts, social sciences and humanities should be available to young men and women having talents in them. All are required for authentic national growth. These need not, and in fact should not, be financed on an equal basis, but national manpower policy should recognize and provide facilities for the intellectual, the scholar, and the artist along with the engineer, soil scientist, and administrator. To restate the point briefly, national policy with respect to investment in education should be formulated in terms of national goals. These include increases in production, in gross national product, and in *per capita* income, but extend beyond them to the whole complex of national endeavours requiring manpower and specialized skills. These include, to be sure, a wide range of modern technological skills. But equally essential to true national development is the modernization and application of scholarship in the social sciences and humanities—in creating or re-creating a culture and society supported by a durable structure of modernizing ideas and institutions.

Development of present labour force

Any realistic national strategy must face the fact that success or failure in the development programme for the next five to fifteen years rests mainly with men and women who have already left school. The inescapable truth is that active, intelligent development of the skills and motivation of the present labour force is, in the short term, more important to successful educational system. As nations emerge into independence, their administrators must administer, their managers manage, their teachers teach, regardless of their level of training and experience. From the standpoint of manpower policy, this should signal a vast programme of self-education and on-the-job training in every government ministry and institution and in every industrial enterprise.

However, in most developing countries (in fact in all countries) there is a considerable legacy of manpower policies and practices from the period in which accelerated national development was not an objective. Hiring and promotion practices often are restrictive. On-the-job training is often resisted or unduly prolonged by supervisors and technicians. At the professional level, job opportunities and degrees are equated to such an extent that development does not open up the opportunities which development should confer. The widespread practice of highly trained persons holding a half dozen jobs tend to reduce seriously their effective contribution in any of them. The matter of wage and salary policy becomes crucial, particularly in those countries which have undertaken development through socialization of industry. On the one hand, there is the goal of correcting the great inequalities which have traditionally existed, and, on the other, the goal of sustaining and improving the morale of the top professional and managerial classes. In this case, national policy tends to point in contradictory directions.

Whatever other factors enter into the motivation of men and women, and there are many, there is no doubt that achievement of an adequate and growing income is an important one. This is true at all levels of employment, and yet there is a limit to what the national wage budget can afford. In this case it is not easy to determine what policy a nation can afford to pursue and what policy it can afford not to pursue. But one thing seems certain: that unless wage and salary administration is so conducted that it sustains or improves the motivation and morale of workers at all levels, the development programme is in serious jeopardy. Closely associated with the problem of sustained motivation is that of meeting serious manpower shortages in critical occupations. Not infrequently, countries are inclined to meet these problems by such policies as 'assignment', compulsory service or other forms of coercion. Experience of the last quarter century has clearly revealed that such policies are self-defeating and particularly so with workers whose product is mainly intellectual. While there may be no final and complete answer to this problem, the best approach to it seems clearly in the direction of measures to increase opportunities and incentives for better performance and effective measures for improving the efficiency of the supply. These are now well known and need not be detailed here.

Short of application of compulsory service, there are other restrictions upon manpower mobility which reduce morale and effective performance. For example, some countries require the agreement of the present employer before an individual may accept a different post— even a higher one sponsored by the government. While it is no doubt necessary to inhibit excessive job shopping in a period of development, the fact is that development by its very nature demands an increase in both the vertical and horizontal mobility of labour. Where such inhibitions are imposed, it would seem there should be some national agency established to adjudicate disagreements promptly rather than to make the individual employee the victim of a tug–of–war, or to be denied arbitrarily what he regards as a change advantageous both to himself and to his country. In short, a second main policy in national manpower strategy must be a systematic study of the problems of the existing labour force and a greatly enlarged investment in developing its skills, health and morale.

Full employment

There is perhaps no country which has not either adopted full employment as an explicit national manpower policy or as an eventual goal of development. Nevertheless, there are many economic, technical and policy problems which stand in the way of progress towards this goal. Policies of industrialization increase urbanization and therefore increase the needs for urban employment, usually faster than such jobs are created. Measures for improved land use often create less rural employment rather than more. Above all, a policy of universal, or, at least, rapidly increasing, education creates both an expansion in the number of persons seeking wage employment and significant changes in the attitudes, skill composition and job expectations of the labour force. It is in the face of such problems as these that a national policy approach is required rather than one geared to economic development alone.

Rapid changes in the social, economic and technological character of a country usually produce for a period of years serious imbalances in the relationships of the skills of the labour force to the job requirements brought about by development. This tends to create or maintain high levels of general unemployment or underemployment and also to create specialized unemployment problems such as the large scale unemployment of educated persons. These in turn create economic, social and political problems which require overall national policy. At the opposite end of the scale, as has been noted, for that part of the labour force having needed skills, there develops a condition of over-employment, creating inefficiencies in the utilization of manpower resources. In these circumstances, also, there is no single or completely satisfactory solution to the problem. To the extent that solutions are to be found, they lie in a complex of integrated actions derived from a careful study of the problem as it relates to the total programme of national development.

Employment of women

One of the most important and complex problems involved in national manpower policy is that of womanpower. The demographers have finally convinced us that, numerically at least, women constitute approximately half of the human race. At the same time, every progressive government has adopted measures for the increased education of women and for their fuller participation in the national life. Rendering effective such a decision is usually difficult even in a labour shortage economy. In most of the developing countries, both urban and rural unemployment are a pervasive fact, even when only the male labour force is considered. How do we manage the 'female revolution' which is being inexorably created by the education of women?

At the very heart of this issue, and perhaps our most crucial problem, is that of limitation of population. Whatever chemical, biological or mechanical discoveries may be made, it seems likely that they will be made widely effective only to the extent that the world's women are increasingly educated and take their place as partners in the great constructive endeavours of our time. In doing this, however, there must be created in many countries revolutionary changes in education and employment and in the whole fabric of social and economic life. Great wisdom and courage will be required to forge a strategy which can accelerate the development of women and not create serious disturbances in overall development.

These are only a few of the manpower problems on which intelligent and timely decision must be made and on which success or failure in national development may well turn, and these problems are so closely interwoven that none can successfully be dealt with in isolation from the others.

Toward national manpower policy

In the preceding pages, there have been posed four manpower problems in the general context of national development. No solutions have been offered, and, indeed, it is questionable whether there are single or unitary solutions to any of them. And they are only suggestive of a longer list confronted by every nation undertaking accelerated national development. The essential point is that even amelioration of these problems require that they be arranged in a systematic way, and dealt with as a matter of national strategy, for the one indispensable resource of every nation is its men and women. It is the resource that is at once the architect, the means and the reason for national development.

There are no doubt many ways of approaching such a strategy. But first let us define the reasons for an explicitly stated manpower policy. Such a policy would seem to have four main objectives:

(a) Provide an integrated and systematic statement of the nation's commitments with regard to human resources development, rather than a patchwork of *ad hoc* policies;

(b) Serve as a firm base for establishment of institutions and taking of actions to effect national policy;

(c) Permit evaluation of manpower administration as it actually relates to the goals of national development; and

(d) Permit conscious changes of policy for improvement or to meet changed conditions.

Fortunately, Nigeria is one of the countries which has already taken important steps toward achievement of integrated manpower policy. The establishment of the National Manpower Board and Secretariat represents a crucial first step. But organizational arrangements alone are not sufficient—the way in which manpower goals are formulated determines the policy issues which the Board may be called upon to consider. All the problems mentioned above must be resolved in some manner by the Board. And there are many others. For example, an important policy question implicit in the report on Nigeria's High-Level Manpower 1963–70 is: 'Do we have no requirement for highly trained social scientists?' The projected requirements show no need for sociologists, anthropologists, psychologists, political scientists, archaeologists, linguists or legal scholars. Yet all these fields of scholarship have been discovered to have great value in accelerating national development. As further examples of policy questions which are interwoven and which are implicit in the report are: replacement of expatriates with Nigerians, overseas training for sponsored and unsponsored students, advanced study in selected occupations, training and upgrading of the present labour force. There are many others. The National Manpower Board, therefore, must be enabled to consider the right problem, in the clear context of national objectives.

A further requirement is the authority necessary to implement policy decisions. It is not entirely clear how this is contemplated but would appear to require either a Cabinet Committee or a statutory authority vested in the Board for implementation of its policies. Finally, the nature of national manpower problems and policies should be made as widely known as possible. Manpower is people—and people have a deep and proper interest in matters that affect them. In addition to day-to-day activities, the Board should render annual reports to the

Head of State, the Parliament and the people. In this way, the formulation and execution of national manpower policy can be derived from the established national goals and integrated with the overall strategy for achieving those goals.

4

New Markets for Manpower Planning

George Tobias

INTERNATIONAL BANK FOR RECONSTRUCTION AND DEVELOPMENT

The nearly universal acceptance of the importance of human resources development to general economic development has placed new and urgent responsibilities upon manpower planning. My theme is that the profession of manpower planning is sufficiently developed in its technical equipment to assume those responsibilities, to shift to a more active role in manpower administration, and to switch from the research laboratory to practical application of its knowledge. Further improvement in statistical technique and theory will develop best as theory and practice serve as two hands washing each other—new principles will evolve from solving practical problems of manpower administration.

Manpower programme and allocation

Manpower is people, humanity, society with all of its aspirations, needs and capacities. Manpower, considered as an economic resource, represents the aggregate of skills and attitudes resulting from education plus training that equips a labour force with the capacity to plan, organize and carry out economic processes when properly allocated. 'High-level manpower' includes the executives, administrators, technologists, professionals, technicians and long-trained craftsmen, the 'produced producers'. This is the 'human capital' that must be matched with other forms of capital in a continuous process of allocation between alternative uses. Allocation of manpower between alternative uses takes place continuously because the supply is scarcer than the needs; a sharing of shortages, deliberately or accidentally, results. There is an allocation every time a student makes a career choice, a university changes its curriculum, an enterprise makes a capital commitment, or a basic wage decision is made.

A manpower programme provides logistics support to an economic development plan. If there is no economic development plan, a manpower programme is isolated and indefinite. In the absence of a controlling economic development plan, however generalized and incomplete, a detailed manpower programme may actually lead the labour force in the wrong direction. It should never be the responsibility of the manpower planner to determine his own directions and levels, but rather to act as a staff service to the executive centre responsible for the economic and political decisions of economic development. Hence, there must not be a manpower strategy independent of the development strategy of which it is only, however important, a part. Within that larger context, a balanced manpower programme has seven aspects.

1. Recruitment
2. Deployment
3. Motivation
4. Education
5. Training
6. Utilization
7. Stabilization

The labour market is *continuously and simultaneously* affected by these seven impacts. There is no significance in the sequence in which these aspects are here set down; they occur in what physicists call a 'time-space continuum'. No matter where or how lightly we touch the labour market, every one of these pieces in it jiggles. The tools of manpower planning—even its terminology—were developed within the last thirty years. In 1936 there did not even exist an occupational dictionary to describe the jobs that make up the labour force. It is therefore essential at this stage to define the above terms clearly. *Recruitment* includes mobilizing and matching men and jobs—informing workers and employers of labour market facts; counselling workers who are changing jobs or students choosing careers; testing the worker's capacity against job requirements; determining the real requirements to perform a given task which, in turn, set the training and education appropriate to the job. Recruitment involves the forecasting of manpower requirements and resources, analysing present and historical labour force data, and relating the economic outlook with the population and labour force outlook.

Deployment of the labour force takes place to improve its balance as between areas, industries and occupations, to transfer and transform surplus workers so as to provide for growing economic needs and to give the worker a better chance at a job. Agricultural reform, area redevelopment, government activities to encourage new industries in old areas and social, economic and political problems of urbanization affect manpower deployment.

Motivation programmes encourage and give incentives to workers to assume, learn and stick with new kinds of tasks. They provide programmes of wage incentive and control and establish social values in support of economic development in lieu of those which inhibit economic progress—all the while avoiding compulsion upon the individual to work only in a given job and place.

The *education* aspect of a manpower programme includes setting goals, requirements and resources of educated people, reviewing and perfecting school course content, and expanding and revising enrolment and curricula of schools in support of economic development, compatible with other educational objectives. Assuring an adequate source of apt students and able teachers is part of this aspect of manpower planning.

Training programmes prepare the worker for efficient labour force participation with respect to a given occupation. Training programmes require the support of the employer, the community, professional groups and trade unions.

Full *utilization* of the labour force involves the manpower planner in identifying problems of underemployment, planning of plant organization and layout, productivity improvement, job relationships and providing sufficient middle-level workers to support the highest skilled personnel.

Stabilization of the labour force involves, for the manpower planner, programmes of social protection, housing, community facilities, industrial relations and other activities that help reduce wasteful turnover.

The nature of manpower planning

Economic management of the labour market in Western Europe, the United States of America, the Soviet Union and Japan was a necessary concomitant of World War II. Manpower economics discovered its tools and rules in the necessity to use scarce professional and skilled workers where they could contribute most to the war effort. Practically every one of today's manpower practitioners of the appropriate age in the United States learned his trade in World War II. Many of them were brought back and retreaded for service in the Korean War. Many wartime experts, like Tommy Atkins, have spent the post-war years honing their bayonets and oiling their rifles, waiting for the call which is now being heard for manpower planning. The United States of America, Western European countries, India, Egypt, Pakistan, Mexico and Nigeria, among others, now share a common awareness of labour market problems resulting from planned change.

All social and economic planning is approximate and experimental by its nature, and manpower planning is no exception. It is not possible to anticipate perfectly the manpower requirements and outputs by occupation area and industry, to assure full utilization of the present labour force in balance with the needs of economic growth. Development plans flow from a series of successively closer, complementary estimates. Erected on partial and sometimes contradictory data, development plans are often advocated on the basis of unproven social and political theories, assumptions and hopes. Proposed by social scientists, they are disposed of by politicians. Typically, funds for the plan's fulfilment are frequently expected to come from external credit revenues hitherto untapped or not yet written into law. The plans are to be implemented by private enterprise and by government administrators and professionals of all types who are not yet trained and who will always be in short supply. Many of the agencies supposed to carry out the plans either are not yet established or are sadly in need of reform. And yet, economic plans are being put together by—and for— capitalist and socialist countries, primitive and sophisticated societies, more developed and less developed economies, with high hope and with dogged determination.

The three elements of administering anything are planning, execution and control—planning is a staff service in support of administration. The manpower planner, in a staff capacity, anticipates questions that already plague the administrators, as well as those which the planner knows the administrator will encounter in the future. In addition, the planner seeks out answers to problems which the administrator is sometimes not conscious that he has—but which the planner believes have to be tackled for successful manpower programmes. Such problems are clearly manifold and cannot be covered within the compass of this paper. The rest of this chapter will, therefore, be devoted to a few of the most important areas in which economic development requires guidance from manpower planners.

Setting employment objectives

Within the limited financial and other resources at hand, a wide variety of targets for economic development present themselves. What kind of a country is wanted? Can the country afford the heavy costs of industrialization, especially if it risks stranding in a backwater the probable majority of the labour force which cannot be employed in industry? 'Full employment' is always an appealing objective. But full employment is meaningless unless the full employment is productive, with the employer free to choose and change his workers, with the worker free to choose and change his employment and to advance within the limits of his ability. The dual goals of maximum labour mobility and highest labour productivity may not be easy to reach simultaneously.

The choice between labour intensive and capital intensive industries cannot be resolved in purely economic terms of realized net return. Few societies can risk the political turmoil that results if only a small *élite* enjoys the benefit of highly productive investment, with the majority left in an undercapitalized *status quo*. Furthermore, once high capital input industry is chosen, an inexorable arithmetic of compound interest sets in, with continued capital increments having to go to modernize and maintain both production and distribution. Yet, paradoxically, some of the greatest success stories in underdeveloped countries are those of the industries of smallest labour input. The greatest difficulties have often beset industries of high labour use. Telephone service or highway transportation investment, for example, in which labour input after construction is extremely low, have shown high, trouble-free returns. The greatest difficulty has been encountered in such activity as irrigation and land resettlement. The reason is the shortage of high-level manpower, the executives and organizers for large-employing enterprises. This is especially true in agriculture where problems of agrarian reform, community development and directing a large, raw labour force have to be faced simultaneously.

Manpower is more than numbers

Preoccupation with forecasting of the size and composition of the labour force and of the kinds and numbers of occupation needed over the long term has given an unfortunate mathematical tone to the profession. It is not necessary here to recount the statistical methods employed in long-range forecasting. But it is appropriate to warn against methods which assume rigidity of the labour force and scientific precision in occupational requirements.

No element of production is so highly substitutable as is manpower. Tinbergen, among others, surprises many by going so far as to say that a given expenditure for education and training yields about the same economic advancement, no matter what the training and education might consist of. It is clear that, in many cases, one kind of education and experience can be made to fit the requirements of a new job in a short time, even at the highest technical and executive level. In developing employment objectives, planners should anticipate the greatest lateral occupational mobility, encouraging workers to shift as opportunity and balanced resource allocation demands, from one activity to another.

The behaviour of the labour market, more than the rigidly defined requirements of a job, determines the specifications which employers actually use in their hiring. Specifications change as the labour market changes. Americans over fifty years of age can recall from their own experience a time when Macy's did not hire salesgirls without university degrees (Hunter College preferred). Ten years later, any young lady with a discernible pulse was readily hired for the same job. Had the job specifications really changed? Not at all—the labour market had changed. What, then, were the 'real' requirements of education and experience for the job? Typically, the employer (or his collaborator, the educator) insists upon the highest educational requirements *at the time of hiring*. But later, when wages are bargained, the experience and education, highly valued and much demanded by the employer when he hired the man, are of much less worth than the worker's proven adjustment to the job. It is evident that there is a great difference in pre-employment education (and experience) among successful men even in high-level occupations.

Equally, it is not true that an industrial process requires a fixed, rigid and invariable percentage of each occupation in order to operate efficiently. Nor can it be shown that an economy's industrial evolution follows a rigid and predetermined rate and pattern. There is not a proven, mechanical relationship in the balance between occupations within an enterprise. Thus, if inter-industry matrixes mechanically ascribe for a given level of economic activity the specific kinds and numbers of occupations necessary, they are likely to be far off the mark. Experience shows that the labour market best meets production requirements (and increases the labour force's total skill level into the bargain) when it encourages the widest latitude of inter-occupational, inter-industry and inter-area shifts, with intensive on-the-job training after the worker enters the specific job.

Worker productivity and social adjustment

The key to improving worker productivity is to facilitate shifts to new areas, industries, occupations or processes, to equip the worker with new attitudes and attributes that raise his output and reduce his lost time and motion, and to do so as quickly as possible. Improved work-organization within the employing organization assures that the highly qualified are kept working at the peak of their skill, assisted by technicians and helpers. The manpower planner can contribute to these programmes by engaging the participation and support of the business community, trade unions, teaching institutions and government. Manpower programmes help by:

  simplifying the job;
  speeding the training on the job;
  introducing technicians and other single skill practitioners to
    share the lesser tasks; and
  permitting each to work at the peak of his skill.

There is an important personal dimension to persuading the labour force to accept new techniques of production to improve output. Automated machines with electronic controls now have what amounts to a high school education. Machines may soon displace workers with less than a high school education in repetitive, mechanized manufacturing processes, and the machines work at a wage that will not support a family. The problem of introducing automation into a work force is a challenge to the manpower planner who must retain the co-operation and acceptance of those very workers whose jobs are disappearing. Technological indigestion shows up in the form of 'feather bedding', not because workers do not want to work but because they do want to maintain their place in the labour force. The only place the worker can maintain, he feels, is the place that he has known. Manpower planners are faced with the challenge of retraining, re-equipping workers for their new roles, of retaining their support, and of demonstrating the benefits, even though surplus workers may have to make personally painful shifts to new jobs. It is possible that perhaps, automation, the *nouvelle vague* for organized worrying, has been overdone. Only relatively few kinds of large-scale *and repetitive* processes may ever achieve the economy of mass production that auto-mation promises and threatens. Servo-mechanisms may have to find their place in the battery of technology as has every previous invention since the wheel, and the human being's capacity will continue to play the central role in production.

Education

As early as the seventeenth century, the economic value of an educated and trained person was investigated by Sir William Petty, perhaps the world's first econometrician. He calculated that there were measurable differences in the output of individuals traceable directly to the preparation they had had for their jobs. But he did not stop there. He proved, to his satisfaction, in 1687 that the value to society of a trained mill hand was £90 per annum in England and only £70 in Ireland and that, for the advantage of both the Irish worker and English manufacture, migration should be encouraged. He also cal-culated the economic value of resettling in a healthy area, workers who lived in the path of a plague. He found that the yield was 84 times the estimated costs of the investment. A century later, Adam Smith was captivated by the cost-benefit ratio of investment in human capital. Indeed, he built a whole thesis on the need to husband resources and argued for improving labour productivity through training. David Ricardo concluded that workers' outputs vary in accordance with acquired as well as natural capacities, and that their rewards vary accordingly. In today's idiom, Galbraith puts it that 'nowhere in the world is a well-educated person really poor'. Education is the biggest user of high-level manpower in both developed and undeveloped countries. Indeed, it is the biggest 'industry' in terms of employment, payroll and investment in plant. Problems of how best to supply and utilize teachers and administrators are present in all countries. Ques-tions of how much education can be afforded, of what kinds, toward what labour market objectives are real and current everywhere. Technical education, fitting workers only for single, narrowly restricted occupations, can be overdone. Theoretical education gives the worker greater mobility and adaptability to change his occupation and industry, and perhaps should be encouraged more than narrow single-job technical education. For the newly developing country whose precise future occupational needs are uncertain, too precise technical education is risky in that it may turn the young into very limited job specialists. Not all highly developed countries educate their traditional-craft learners, such as carpenter, mason, etc., to secondary school level, nor do they need to do so. The traditional method of acquiring skill on the job should be counted on to supply the labour market for some years to come in most underdeveloped countries.

There is always the risk that long-term educational forecasts and estimates of skill requirements may mislead young people into blind alleys if patterns of employment and production change. In 1944, one of the most complex mechanisms ever developed in the United States was the manned heavy bomber—enormous investment in skills, materials and machinery for its production and use was anticipated for the future. The last of the heavy bombers was on its way to the scrap heap in 1964. What provision was made 15 years ago for missile production, space exploration, telemetry, solid fuel production? If previous generations in that country had acted with the greatest wisdom they possessed to assure the future of useful occupations, they would have provided a substantial whaling industry for lighting oil, and hickory farming for wagon components, and the education to go with it. Plainly, in educational investment, plenty of latitude should be left for human, social and personal attitudes. Keynes, in his *General Theory*, put it this way:

> 'If human nature felt no temptations to take a chance, no satisfaction (profit apart) in constructing a factory, a railway, a mine or a farm, there might not be much investment merely as a result of cold calculation.'

The last element added to any investment appraisal is intuition—and that is more true in investment for education than anywhere else.

Training on the job

Ultimately, every worker, both at professional and craft level, learns his job by doing it. The best friends of educational investment often weaken their own case by claiming too much for education. As a capital asset, as a tool of production, formal education and training in the classroom represents only one segment in the spectrum of human resources development. Formal education has done its job if it makes the student a 'trainable' individual, more apt to perfect his professional and technical competence in the labour force than he would have been without such formal education. Preparation for effective labour market participation begins with the child at home and is carried no more than one long step forward by his educational experiences and the discipline of reckoning and reasoning acquired in the classroom. But it is from his colleagues and superiors that the worker ultimately acquires competence in his trade or profession. A surgeon must have had classroom instruction in anatomy; and yet doctors and surgeons equally must complete internships and residencies before they are ready to practise on the public. Lawyers must complete clerkships. Engineers pass through apprenticeships, under one name or another, executives and administrators are 'finished', and competence in making decisions and in directing a staff is acquired only after years of supervised control and on-the-job training.

The mark of a profession is the requirement that the practitioner pass through successive levels of attainment after entering the profession, based on the judgement of his peers, after training by his peers. If it is correct that individuals attain professional competence by doing the job after pre-employment education, then it follows that the employer has a key and vital role in manpower development. It is the responsibility of the manpower planner to involve the employer deeply in carrying out that role efficiently. The state's prime role in manpower training is that of exhorting the employing community, suggesting training methods, helping to choose those for employment as trainees. Some governments have found it desirable to encourage by subsidy or require by penalty that employers 'overtrain'—by training above their foreseeable needs so as to enrich the general labour market. Many states operate training institutes of one kind or another for their own employment needs. But when the state undertakes technical and vocational education and training for other employers, experience shows that many mistakes can be made by training the wrong people for the wrong jobs in the wrong way.

Ultimately, an economy builds up for itself a supply of qualified workers in a given occupation large enough to carry out its production obligations and to train newcomers. Until that 'critical mass' is attained, large enough to sustain a chain reaction that automatically produces additional qualified workers as a by-product of the process of production, the state may need to operate vocational training facilities as an auxiliary aid to employers' own training capacity. The state's role might well be restricted to the *new* technical occupations not found in that economy in earlier times. Not much is added by state training in the traditional crafts which have always been filled one way or another and which had better be left to the employer. On-the-job training equips the worker to work on a particular product of the employer, with the tools he will continue to use, within standards, tolerances and disciplines peculiar to the shop. Such in-service training is focused on the worker who has already made his job choice, has taken on a commitment, and is working side by side with his colleagues at a wide range of skills. Training by the state off-the-job can seldom reproduce the environment needed for such precise attainment.

Many countries enrich the compulsory military experience of their young people with training that has civilian uses—training in a real production context, supervised by qualified practitioners. Indeed, training is endless—so long as a man works, he learns and teaches others at all levels, from the executive and scientist to the technician and foreman. How to harness this abundant, free, universal training energy for human resources development constitutes one of the major problems confronting the manpower planner.

High-level staffing

Many governments and lending institutions have often gone through the experience of creating new industrial enterprises only to find them under-utilized or idle because the entrepreneur had not planned in detail for his manpower needs—especially at the highest levels of decision making, organizing, direction and supervising. Enterprises in the highly developed countries discovered only in the stress of full employment that human resources need to be planned for on a plant-by-plant, job-by-job basis, even longer ahead than material or financial resources. In many less-developed countries that lesson has yet to be learned. With the executives and technologists provided for, craftsmen can usually be trained or recruited or imported or borrowed. But if the cadre is not there, the enterprise will not run. It is essential that the manpower planner should do everything possible to help employers grasp this fact, and to develop effective methods of recruitment, analysis, and timely hiring for training at top-most levels. It should be possible to make it obligatory that every new project, financed by private or public banks, be accompanied by a detailed recruitment commitment for the high and middle level jobs—as a condition of the credit—with the source clearly indicated for each needed executive, technologist and technician, or a plan for developing him which incorporates an educational development plan.

Agriculture

Probably 70 per cent of the people in the world earn their living on the land. That percentage may not shrink appreciably within this century, despite all of the hopes for speedy industrialization. In many countries of the world, adding 200 calories per day to the average diet would be development enough. In addition, agriculture is going to have to supply an exportable surplus to generate foreign exchange, to buy the imports and to service the loans from which industrialization may grow. Furthermore, as technology is introduced to agriculture it carries in its train the improvement of skills generally, of technical awareness of industrial discipline, of a will to work and to work together. There is the problem of recruiting and training the farm leadership. Often, under-developed countries are not able to offer the farm boy as high a level of education as the city boy. Many an extension worker has a city background. If that betokens his real dedication to the land, he should be welcomed. But if it simply means that the city boy could not find any place open to him for higher education than that provided in a mediocre agricultural school, he may turn out to be only a technician without the complex of attitudes, traditions and social awareness that make it possible for him to work with farmers effectively.

Yet we ought not to try to keep farm boys exclusively on the land. Isn't there an inconsistency when manpower and educational planners demand more and better education to 'take the youths out of the jungle of the city slums' if, at the same time, they are suspicious of education that might take the youth out of the jungle of rural slums? Manpower programmes, to supply the technical and societal leaderships for agriculture, will have to bring together the forces of economists, agronomists, health experts and sociologists, if rural life in underdeveloped countries is ever to be more than 'dull, brutish and short' for that three-fourths of the world who will continue to live out their lives on the farm.

Development programmes to increase jobs, especially in rural areas, are an aspect of productivity improvement to use local labour. State-assigned purchasing on a preferential basis to a distressed area, and state construction projects carried out on a barter basis of food-for-labour have been successful in many countries to mobilize surplus agricultural labour. Underemployment characterizes agricultural societies both because of the absolute redundancy of workers and because of seasonal idleness. The underemployed are more readily concealed in agriculture than in industry because in the latter there is a closer watch kept on the connection between prices, costs and wages. The greatest publicity has been given to labour market imbalances in market economies. But the absence of statistics on rural (and urban) unemployment and under-employment in planned societies does not prove the absence of the problem. For example, one authority on the U.S.S.R. has said that:

> 'the number of people working on a given farm is not the minimum necessary to till the soil, cultivate the crops and raise farm animals and poultry. Rather it represents the number of able-bodied collective farmers in the given co-operative. We cannot allow a state of affairs in which some members of the co-operative work, while others are deprived of the right to work.'[1]

Wage policies

If the manpower planner is to be successful in restructuring the labour market, he is going to have to use all of the implements at his hand. One of them is wage and salary policy in which every government has an interest and most governments have a direct responsibility. Government wage policy directly affects a substantial portion of the labour force in every country and its effect ricochets throughout the economy. Of course, setting wage levels and perfecting wage relationships cannot be counted on alone to redirect the labour force in even the simplest of societies—too many non-wage elements enter into choice of career and choice of job. But it would be a mistake if the manpower planner did not use the wage device for its fullest effect, with caution. If wage movements can induce labour market shifts that are desirable, so can they produce undesirable ones. Indeed, there is almost a perversity in the way salaries rise for just those occupations that economic development want to suppress—more tobacco salesmen turn up where we want more agronomists. Yet government administrators, or school teachers,

[1] N. S. Khrushchev, *World Without Arms, World Without Wars*, Book 2, p. 260, Moscow, 1959.

or agricultural extension workers are not always underpaid in poor countries. High-level manpower in the underdeveloped country can charge a monopoly price which it cannot get in a country where skills are more abundant. In the United States, a secondary school teacher earns three times the *per capita* national income—in Tanganyika he earns forty times or even more.

Rough and ready adjustments to clear the labour market only in a certain direction may generate just enough inflation to discourage development. Too often, correcting gross inequities between occupations in a wage structure has been immediately followed by demands to restore historic differentials between those same occupations, so chasing each other up the wage spiral to everyone's loss.

A challenge

In conclusion, it might be useful to list here a few typical questions representing manpower planning challenges on which administrators need help and advice.

What are the probable consequences, politically, socially and economically, of industrializing as rapidly as possible? What are the relative advantages of low labour input, high capital input activities to the political stability of the country as opposed to high labour, low capital input activities? Inasmuch as all under-developed countries are agricultural and will probably remain so for several generations, what are the employment implications of investment to raise agricultural output as opposed to industrial output? What place in employment objectives should handicraft, co-operative and cottage industry production have, in order to raise the productivity of workers with the least capital input?

What are the employment, social and political implications of land reform in a country like India where more 'rational' use of the land in Western terms would probably displace peasants from their tiny holdings? What are the implications of land reform for countries like Peru where the end of latifundia would require vast training, development and redeployment of manpower into agricultural pursuits to cultivate the land thus released?

Where are executives, professional and technical personnel to come from in the short run? Shall we encourage employers to bring them in from abroad? How establish training centres for executive, professional and technical personnel—in each underdeveloped country? Should this, for example, be done on a regional basis?

Should new industries be located close to their labour supplies or close to their other resources? What are the cost problems and the social and economic implications of resettling the work-force near the production sites? Does meeting the employment objectives require new institutions? Are employment exchanges needed? What is the role of the labour union in increasing productivity, acquainting new workers with industrial discipline, group production methods, occupational specialization, team operation, etc? Is there a necessary conflict between full employment and freedom of decision by workers and employers? What are the social costs of partially immobilizing the labour force in order to ensure full employment (even at very low real wages which may be the consequence of redundancy, low investment and under-utilization)?

How can marginally attached workers, agricultural workers of low productivity and others be brought into the labour market? What social protection do they need during transition? Should their earnings be subsidized during transition by pay in kind rather than in cash?

These questions are simply illustrative. They are bound together and require answers that transcend particular narrow statistical approaches. In finding the answers and in getting them adopted, the manpower practitioner could well follow the advice of Benjamin Franklin for the diplomat who, he said, must have 'sleepless tact, unmovable calm, and patience no folly, no provocation can shake'.

5

Summary of Discussion
and Conclusions (I)

I. *The objectives of economic development*

1. If the good things of life were abundant for the taking, there would be little interest in economic development or planning for it. Man, in his natural state, living in an Eden of plenty, need take little heed for the future. But in a modern society, peopled by a lively citizenry aware of its worth, conscious of its destiny, miserably mindful of the physical and social shortcomings of its present life, forethought and action for a more abundant future is the keystone of every political and economic attitude. Awareness that life is richer elsewhere and can be better everywhere, translates into dissatisfaction with the present, which in turn raises aspirations and expectations. A people sensible, peaceable and disciplined enough to have reached that level of rising expectations, is prepared for the next step in its fulfilment—organized planning and affirmative action for economic development. The principle of *laissez faire* or non-interference in economic matters, has everywhere been modified or abandoned. Today there is hardly a country in the world where economic planning of one type or another is not being done by the body politic.

2. It is plain that the ultimate objective of economic development is the satisfaction of the citizen's consumer needs. Put most simply the end of economic development is improved real consumer income for the individual, real income in goods and services of all kinds, chosen by the consumer to his taste and within his capacity to buy. It is most essential to keep this ultimate objective in mind if the society and its responsible leadership are not to confuse means and ends. There are inevitable antecedents necessary in supplying the capital goods, the social infrastructure, the marketing system to provide higher real consumer income, and the opportunity of productive employment for all who seek it.

3. Now, these generalizations apply to developed and under-developed countries alike. Every society, except on those occasions when it is diverted from its objective by natural catastrophe or war, is prepared to do what is timely and necessary to improve the lot of its people as consumers. And they all realize that it is necessary to create the preconditions for such increased production by providing for the capital goods and basic services which in turn would provide that improved level of life. But for the poor and under-developed country, using up all or most of its current product for current consumption, there is little or nothing to be set aside for building capital goods. Nor is it easy for under-developed countries to obtain capital from abroad, because they must compete with other capital-short countries which are already well advanced, which are, as it were, 'better risks', and which can give better evidence of an ability:

(a) to utilize the imported capital wisely; and
(b) to service the debt promptly.

4. It is one of the characteristic features of an under-developed country that it is at one and the same time plagued with all sorts of economic problems. There is low 'per capita' income, unemployment or under-employment, lack of technical, industrial, professional and scientific skills, over-dependence on imported manufactured goods and inelasticity of the supply of its own predominantly primary production. This confronts the planner with several competing economic challenges. Accordingly, economic development (like any other economic situation) poses the problem of choice-making, of rationing, of allocation. Four main steps are necessary to making those choices rational:

(a) an inventory of resources and capacities, in men, materials, production capacity and credit, including available domestic savings;
(b) identifying imbalances between resource sectors;
(c) deciding, on the basis of political, social and economic factors, which of the shortage sectors will have priority in allocating available resources;
(d) organizing the controls and machinery, public and private, to carry out the decisions and manage the economy.

5. To the harrassed administrator in a developing country, assailed by insistent demands on all sides for 'more', the fact that there is not

enough of anything is painfully obvious. Yet there is an exception. The one resource that is abundant in most under-developed countries is the human resources—perhaps raw and untrained but eager and willing. That very abundance, indeed, can be one of the reasons why those countries are under-developed! The economic development planner is well advised, then to concentrate as much as possible of his investment effort on improving and utilizing that one abundant resource for economic growth and stability. In summary, the goals of economic planning are:

(a) to achieve progress in raising standards of living, by providing jobs for the growing labour force, and ensuring that the real incomes of the population in *per capita* terms increase; and

(b) to promote long-run and steady development, by fostering agriculture and encouraging new industries, improving the variety and quality of goods produced, assuring their economical distribution, providing import-substitution, export-promotion and the satisfaction of the growing demand both for consumers and necessary supporting producer goods.

II. *Planning for economic development*

6. Manpower planning is an integral part of economic planning because manpower availability is both a pre-condition and a prime test of feasibility of an economic plan and, also, because the goal of economic planning is to improve the lot of man himself. Considerations of manpower needs and availabilities thus play an important role in constructing a comprehensive plan of economic development, for both the public and the private sectors.

7. The most important parameter of such a plan is the average annual rate of growth of the national income. Governments will of course aim at fixing it at the highest attainable level. But the higher the rate of growth planned, the more investment capital will be required to attain it. Excessive emphasis on such investment would depress current consumption and investment on social overheads in the short run, even though, in the long-run, such a high rate of investment might contribute to an increase of the standard of living. The attainable rate of growth, furthermore, is often limited:

(a) by considerations of foreign trade balance and the difficulty of financing the imports of producer goods required by a higher rate of growth;

(b) by the rate of growth of supply and distribution of food which, in the developing countries, is the basic wage-good;

(c) by the availabilities of high level manpower of the kind required by the nature of the type of production postulated by the plan; and

(d) by financial considerations, arising from the difficulty of attracting private investment to projects of high social priority; and the difficulties involved in diverting national income to productive investment via taxation because of political and social obstacles in the way of establishing a progressive direct tax system and an equitable indirect tax structure.

8. The first step in the construction of a plan should consist in drawing up a crude outline *assuming* a rate of growth which is considerably higher than the past performance, but which eventually may have to be scaled down at further stages of plan elaboration, after testing for feasibility of attainment. Next we have to make assumptions, again as a first approximation to be corrected afterwards, about the capital co-efficient relative to productive investment, and the rate of increase of inventories. Then, by deducting productive investment and the increase in inventories from the prospective national income, we determine as a residual the sum of consumption and of funds available for investment in social overheads. Splitting of this total into the two components above, may need to be done somewhat arbitrarily, on the basis of a thorough knowledge of the political and social situation prevailing in the country and of the people's non-deferrable needs in education, health and housing arising from the general goals pursued by the plan. The next step is to establish, in general, the industrial structure desired for the national income, on basis of assumptions about the likely or the desirable pattern of consumption, as well as of the prospects of foreign trade.

9. At this still preliminary stage the supply of, and demand for, manpower must be examined in detail in order to check:

(a) whether the supply of skilled or semi-skilled labour will meet the demand created by the economic expansion as postulated in the plan; and

(b) whether the employment opportunities provided in the plan are consistent with its goals. Such an examination may prompt conclusions, leading to a revision of targets outlined in the plan, to adjustments in the sectoal allocation of investments, as well as to recommendations about the choice of techniques to be adopted within the possible range of substitution of capital by labour.

10. The above exercise should be repeated several times, each stage differing from the previous by the adjustments made in the light of inconsistencies or infeasibilities detected at the previous stage. By successive approximations it is possible to arrive in this way at a consistent variant of the plan. To make easier the task of the politicians, who will take the final decision, it is usually advisable to present more than one variant of the plan. In particular, it might be rewarding to build two to three alternatives with different employment and other targets.

11. Thus, considerations of manpower policy play a crucial role in the different stages of construction of a comprehensive plan: at the stage of formulation of general goals, at the stage of checking the consistency of the plan and at the stage of formulating concrete recommendations on productive investment. It is necessary to state in the plan all the manpower implications of the assumed rate and pattern of growth. At the same time it is necessary to include in the plan an action programme for manpower, and to arrive at decisions about the necessary and appropriate investment in social overheads.

III. *Integrating manpower planning with overall development planning*

12. To reiterate what has gone before, manpower constitutes both the means of, and reason for, economic development. Hence, planning for manpower resources must be an organic part of overall planning. There are several reasons why this is necessary. Firstly, the numbers and skills of the labour force determine the extent to which other resource potentials may be put to work. Secondly, manpower is the resource that lends itself to the greatest adaptation to meet development needs. Through foresighted education and training, manpower can be developed to meet almost any conceivable development problem. Thirdly, the preparation of manpower for technical and skilled occupations requires more lead time than any other aspect of development. The building of a steel plant or a dam requires a relatively brief period of time as compared with the training of a metallurgist or a highly qualified engineer.

13. For these reasons planning for manpower resource development must begin when overall planning begins or even earlier, and remain

continuously interwoven with it. Organizationally, manpower planning should be a major wing of the overall planning machinery. This is necessary for purposes of plan integration and co-ordination. Each ministry, public organization and private industry should be directly responsible for manpower planning within their respective areas of responsibility. However, this planning must be brought together and woven into an overall manpower plan in order for it to be integrated into total national planning. Functionally, there are four main ways in which manpower planning should be integrated with overall planning:

(a) participating in determining plan targets with regard to magnitude, distribution and timing of employment;

(b) helping to determine the manpower feasibility of overall plans for economic and social development, in terms of skills, numbers, location and timing;

(c) assessing the resources required for manpower development to meet plan needs. These include resources for educational and training institutions, economic incentives, housing, health, etc.

(d) monitoring the year by year progress of manpower programmes as they relate to the overall development programmes. This involves adjusting manpower plans to the evolving requirements of the overall plan, or recommending modifications in the overall plan which may be required for manpower reasons.

In this way, manpower planning contributes both to the formulation and the implementation of the economic development plan.

IV. *Observations in respect of Nigeria*

14. Ideally manpower planning should be comprehensive. It should include in its purview not only a review of the manpower requirements of the country but also the education programme, the in-service training of workers and the provision of incentives to get people into important areas, industries and occupations. On the other hand, economic planning should have as its main theme the mobilization of the resources of a country, both human and material, in such a way that the highest increase in national income is obtained—consistent with the general goals of the plan.

15. Comprehensive economic and manpower planning are relatively new undertakings in Nigeria. There has not yet been the opportunity for the full exchange of views and problems in a reciprocal fashion

between economic and manpower planners. Successive economic plans should be devised to give more specific attention to the manpower dimension and the capability of the labour force to carry out the plan. Education in Nigeria, for example, is not specifically or consciously planned to meet the requirements of economic development as set down in the Six-Year National Development Plan, 1962–8. The educational system is primarily geared to provide general education rather than to emphasize functional, technical and vocational education.

16. Similarly, forecasting manpower requirements has not been done within the context of the general economic development plan. The tentative forecast of manpower requirements made by the Manpower Secretariat and discussed by the Seminar, was based on the assumption of full employment of the entire Nigerian labour force by 1968. That goal is obviously unattainable and not consistent with the investment, production and consumption levels adopted for the Economic Development Plan which does not itself contain specific provision for employment targets. When there is more nearly perfect relationship between manpower planning and general economic planning, such future manpower forecasting should be made within the context of the Economic Development Plan and designed as a complement to that plan.

17. The drawing up of the successor to the 1962–8 plan should be used as a grand opportunity to review the entire position of manpower in Nigeria. The present plan did not take full account of the manpower implications of its main objective—the growth in national income of 4 per cent per annum. Even though references were made to the scarcity of skilled manpower and the need to create more employment opportunities, the plan did not give the lead as to how to tackle these problems. Future economic plans should examine what the manpower implications are and, if possible, make arrangements in good time for the provision of appropriate numbers of high-level manpower, having regard to the effects of the plan on both the public and private sectors of the economy. If scarcity of high-level manpower is a bottleneck to economic development, as it has been in Nigeria, the realization of a desired rate of growth in the economy may be frustrated by inadequate attention to the manpower problem.

18. In aiming at raising national income by 4 per cent per annum, it had been assumed that the rate of population growth should continue at about 2 per cent. But the result of the recent population census implies that the 1963 population was higher than assumed and increas-

ing at a rate higher than 2 per cent per annum. Hence, a 4 per cent national income rise would yield a lower *per capita* income than had been expected, and the danger of growing unemployment, which is already noticeable, would become more acute. Unemployment and under-employment are twin problems which have bedevilled Nigeria for some time. Future plans should pay more attention to employment objectives—stating how many employment opportunities are to be created each year and which techniques would make the realization of the employment objectives possible. The manpower office should be charged with devising and recommending proper methods of manpower development, deployment and utilization.

V. *Recommendations*

19. In view of the foregoing discussion, the following recommendations are proposed:

(1) Organizational arrangements should be made now for assuring integration and complementarity of manpower planning with overall economic planning in Nigeria.

(2) Manpower administration includes planning, execution and control; the manpower organization must, therefore, maintain a continuing review of progress, identifying and anticipating failures to meet the plan and recommending remedial changes, if necessary.

(3) Checking of the employment potential of the present plan and making a study of the employment prospects in the public and private sectors including the agricultural and non-agricultural sectors must be speeded up. Maximization of employment should be taken as a keynote of plan development. Planning is a continuous process and, therefore, such an inquiry will, in any case, be necessary for the elaboration of the next plan. The results should, therefore, be known before 1966, on the assumption that the elaboration of the next plan should start in 1967.

(4) The participation of public, professional, educational, business, and labour groups in developing the next plan and in carrying it out, should be provided for with urgent priority.

(5) Manpower planning should reflect a comprehensive concept of high-level manpower. The needs of national development include the competent professional people in the physical sciences,

engineering, administration, craft skills and social sciences and humanities.

(6) More resources should be invested in the training and upgrading of the employed labour force, especially by employers, on-the-job.

(7) As planning of manpower training involves a time horizon of up to as much as 15 years, a projection (or a set of alternative projections) is needed of the economic development of Nigeria up to 1980 in terms of:

(a) national income and its industrial origin:

(b) structure of employment, confronted with the projections of labour force.

Such a set of projections should be worked out in collaboration between the manpower office and the Ministry of Economic Development.

(8) In view of the mounting demographic pressure, growing urban unemployment, rural and urban underemployment, and excessive urbanization, special attention should be devoted to the study, on a regional as well as a national basis, of the possibility of creating jobs in the villages by itensifying and diversifying agriculture, improving the infrastructure and expanding food processing and other consumer goods and other industries. The opportunity for using labour intensive techniques in development schemes should be fully examined.

(9) To meet the growing needs of employment in the future, it should be a part of planning to emphasize the setting up of basic industries consistent with the natural resources of the country.

Part Two

Machinery and Methodology of Manpower Planning and Forecasting

6

The Objectives, Machinery and Methodology of Manpower Planning

Frederick H. Harbison

PROFESSOR OF ECONOMICS, PRINCETON UNIVERSITY

This paper deals with three aspects of manpower or human resources development: I. Objectives; II. Machinery; and III. Methodology. It stresses in particular the problem of newly developing countries with partially planned economies. In many aspects, it reflects the basic approach and philosophy of manpower development which appear to be emerging in Nigeria and some of the other new nations of Africa. This particular paper is part of a more comprehensive treatment of the subject which may be found in the book entitled, *Education, Manpower and Economic Growth*, by Frederick Harbison and Charles A. Myers.[1]

I. *Objectives of Manpower Planning*

The central objective of manpower planning is to construct a strategy of human resource development which is consistent with a country's broader aims of social, political and economic development. At the outset, let us be clear about the scope of manpower planning. At the very minimum, manpower planning includes planning of the formal education system, planning of in-service training and adult education, analysis of the structure of incentives and the utilization of manpower, as well as surveys of manpower requirements. It should also include the analysis of unemployment and underemployment and appropriate measure for alleviating them. All of these things, I am happy to note, come within the broad jurisdiction of the National Manpower Board in Nigeria.

In more specific terms, I would suggest that the objective of a man-

[1] Published by McGraw-Hill Book Company, New York, 1964.

power or human resource development strategy is to arrive at an effective balance in choices of policy objectives. Some of the critical areas of choice for the partially planned economy are the following:

(a) In all areas of formal education, the relative emphasis on *quality* versus *quantity*.

(b) In secondary and higher education, the stressing of science and technical subjects versus law, arts and humanities.

(c) In skill development, the relative reliance on pre-employment formal training versus in-service or on-the-job training.

(d) In building incentives, the conscious manipulation of wage and salary structures versus dependence on market forces.

(e) In the general rationale of human resource development, consideration of the desires of individual versus the needs of the country.

A newly developing country is compelled to make difficult choices, and it should make these choices on the basis of rationally determined priorities.

The choice between quantity and quality in educational development may take many forms. In some countries it is necessary to choose between primary education for all or high-quality secondary and university education for a smaller number of potential leaders. There is always a choice between educating fewer students with better-qualified teachers and larger numbers with unqualified teachers; and there is also the choice between a good but a costly curriculum and a poor but cheaper one. In general, political and social pressures make for emphasis on quantity, whereas the achievement of rapid economic growth makes it imperative to emphasize the quality of high-level manpower required for development.

The choice between science and technology versus the law, arts and humanities in secondary and higher education is a difficult one for all nations. In a country such as Nigeria, there are critical shortages of technical manpower. There are also pervasive shortages of good teachers, managers, administrators and social scientists. But there are also needs for artists, writers, musicians, jurists, historians and students of African culture. In part, the choice is one between expensive education and cheap education, as we have noted above. But, in important respects, it is also related to the values and ideals of the nation. Social and political pressures tend to stress the importance of the more liberal, non-scientific type of education, whereas economic considerations demand greater concentration on science and technology.

In building technical skills, particularly at the craft level, countries may choose to place primary responsibility for training on the formal education system or they may attempt to shift most of the burden to the employing institutions. In practice, training and retraining is a continuous lifetime process of human development, and thus the employing institutions cannot escape responsibility for some training. Ideally, the role of the schools, particularly at the secondary level, is to produce broadly-educated persons who are readily trainable. But some training probably must be provided, prior to employment, by the schools and more can be offered through various kinds of 'sandwich', extension and part-time courses for those already employed. A strong case can be made, of course, for pre-employment sub-professional and professional training in higher education, but an equally strong argument can be made for continuation training and retraining conducted by joint efforts of employers, labour unions and educational institutions. In this area, the rational choice are essentially technical in nature, but they are also influenced significantly by social and political pressures. For example, in some countries labour organizations have not only developed leadership training and worker education programmes, but have also pressed for broader access to formal education.

No country today can rely completely upon market forces to provide the incentives for its people to engage in the kinds of activities most critically needed for development. In some cases, the status and compensation of engineers, scientists or agricultural specialists are too low. In nearly all countries, the pay of teachers is inadequate, and the rewards of sub-professional personnel and technicians are far from sufficient to attract the numbers needed. The preferences for urban living, the forces of tradition, and historical differentials, all tend to distort the market for critical skills. Thus, all countries must take some deliberate measure to influence the allocation of manpower, and these measures may range from outright compulsion to various kinds of financial and non-financial inducements. In general the more rapid the pace of planned development, the more deliberate these measures must become.

Finally, there is the crucial choice between the interests of the individual and the interests of the state in virtually all phases of manpower development. Does the state exist for the individual, or the individual for the state? The answer is never simple. A manpower strategy may have as its central goal the enhancement of the freedom, dignity and worth of man, but man has some obligations to help build the kind of economy which can provide decent living standards and protection of basic freedom. In all societies, therefore, there must be some compromise, or perhaps blending of the interests of the state and the individual. The actual blend will vary with the political and ideological character of the society.

As already noted, the objective of a manpower strategy is to strike the right balance in these critical areas of choice. The nature of this balance depends upon the goals of a society, its level of development, and its leadership. A country which fails to achieve a proper balance will produce the wrong kind of high-level manpower; it will invest in the wrong kind of education; it will allow the perpetuation of the wrong kind of incentives; and it will emphasize the wrong kind of training. In reality, no society achieves a perfect balance, the forces which make for an effective balance are constantly changing, so there must be a continuous process of successive adjustment.

II. *The Machinery of Manpower Planning*

There is now emerging some experience in the establishment of governmental machinery for manpower planning. Among the non-communist countries, India has probably done more in this field than any other country. Ghana, Nigeria and Tanganyika and one or two other countries are in various stages of establishing human resource planning boards. The time has come for more intensive study of this process as well as exchange of significant experience.

There are many potential participants in both the formation and the implementation of a strategy of human resource development. Within the central government the ministries of education and labour obviously have major roles to play. Many other ministries, however, are vitally concerned with education, training and development of particular categories of manpower. The government establishment office is concerned with personnel in the public sector; the public health ministry, more particularly with doctors, dentists, nurses and the medical technicians; the agriculture ministry, with agronomists, veterinarians, foresters and their various assistants; the ministry of industry and commerce, with manpower for private and public enterprises; the armed forces, with military personnel; and so forth. In addition, employer organization and labour unions are intimately concerned with manpower problems. This diffusion of interest and responsibility—for human resources development highlights the needs for organizational machinery which will:

(1) co-ordinate the activities of these various bodies;

(2) encourage forward planning on the part of each within its particular area of interest;

(3) assume responsibility for human resource assessments on a continuing basis;

(4) relate human resource programmes to planning in all other areas;

(5) construct and periodically revise a master strategy; and

(6) promote and review the implementation of the strategy which has been agreed upon.

In the newly developing countries, there are perhaps three major components of this machinery. The first is the establishment of a human resource or manpower development board. It should have representation from the appropriate government ministries and also from private employer and labour organizations. The functions of the board should be to allocate responsibility for various aspects of human resource planning to the appropriate ministries or groups, to review their plans and programmes, and to provide for co-ordination. The second is the establishment of appropriate planning staffs within the main participating bodies to shoulder the responsibilities agreed upon by the human resource development board. The ministry of education needs its own planning unit, as does the ministry of labour and perhaps others as well. And employer organizations should certainly be encouraged to set up staffs to work on programmes for training and manpower development. The third is the creation of a general human resource planning secretariat. In most cases, this secretariat can serve the human resource development board. It can also constitute the human resource staff of the national planning organization, if one exists. In any case, the key to success is the competence of this staff, because deliberations of busy and powerful political leaders on human resource or general planning boards can be only as sophisticated as the quality of their secretariat services.

The chairmanship, or location, of the human resource development board and the secretariat serving it are matters which are likely to be determined in different ways by particular governments. In some cases, the leadership of the board is viewed as a logical extension of the responsibility of the ministry of education, and in others it has been lodged in the ministry of labour. Where strong general planning organizations exist, there is a compelling reason to put the human resource planning machinery under its jurisdiction. In a few countries, human resource planning may be undertaken before the creation of general planning organizations, and here a case can be made to put it directly in the office of the prime minister. And in some countries, the staff-work on planning of all kinds is conducted by semi-independent organizations which are removed in part from the formal government machinery. The decision as to where to locate the planning function in a particular country may be made quite rightly in accordance with political criteria rather than with administratively-logical organization charts. In the end, the crucial question is whether the machinery works. The precise location of a planning unit in an organization chart is not a matter of major consequence; it is far more important to link the planning function to clearly identified centres of power wherever they may be. Particularly in the human resource area, the planning process needs to involve the local and regional as well as national government bodies and influential private groups. This is important to create 'systems of consent-building' which are essential if plans and strategies are to be implemented effectively.

The major tasks to be performed by the human resource planning staff, therefore, are not narrowly technical. To be sure, statisticians theoretical economists, engineers, or pedagogical experts may be needed to work on pieces of the problem, but the most critical skills required in the secretariat are organizational and political. The leading figures in the staff perhaps should be experts in their own right in particular fields of knowledge but their principal functions are to act act as 'transmission belts' for concepts, ideas and programmes in all fields of human resource development. They need social perspective, political insight and broad knowledge of their country's economic and social institutions. They must be promoters as well as judges. And above all they must be integrators and generalists. A human resource pro-gramme which consists of unrelated pieces is hardly better than no programme at all. The top staff men in the organizational machinery for human resource development should be strategy-builders rather than purely technical specialists.

III. *The Methodology for Setting Manpower Development Targets*

In order to formulate a strategy of manpower development for a particular country, it is essential to make a systematical assessment of its human resource problems and requirements. Such an assessment is much more comprehensive than a manpower survey or a study of formal education. It should include, at the minimum, an analysis of manpower requirements; the system of formal education; institutions for in-service training and adult education; and, the structure of incentives and the utilization of high-level manpower. It might also include some appraisal of problems of health improvement and nutrition. And, of course, it must be based upon an analysis of demographic trends and be related realistically to the social, political, and economic environment of the country.

In assessing the problems of human resource development, the most difficult task is estimating the future requirements for manpower. If these can be specified, it is then possible to plan programmes for the building of educational and training institutions and to estimate the costs involved. Also, if net requirements for manpower are estimated, it is possible to calculate the annual rate of withdrawal from the labour force because of death, retirement, or other causes during a planning period, thus arriving at figures for gross requirements. In the discussion which follows, therefore, it is assumed that the policy planner is in position to handle such tasks, and that his major problem is the estimation of future manpower requirements as a basis for the other decisions which he will have to make. Stripped to its essentials, the estimation of manpower requirements involves, firstly, a reasonably comprehensive analysis of the present situation, and secondly, using this as a base line, a forward estimate of long-run requirements for a period of perhaps 10 to 20 years. We shall discuss both in some detail.

The analysis of the present situation

The assessment of present and short-term manpower requirements, while fundamental as a basis for longer-range estimates, presents few serious methodological problems. Short range is considered here as a period of one to three years. The essential elements are:

(a) an inventory of employment and short-term requirements for manpower;
(b) a general appraisal of the educational system;
(c) a survey of existing programmes for on-the-job training; and
(d) a brief analysis of the structure of incentives and the utilization of high-level manpower.

An analysis of the present situation starts with a review of the available facts about the population and an inventory of the existing labour force. Where possible the probable or actual labour force participation rates for males and females should be obtained. Then an inventory of employment and short-term requirements should be made for each major sector of the economy. These should include as a minimum: agriculture, construction, mining, manufacturing, public utilities, transportation and communication, trade and commerce, education and government services (exclusive of education). Where appropriate, a more detailed choice of sectors can follow the classification used for the national accounting system or the economic development plan.

Within each sector, an estimate should be made of total employment as well as the extent of unemployment or underemployment.[2] In addition, employment should be broken down by major occupational categories in order to identify various classes of high-level manpower. Here the following categories made by Parnes for the 'Mediterranean Regional Project' of O.E.C.D. are useful.[3]

Class A: includes all occupations for which a university education or an advanced teachers college degree or its equivalent would normally be required.

[2] For a good description of the process, see Herbert S. Parnes, *Forecasting Educational Needs for Economic and Special Development*. (O.E.E.C., Paris, 1962) Section II.

[3] Parnes, ibid., Appendix B, pp. 77–87. An alternative approach using six occupational levels with educational requirements, has been used by the French Manpower Committee, Raymond Piognant, 'France' in *The Planning of Education in Relation to Economic Growth*, papers presented at Policy Conference on Economic Growth and Investment in Education, Part IV, Washington, 16–20 October 1961, Organization for Economic Co-operation and Development, Paris, February 1962, pp. 19–20.

Seven occupational-educational requirements categories are used in Czechoslovakian manpower, planning. Jan Auerhan, *Problems of Forecasting of Skilled Manpower Requirements*, mimeographed paper at Regional Seminar on Problems of Planning the Labour Force and its employment, Cairo, 11–22 March 1963 (organized jointly by the International Institute of Labour Studies, Geneva, and the Institute of National Planning, Cairo).

Class B: includes occupations for which two or three years of education beyond the secondary level (12 years) or its equivalent may be required.

Class C: includes occupations for which a secondary school education (either technical or academic) or its equivalent would normally be required.

A fourth category, Class D, encompasses all occupations not included in the above three classes. Parnes had grouped all of the 1,345 occupations defined in the International Standard Classification of Occupations into these four classes.

There are, of course, obvious difficulties involved in the use of this or any other system of occupational classification which attempts to relate occupations to formal education requirements. For example, the educational requirements for a graduate engineer, a physical scientist, an agronomist, or a doctor are reasonably clear. But those for teachers are not. In an advanced country, most primary school teachers would fall into Classes A or B since they would have a minimum of 14 to 16 years of formal education. But in many underdeveloped countries, the majority of elementary school teachers may have no more than a primary school education. In this case, they would fall in Class D and would not appear in the high-level manpower categories. The requirements for managers, technicians and foremen likewise are difficult to define in educational terms. Indeed, the educational level of persons in a wide variety of high-level occupations depends in part on the available supplies of educated manpower. In a relatively advanced country, employers can and do insist on higher standards of formal education than in less developed countries. In making the employment inventory, therefore, it is desirable to ascertain the actual educational attainment of the major categories of the labour force. Where this is impossible, one must rely on experienced judgement.

Within the three classes of high-level occupations described above, it is necessary to distinguish those requiring pre-employment technical training and those requiring largely general education. And in Classes A and B it is necessary to further subdivide the occupational categories so as, at least, to be able to distinguish managerial and administrative jobs from professional, scientific and technical occupations. An even more detailed breakdown, of course, is desirable if the information can be obtained.

The methods for making manpower inventories are now well-known.[4] They may be based on special or general census data, if available, or upon establishment surveys. The sample establishment survey, using interviews to supplement questionnaires, is perhaps the most reliable method, and it has one additional advantage of great importance. The establishments surveyed may be asked to report existing shortages as well as anticipated short-term needs for one to three years. They can also be asked to report on existing or desired qualifications of the labour force. Many of the recent manpower studies conducted in newly developing countries have in fact been based on some sort of establishment survey, and the inherent advantages of this method would warrant its use even where general census data is available.

The inventory of employment and short-term requirements, if conducted properly, serves three major purposes. It identifies immediate, short-range needs; it provides a base line for comparison with other countries and for making forward estimates; and it establishes a framework for making subsequent periodic inventories of manpower requirements. The manpower inventory necessitates collection of considerable statistical data, and it requires the use of experienced judgement (particularly in relating occupations to education).

The conceptual and methodological problems, however, are relatively simple.

The task of appraising the existing educational system is reasonably clear-cut. Data are needed on enrolments by age groups for the various grades in each educational level, the numbers of teachers by level and by qualification, the teacher-student ratios, wastage or drop-out rates, and school completion rates for each level. The curricula at each level should be evaluated in terms of immediately needed changes or improvements. Capital and recurring costs should be estimated for each level of education, and within each level for various types of education such as academic, technical, teacher training and others.

[4] Note the reference already cited on handbooks or manuals. By the middle of 1962, a sizeable number of manpower surveys had been made by experts from I.L.O., U.S.A.I.D., the Ford Foundation, and other organizations providing technical assistance in this field. Many others are planned or in process. Although actual publications setting forth methodological procedures are few, those persons who have made surveys can and do instruct others in the techniques involved. See also papers submitted to the *United Nations Conference on the application of Science and Technology for the Benefit of the less Developed Areas*, Geneva, 1963. (Section B-2: Techniques of Manpower Assessment and their Implications).

In many countries, specialized quantitative and qualitative studies are made for each level and type of education. Thus there may be surveys of primary schools, secondary schools, or post-secondary and higher education. Often technical education is singled out for special attention. Unfortunately, however, an analysis of training on the job or the structure of incentives is often lacking. Educational assessments should be made as part of a broader analysis of human resource problems, and the failure to do so makes it difficult subsequently to construct realistic long-range targets for development.

Human capital formation may start with formal education, but it does not end there. Most managerial, technical and craft skills, for example, are developed on the job much more effectively than in vocational schools. Indeed, in many countries, vocational or trade schools are quite inefficient and wasteful instruments of human capital formation. Better craft training would result from shifting more responsibility for skill development to the employing institutions. But in any case, it is just as important to make an analysis of the processes of skilled development of employed manpower as it is to make a survey of formal educational institutions.

In particular, attention should be given to programmes of administration and management development, supervisory training, craft training and apprenticeship. It should cover experience of large and small establishments of both government agencies and private enterprise. And, indeed, the discovery of the lack of concerted on-the-job training efforts is in itself important. An attempt should be made also to ascertain the degree of co-operation between the employing institutions and the vocational schools, the judgements of employers with respect to the usefulness of such pre-employment training, as well as the costs of in-service training programme.

Closely related to on-the-job training are programmes of general adult education, fundamental education as part of community development projects, and agricultural extension projects. A general study of the existing and possible roles of such activities is, of course, an essential part of any comprehensive human resource assessment.

Another significant but commonly neglected facet of the assessment of the current situation is the structure of incentives. Ideally, it would be desirable to have in every country a nationwide survey of wages and salaries coupled with analysis in depth of non-financial incentives which motivate persons in the various occupational categories of the labour force. Few countries can afford to make such a comprehensive survey. Nevertheless, it is possible to make an examination of a small number of critical occupations. If there are critical shortages of engineering technicians, for example, the differentials in compensation between sub-professional and fully qualified professional personnel might be explored. The differentials between certain administrative and technical jobs can be examined in cases where there is evidence to indicate a shortage in one and a surplus in another. The relative preference of persons for jobs in the city as compared with the rural areas should be noted, as well as the existence of unfilled places in agricultural and junior technical training centres. In many countries, furthermore, there is wide-spread under-utilization of certain kinds of highly skilled manpower, and the reasons for this should be determined. In most countries, the problems of incentives and proper utilization of manpower are well known to informed people in government and private enterprise. Admittedly, it may be difficult to quantify such problems. But to overlook them completely in a human resource assessment is a serious conceptual error.

The time available for surveys of the present situation may be short or long, and the staff may range from a single person to a large team of experts. As a practical matter, the human resource planner must do the best he can with the information he is able to get within prescribed limits of time and budget. Nevertheless, a preliminary survey, even if it is superficial, is better than no survey. The availability of statistical data is a great asset, but at the same time it is often necessary to make assessments even when statistics are poor or non-existent.

The manpower assessment, no matter how superficial or tentative, should cover the four areas described above. A survey of formal education by itself, or an assessment of present and short-term manpower requirements, without adequate consideration of on-the-job training and the structure of incentives, can be quite misleading. It may be necessary, of course, for several experts to collaborate in making an assessment of broad scope, but the net result should be an integrated rather than a one-sided analysis. It is far more important to aim for comprehensiveness than thoroughness in initial surveys of human resource development problems. For if the scope of the assessment of the present situation is too narrow, responsible programming for future development becomes quite unrealistic.

Procedures for estimating future requirements

The most difficult aspect of manpower analysis is the determination of long-term future requirements. Because of the long lead time required for human resource development, requirements must be estimated for a minimum of ten years and preferably for two decades in advance. This is obvious when one considers the time required to build schools, to train teachers, and to fill the education pipe lines in primary and secondary schools in order to expand the number of university graduates. For example, most of the potential university graduates for ten years in advance are already in secondary schools. Children now entering primary school will not emerge as secondary school leavers for approximately 12 years, nor as university graduates for at least 15 years, a longer time perspective than that encompassed in most economic development plans.

There is no generally accepted methodology for estimating future requirements. Nor is there a clear concept of the meaning of the term 'future requirements'. Some people talk about 'predicting' or 'forecasting' manpower requirements; others contend that they are making 'projections'. And still others emphasize the process of forward 'target-setting'. Let us briefly examine some of the more common approaches which are in current use.

A rather simple method of estimating future requirements is to ask existing establishments to specify them. This will provide an informed judgement of short-term requirements, it is quite unreliable for long-run estimates. The establishments which may be in existence 10 or 20 years hence may not be at all the same as the present ones. Furthermore, most employers are unwilling or unable to estimate what employment will be in the long run. As one exasperated owner of a business in Jordan is reported as saying, 'Such guessing is an impious act, for only Allah knows what the future may hold.' For these reasons, I consider that forecasts made by individual establishments are essentially part of an assessment of the present situation rather than a practical means of long-run estimates.

Another method is to use past trends as a means of projecting future requirements.[5] This method has been used in some advanced countries

[5] See Harold Goldstein, *Methods of Forecasting Demand for and Supply of Scientists and Engineers*, O.E.E.C., S.T.P. (58) 1 June 1958 (mimeographed) for description of this and other methods of projections in European countries. Also, see *Forecasting Manpower Needs for the Age of Science*, O.E.C.D., Paris, 1960; S.O. Doos, *Forecasting Manpower*

to estimate needs for high-level scientific and engineering manpower as well as for teachers. The procedure is to extrapolate past trends in the growth of the number of persons in the particular occupation, and then correlate this with total employment, production, population, Gross National Product, or some combination of such variables. The regression table thus obtained is then used to project future requirements for each occupation. This projection method has the advantage of simplicity, but its usefulness is limited. In many countries it is impossible to get past data for an adequate time series. And even where the data may be available, the assumption that future relationships can be derived from past trends is open to question. Actually, the concept of forward planning usually implies that the future will be different from the past. In some cases, however, the projection of trends may be useful as a check, along with other exercises performed in the process of constructing forward targets.

A more complicated method is what Beckerman and Parnes described as the 'manpower requirements approach to educational planning'.[6] Here the estimation of changes in productivity is the critical factor. The steps in this approach are the following.

The analysis of the existing manpower structure is made along the lines which were described earlier. The patterns of output for the various sectors of the economy are projected for the forecast year, usually as set forth in an economic development plan. Then total employment for the economy as well as for each sector is estimated on the basis of some assumptions about productivity. For each sector, the total employment for the forecast year is allocated among the various occupations according to the occupational classification system which has been chosen. Then the requirements for each occupational category are aggregated from the various sectors to give the total stocks required in the forecast year. Here, however, allowance must be made for the effects of increases in productivity on the occupational structure. As productivity increases, of course, the proportion of persons in high-level occupations increases relatively to those in the lesser skilled jobs.

Requirements by Occupational Categories, prepared for Training Course for Human Resource Strategists, Frascati, Italy, 1962. Directorate of Scientific Affairs, O.E.C.D., Paris (mimeographed); and National Science Foundation, *The Long Range Demand for Scientific and Technical Personnel*, A Methodological Study, Washington, 1961.

[6] See, Parnes, op. cit., and also Wilfred Beckerman, *Methodology for Projection of Educational Requirements*, Mediterranean Regional Project (StP.–22), Directorate for Scientific Affairs, O.E.C.D., Paris, 1962 (mimeographed).

In practice, however, one must make assumptions regarding the influence of productivity increases on occupational structure, since there are very little reliable data on which to base objective calculations. The supply of personnel with each major type of educational qualification is estimated for the forecast year on the basis of present stocks, anticipated outflows from the existing educational system as presently planned, and allowances for losses due to death, retirement, and other reasons for withdrawal from the labour force. The estimated outputs from the educational system are compared with the required outputs as thus determined. And, finally, the orders of magnitude for expansion of the educational system are then established to close the gap between anticipated requirements and presently expected supply.

This method, perhaps, has the greatest appeal to economic development planners, and with modifications has been used by most of the countries in the Mediterranean Regional Project.[7] It links manpower requirements to productivity; it is designed to identify high-level manpower bottlenecks which could hamper production; and thus it appears logically to relate human resource needs to economic requirements.

This approach, however, has some shortcomings. Although the productivity criterion may be appropriate for the manufacturing, construction, mining and transportation sectors, it is not so useful for estimating high-level manpower requirements in public health, general activities of governments and many kinds of services. It is questionable also whether in agriculture it is possible to estimate future employment by predicting what productivity will be, particularly in countries where there may be extensive disguised unemployment and under-utilization of labour on the land. Some countries, of course, merely assume that the labour which cannot be employed in other activities will have to be retained on the land. But, in any case, a simple estimate of future productivity is unlikely to provide any clues about the quantity and quality of high-level manpower needed in agriculture.

Perhaps the most troublesome problem is the lack of empirical data on which to base estimates of expected increases in productivity and the bearing of these on changes in occupational requirements. In practice, one can do little more here than to make general assumptions.

[7] This is a co-operative education planning effort by Turkey, Greece, Yugoslavia, Italy, Spain and Portugal, which was organized by the office of Scientific and Technical Personnel of the Organization for Economic Co-operation and Development (O.E.C.D.).

For example, one may assume that in the forecast year the average productivity of all factories in a particular sector will equal the present productivity of the most modern ones. Or, one can assume that average productivity of the manufacturing sector in Country A in the forecast year will approximate present productivity of a comparable sector in Country B which is somewhat more advanced.[8]

Another problem inherent in this approach as well as in most others, is the determination of required educational qualification of high-level occupations for the forecast year. To a large extent, these may depend upon the supply structure of educated persons at that time. Here again, one is forced to make assumptions, and these are often made on the basis of comparisons with other countries.

Another possible criticism of the manpower requirements approach is that it gives an impression of making forecasts or predictions about a future situation. Because of the complexity of economic, social and political events, predictions are dangerous. However, the manpower requirements approach need not be linked to forecasts and could be used as a method for target setting, a concept which we shall discuss shortly.

In the end, the validity of the 'manpower requirements' approach rests upon the reasonableness of the assumptions made about productivity, and these assumptions, in most cases, must be based upon international comparisons. Some countries, which have adequate time-series data, may make projections on the basis of past trends, and for some manufacturing sectors it may be possible to estimate both productivity and occupational requirements where the precise future technology of production has already been determined. Nevertheless, it is quite misleading to think that future manpower requirements based on productivity analysis are less subject to arbitrary judgement than other approaches.

Beckerman and Parnes also have described an alternative approach

[8] For example, a Puerto Rican manpower survey made in 1957 assumed that industrial productivity in that country would rise by 1975 to the level of the United States in 1950, and that paralleled occupation groups should have equivalent educational requirements.

The survey of manpower and education requirements in Italy made its productivity calculation (except for agriculture) by assuming that in 1975 productivity would reach that attained by France in 1960.

For further discussion of problems of productivity assumptions, see Parnes, op. cit., and Michel Debeauvais, *Methods of Forecasting Long-Term Manpower Needs*, paper prepared for Training Course for Human Resources Strategists, Frascati, Italy, 1962, O.E.C.D., Paris.

which they call 'the social objectives method'.[9] Unlike the manpower requirements approach which attempts to define education needs in terms of productivity and a given pattern of economic growth, the 'social objectives' approach recognizes that education serves more than economic ends.

It assumes that a more educated labour force will itself tend to promote economic growth, and that it is neither necessary nor desirable to attempt to measure specific manpower requirements for economic objectives. This method concentrates, therefore, on identifying deficiencies in the present educational system in the light of social and educational objectives, and it projects future needs in terms of estimated population increases and the desire of persons for education at various levels. Certain goals are taken for granted such as elimination of illiteracy, increasing enrolment ratios in secondary education, decreasing the student-teacher ratios to desirable levels, lowering wastage rates, and improvement of standards. These goals, in effect, are suggested by making comparisons with other countries. Then the targets for future development are based upon a statistical calculation of the logistics and costs of satisfying these goals in varying periods of time.

This approach has been favoured traditionally by educators. It bypasses completely the difficult determination of occupational requirements. But at the same time, it overlooks essential economic problems. If this approach is used, there is likely to be little integration of the work of the educational planners and the economic planners, and in the end the latter are likely to recommend that expenditures for education, along with other social activities, be given a lower priority than investments in projects which are clearly productive and appear to contribute more directly to economic growth.

Other methods of estimating future manpower and education needs have been suggested, including the very imaginative Tinbergen-Correa model.[10] Using what they call a simple model of the input-output type, the authors attempt to relate directly needed secondary and higher education outputs to given rates of economic growth, without using the intermediate step of calculating occupational requirements. Essentially, the number of persons required from each educational level

[9] See Parnes, op. cit., and Beckerman, op. cit.

[10] Tinbergen, J., *Quantitative Adaption of Education to Accelerated Growth*, paper prepared for Training Course for Human Resource Strategists, Frascati, Italy, 1962. Directorate for Scientific Affairs, O.E.C.D., Paris (mimeographed).

is calculated from a series of linear difference equations which relate the stock of person completing a given level of education and the number of students in each level to the aggregated volume of production. Its purpose is to suggest what structure of the education system is needed in order to 'let the economy grow at a certain rate', and how that structure should change with changes in the growth rate.

Certainly, the mathematical formulation of this model offers no grounds for criticism, but the assumptions implicit in the use of certain technical coefficients are open to question. For example, it is assumed that the number of persons with secondary education and also with higher education is proportional to the volume of production in the same time period. Such an assumption is based upon judgement pure and simple. Likewise, the coefficients expressing teacher-student ratios are based upon rather questionable assumptions, those actually used being derived from United States experience. Depending upon one's judgement, of course, coefficients derived from other countries could be used, or perhaps they might even be artificially constructed.

Another implied assumption in the Tinbergen-Correa model is that in the present situation the number of persons with secondary and higher education is the correct number for the existing level of aggregated production. In practice, however, there are usually acute shortages or even sizeable surpluses. Moreover, implicitly, this model assumes that technology and productivity in the time period remain constant, and it thus completely overlooks what effect such factors might have on required occupations and hence required educational qualifications. Finally, the model as presently developed draws no distinction between types of education (technical or academic), makes no allowance for qualitative imbalances in school curricula, and fails to distinguish between the major economic sectors of the economy.

In conclusion, the practical use of the Tinbergen-Correa model, as well as other approaches, depends upon the validity of the assumptions made with respect to empirical facts. To the extent that empirical evidence is unavailable, one must make judgements. Thus this model, although giving the appearance of methodological precision, is actually no less dependent upon guesswork than any other approach. To be sure, when empirical evidence becomes available, the assumptions regarding the technical coefficients may be changed accordingly. Likewise, the model can and should be expanded to include other variables such as increases in productivity, and with refinements it could be used to make estimates for educated manpower by occupation and by sector. But at present it provides no substitute for the use of experienced judgement, and is no more objective than any other approach.

Before proceeding to outline some of my own suggestions on methodology, it may be useful to summarize my views on the existing methodology. Firstly, there is confusion about *the concept* of estimating future needs. Is the aim to make forecasts, to construct projections, or to establish targets? The distinction is important. In the modern world, it is really impossible to predict what is going to happen in particular countries or regions, regardless of the techniques which may be employed. Here I find myself in agreement with Beckerman who has said:

> People who believe that economists should be capable—provided they are smart enough and provided they equip themselves with the necessary gadgets, such as input-output tables, demand functions, intra-firm comparison, field surveys, etc.—really to foretell the future are, to my mind, in the same category as members of ancient tribes who attributed similar powers to their witch doctors.

Projections, of course, are different from forecasts. They express the logical consequences of assumed courses of action. They are helpful in determining what needs to be done if certain objectives are to be attained, or perhaps what will happen anyway if certain objectives are in fact achieved. Targets, on the other hand, are operational direction indicators based upon projections and reasonable judgements. The methodology of manpower analysis would be greatly improved if both the concept and the term 'forecast' were discarded, and if analysis would indicate clearly when they are making projections or setting targets.

Secondly, the purpose of manpower estimates are too narrowly conceived. Most projection or target-setting exercises aim only at estimates of requirements for formal education. This is important, but forward estimates of human resource development needs should be designed also to identify on-the-job training needs, required changes in the structure of incentives, and measures for better utilization of high-level manpower. In this respect, the Tinbergen-Correa model, which ignores the estimate of occupational requirements, is particularly unsatisfactory. Human resource development should never be equated exclusively with formal education development, and any methodology which assumes that they are, is inherently deficient.

Thirdly, the validity of all the various approaches depends in the final analysis upon the *judgement exercised in making assumptions*. Empirical evidence upon which to make really objective findings is not now available, nor is it likely to be in the future. The development of mathematical models, though useful in giving a systematic view of possible relationships, will not itself bring about greater accuracy or precision in forward estimates.

Fourthly, in practice most manpower analyists agree that it is necessary to combine different approaches. For example, the so-called 'social objectives approach' which stresses enrolment ratios and comparisons between countries can be combined with the manpower requirements methods which establishes a relationship between education and economic growth and identifies skill bottle-necks which may seriously impede economic progress. And similarly the use of mathematical models is appropriate if one is clear about what he should solve for as well as about the range of the assumptions he is making.

Fifthly, once the task of estimating future requirements is completed, the problems of determining the costs of expansion of educational institutions are not serious. Data on costs are usually available, the methodologies for estimation are reasonably clear-cut, and realistic assumptions are more easily made. Finally, as suggested earlier, the major problems of human resource analysis are conceptual. They involve the purpose of manpower estimates, the scope of assessments, and the relevancy of qualitative as well as quantitative data. The problems of methodology, particularly those requiring judgement in making assumptions, are far from solved, but progress here would be more rapid if there were less confusion about concepts.

The lack of empirical data, though admittedly a problem, is not a major roadblock. The development of clear concepts and systematic methodology will ultimately determine the kind of empirical data which is most relevant, and thus perhaps forestall the collection of facts and figures for which there would be little use. In any case, the present dearth of statistical data provides no excuse for failure to develop sharper concepts and more systematic methods of analysis.

The target-setting approach

In estimating forward requirements for manpower, the purposes of human resource development must be clearly understood. Without some kind of normative rationale, any exercise in estimating future needs is futile. Thus the first principle in the analysis of manpower requirements is that goals be specified. This is clearly a conceptual matter. Let us start with the premise that, in itself, an educated, skilled, and reasonably healthy population is an essential condition for economic growth, but at the same time it is an end in itself. There is no reason to believe that the people of the free world place a higher value on an increase in material wealth than on an increase in health, the expansion of educational opportunities and the opportunity for self-development of their innate capacities. They want all of these things and more.

In more specific terms, the goals of a society are often expressed by its leaders, sometimes with or without the consensus of the population. For example, the leaders of a newly developing country may propose goals such as the following: land reform and improvements in agricultural production, universal primary education, rapid industrialization, a position of leadership in the struggle for independence against new colonialism, the rapid replacement of expatriates in high positions by local national citizens, a huge power and irrigation dam, a steel mill, a television network, an international airline, or an impressive university of spectacular architectural design. Some of these goals are economic, some political, some cultural, and others predominately status symbols. The advanced countries, likewise, have a mixed bag of goals. They may seek expansion of industry and trade, full employment, expansion of higher education, acceleration of basic and applied research, armed forces capable of defence from any enemy, more opportunity for cultural creativity, or the prestige of sending a man to the moon. To achieve any or all of these goals, high-level manpower is required. And it would be very difficult for any country to attempt to make a sharp distinction between the human resources required for economic goals and those required for social, political, or cultural ends.

The manpower planner thus has a difficult problem. In assessing the nature of goals in a particular country, he is aware that some are openly stated, some are simply implied, and others may appear to him to be frivolous or capricious. He must somehow select those which the available evidence indicates are most important and most generally accepted. And he must check the legitimacy of his selections with opinion leaders, politicians, statesmen and others. Obviously, however, if all goals were to be attained within a short time, the costs of developing the required human resources would be beyond the means of any country. Consequently, both goals and requirements may need to be reassessed, and priorities have to be determined by the country's responsible leaders.

The second principle is that major reliance should be placed on making reasonable comparisons both within an economy and with other countries. In modern times, most nations tend to formulate their economic, social and political goals by comparing themselves with other countries. They may seek to follow good examples set by others; they may be intent on following a divergent path from a certain country; or they may wish to avoid particular mistakes which others have made. Similarly, the propensity is strong to compare one region of a country with another. For example, educational goals in many countries are based on the idea that the most backward regions should, in the future, be brought up to the present average standard, or that the general average should be brought up to the standard of the presently most advanced region.

The third principle is that in estimating future requirements the human resource planner should concentrate on *setting targets* rather than on making forecasts. The purpose of target-setting is not to make a prediction of what will take place; nor is it to make projections on the basis of limited assumptions of attainment of one or two specific objectives. Its purpose is rather to *influence* the future course of development. A target indicates a direction for action. Its precise quantitative dimension is far less important than its function of indicating the direction of activity for achievement of specified goals.

If one is clear that he is engaged in a target-setting exercise, no apologies need to be made for basing estimates where necessary on judgement. Of course, the data, the assumptions, the projections and the comparisons on which the judgements are based should be clearly indicated. The target should establish a correct direction for policy, but its location ought to be changed as better judgements are possible. If appropriate, a range of targets based upon alternate assumptions may be presented. But in setting targets, the main concern is to establish a course of action, even if this must be tentative or preliminary.

A fourth principle is that requirements for human resource development be comprehensive. It is not enough to establish a single target for higher education, for secondary education, or even for all formal education. The closely associated targets for on-the-job training, for changing the structure of incentives, for importing expatriate manpower, for better utilization of skills, and for creating adequate employment opportunity should be established along with educational targets. The assessment of human resource development 'in pieces' is perhaps the greatest single deficiency for the manpower and educational surveys which have been conducted in the past. And this deficiency, incidentally, is responsible for much of the difficulty experienced in the integration of human resource planning with general planning for development.

Within the context of the four conceptual principles stated above, the problems of methodology come into sharper focus. Among the more important are the following: the sensitivity of estimates, relationships of occupations to education, the making of comparisons, the construction of 'multipliers', and the interpretation of 'shortfalls'.

The sensitivity of long-range estimates of manpower requirements is governed largely by the analysis of the present situation. The occupational categories, the sectors chosen for analysis, and the problem areas which are identified constitute the base lines for construction of long-range targets. If detailed breakdowns of sectors and occupations are desired (i.e. if great sensitivity in analysis is thought to be important), then the survey of the present situation must be designed accordingly.

It is neither necessary nor desirable to estimate needs for a large number of specialized occupations. In dynamic economies there is a great amount of movement from one occupation to another, and the needs for specialized skills are apt to fluctuate rather sharply. It is necessary, of course, to calculate the number of persons who should have a secondary or higher education or its equivalent, and here a distinction needs to be made between technical and general education. It is not necessary, however, to distinguish occupations requiring very specific training, particularly if much of this training can be acquired on the job. A few examples will serve as illustrations. Certainly, there is no need to calculate separately the long-run needs for carpenters, painters, fitters, welders and so forth. A general estimate for highly skilled craftsmen is sufficient. In the sub-professional categories, principal foremen and technicians in industry may be lumped together, as can nurses and other medical technicians. But, in the higher administrative and professional categories, more distinctions are required. For example, separate estimates are desirable for doctors, scientists and engineers, and if possible the major branches of science and the major branches of engineering (mechanical, civil, electrical and industrial) should be distinguished. In the managerial and administrative category, a distinction must be made between executives in fairly large and complicated establishments and the manager-proprietors of small family businesses. And, finally, the requirements for teachers at the three levels of education should be estimated, with a further designation, if possible, of those needed for the teaching of technical and scientific subjects. In practice, it is very difficult to get reliable information even on the limited range of occupations mentioned above, so that in most cases one is forced to use broader occupational categories.

The conversion of occupational requirements into educational requirements is one of the most perplexing problems in manpower analysis. As we have seen, Parnes made a threefold classification of occupations based on various levels of education or their equivalents. Parnes further points out, quite correctly, that estimates of educational requirements cannot be made mechanically on the basis of the total numbers in each classification. It is necessary to make assumptions, in Class A for example, about the proportions of persons in each group who should be expected to have completed a university education or an advanced teachers' college course, and the proportion who may be expected to fall into this group because of having 'equivalent' qualifications.

Except in the case of a few professions, there is no precise relationship between occupations and educational background. One cannot be sure whether an administrator or manager must have a university education. In many African countries most elementary schoolteachers have only a primary education, whereas in the advanced countries they require completion of some form of higher education. Presumably, skilled craftsmen need a secondary-level education, yet petroleum companies have demonstrated that men who are hardly literate can be trained as painters, carpenters, or welders in less than a year. As indicated already, the supply of educated manpower determines in part the demand also. In similar activities, an advanced country will absorb many more highly educated persons than an under-developed country. And in less developed countries, certain production processes can be designed to utilize effectively persons with very limited education.

Obviously, then, the assumptions about the relationship of occupations to educational levels will differ from country to country. And here again the manpower analyst must rely on judgement rather than on precise data. His estimate may have to be provisional, or even arbitrary. And this perhaps is fortunate, because it underlines the necessity for examining on-the-job training and other means of human capital formation, and demonstrates clearly the dangers of equating human resource development exclusively with the expansion of formal education.

The importance of using inter- and intra-country comparisons to set targets has already been stressed. There are, of course, many problems involved in making both inter-country comparisons as well as regional comparisons within a country. For example, it may be argued that an inter-country comparison is not appropriate unless the social and cultural conditions in the two countries are identical and unless the country with which the comparison is made has satisfactorily met its requirements. This is not so. In the first place, comparisons between countries are best made on a sector-by-sector basis. One compares not entire countries but rather agricultural sectors, industrial sectors, or education sectors. Secondly, it is not necessary to assume that manpower requirements have been met satisfactorily in the country of comparison. For example, if Country B, which is more advanced, has three times the proportion of engineers in its industrial labour force as Country A and still is short of engineers, this fact indicates that Country A may need to increase its proportion of engineers more than three times to satisfactorily attain a comparable level of industrial development. Or, if Country B has an over-supply of engineers, then Country A might lower its estimated requirements accordingly. The same is true in the case of intra-country comparisons between regions. The advanced region does not necessarily establish the desired target for the less advanced regions. The essential point here is that the process is one of comparison of manpower problems as related to sectors at different stages of development. And, as a general rule it is wise to assume that no country has solved its problems in a completely satis-factory way.

One of the outcomes of the comparative approach is the construction of multipliers or ratios from which to construct forward targets. In order to illustrate this point, let us take a somewhat oversimplified example. Assume that a comparison between two countries, A and B, shows the following:

	Country A	Country B
Number of persons with secondary education or more per 10,000 population	25	250
G.N.P. *per capita* in U.S. dollars	$100	$500

Now if, we also assume that there is a high correlation between G.N.P. and stock of manpower with secondary education, we could say that a tenfold increase in educated manpower might be necessary for Country A to have a fivefold increase in G.N.P. The ratio of increase in educated manpower to the increase in G.N.P., therefore, is 2:1. We may turn the example around, of course, and assume that Country A would have to increase its G.N.P. by five times if it hoped to increase its stock of educated manpower by 10 times. In any case, the 2:1 ratio could be used to make an initial estimate of future requirements for persons with secondary education or more.

In practice multipliers or ratios can be calculated for particular occupational categories and for particular sectors. Adjustments are made to take care of existing shortages or surpluses in each country. And the ratios may be constructed after making comparisons not with just one but with several countries. These and many more refinements can be used in a comprehensive assessment. It is important to remember, however, that multipliers or ratios should not be used to forecast manpower requirements in the future. They are a means only of establishing targets which indicate an approximately correct direction for action and a general order of magnitude of required effort. Nor should one forget that the ratios are based upon assumptions rather than upon proven relationships.

Finally, we come to the significance of the 'shortfall'. Most surveys compare estimates of requirements for various categories of manpower with the anticipated output of the educational system as currently projected. The difference between estimated demand and expected supply is usually called the 'shortfall', and targets are then suggested for expanding educational facilities to close the gap. However, the planner should never assume that this gap must be closed merely by expanding educational facilities. He should first explore the extent to which some of the requirements can be met by training on the job, by providing night-school classes for those already employed, by the temporary importation of skilled foreigners, or by improving the organization of work in order to utilize manpower more efficiently. Indeed, one of his principal tasks is the examination of alternative solutions of human resource problems, and in the end to weave them into a broad strategy of human resource development.

IV *Conclusion*

The estimation of long-range human resource requirements is a difficult but absolutely indispensable step in planning for social and economic development. Because this is a new field of interest, the concepts and methodologies of making forward estimates are not clearly formulated. Yet there is no reason to conclude that estimating manpower requirements is a less accurate and rigorous process than estimating the future needs for other resources. All forward estimates must be based upon assumptions, and they are accurate only to the extent that the assumptions are intelligently made.

The target-setting concept, rather than that of forecasting, is the more appropriate one for making long-term manpower estimates. And because most nations tend to formulate their goals for developing by making comparisons with other countries, comparative analysis should constitute the core of the methodology for setting human resource development targets. The targets, together with the policy measures selected to approach them, constitute the strategy of human resource development. And this strategy, in turn, should become part of a country's general plan for economic and social development.

7

Organization for Manpower Planning in Nigeria

T. M. Yesufu

The background

Perhaps one of the most fortunate things that could have happened to Nigeria in the few years immediately preceding independence, was the realization on the part of its leaders that freedom from colonial rule was bound to lead to a revolution of expectations on the part of the people. And since the most visible mark of the new status was the transfer of governmental control to Nigerians, it was obvious that Nigerians would increasingly look to the Governments for fulfilment of those expectations, social as well as economic. With relatively slim financial and other resources, strategic planning of these resources on a hitherto unprecedented scale became a desideratum. The experience gained since the Development Plan of 1945, and the difficulties of Nigerianizing the Civil Services, showed clearly that one of the major difficulties which the country had to overcome, if it were to progress and meet the aspirations of the people, was the development of its human resources, especially through education and training. It soon became clear, however, that the needs for trained manpower went beyond the requirements for Nigerianization for prestige purposes. It was a prerequisite for rapid economic and national development.

But how much education, and what type of training? This question had to be answered quickly and action had to be taken with equal speed. Since 1954, however, primary education had expanded tremendously; the greatest obvious deficiencies, especially in the light of the requirements for economic development and the experience of other countries, lay in the Senior and Intermediate manpower categories. Accordingly, in 1959, the Federal Government appointed a Commission under the chairmanship of Sir Eric Ashby, 'to conduct an investigation into Nigeria's needs in the field of post-School Certificate and Higher Education over the next twenty years'.

The report of the Commission[1] has proved to be more than famous. The recommendations in this respect were those of Professor F. H. Harbison who, on behalf of the Commission, made a survey of Nigeria's high-level manpower needs. In these recommendations, Professor Harbison did not merely confirm the fears about the manpower situation; he revolutionized all ideas and thinking about the manpower factor in economic development. 'The most critical economic factors in the country's development are capital and high-level manpower. The two are complementary. Capital cannot be effectively employed without high-level manpower, and high-level manpower would become redundant without capital. Manpower development, therefore, must be articulated with programmes for capital formation, and planning for manpower development is an integral and indispensable part of general planning for economic development.' Accordingly, the Commission emphasized that, 'the central recommendation' of his report was 'that Nigeria should establish at once appropriate organizational arrangements to assess continuously manpower needs and to formulate programmes for effective manpower development throughout the Federation'.[2]

The National Manpower Board

In 1960, the National Economic Council considered and adopted this recommendation, and in 1962, a National Manpower Board was established. The Ashby Commission in recommending the establishment of the National Manpower Board stressed that it should give full consideration to all aspects of manpower development programmes throughout the Federation with special reference to the following:

1. The periodic appraisal of requirements for manpower in all occupations and in all productive activities through the Federation. In particular, assessments should be made of manpower requirements of all development projects.

2. The periodic analysis of costs of formal education (both capital and recurrent) and the determination of the order of priority in

[1] *Investment in Education* (The Report of the Commission on Post-School Certificate and Higher Education in Nigeria), 1960.
[2] Ibid., p. 67.

expenditures for education to promote the economic, political, social and cultural development of the country.

3. The development of measures for in-service training of employed manpower both in the government service, in private industry and commerce, and in educational institutions.

4. The appraisal of wage and salary scales in the government services and in education in relation to the demand for high-level manpower.

5. The formulation of policy governing scholarships and fellowships for study in Nigeria and abroad. Here, two important elements are involved:

   (a) The use of Regional or Federal funds for scholarships and fellowships.

   (b) The conditions governing acceptance by Nigerians of scholarships and fellowships offered by foreign governments for other institutions outside the Federation.

6. The development of policies concerning Nigerianization in employment, and policies governing the entry and employment of expatriates in both public and private employment.

7. The periodic assessment of unemployment or underemployment in major occupations and activities, and the development of measures to provide needed employment opportunities in particular sectors of the Nigerian economy.

8. The integration of manpower development planning with broader planning for economic, social and political development of the country.

The Commission went further to emphasize that 'as defined above manpower development encompasses the entire field of utilization of human resources for productive activity'. Further details of the work of the Manpower Board as envisaged by the Ashby Commission are contained on pages 67 to 72 of their Report.[3]

The summaries of the terms of reference as approved by the National Economic Council and the Federal and Regional Governments were contained in Sessional Paper No. 3 of 1961 and in Government Notice No. 334 published in the Federation of Nigeria Gazette of 15 February 1963. In the latter Notice which formally established the National

---

[3] *Investment in Education* (Lagos, 1960).

Manpower Board, it was indicated that its terms of reference 'include the determination of the nation's manpower needs in all occupations; formulating, for consideration of the National Economic Council and the Governments of the Federation, programmes for manpower development through university expansion and training, scholarships, fellowships and other facilities; and co-ordinating the policies and activities of the Federal and Regional Ministries primarily concerned with manpower problems. The Board will also be concerned with employment policies including measures to deal with unemployment and the optimum utilization of the Nation's Manpower resources.'

The Manpower Board works under the umbrella of the National Economic Council which is the supreme economic policy formulating body. Since the Council, by its very nature, did not meet frequently, it was decided that its functions with regard to the Manpower Board should be performed by a Standing Manpower Committee of the Council, comprising Ministers representing the Federal and Regional Governments. In 1963, however, before the Standing Committee could meet for the first time, the machinery of the N.E.C. was reviewed and it was decided to abolish the Committee. In doing so, it was decided that the Board might refer special matters to other appropriate Committees of the Council—such as, the Committee on Education and the Committee on the Co-ordination of the Plan. If and when necessary, however, the Board can refer any matter direct to the N.E.C. The Federal Minister of Economic Development is charged with responsibility for the Board.

The membership of the Board reflects its national character and the varying interests involved. It meets under the chairmanship of the Permanent Secretary of the Federal Ministry of Economic Development. All the Federal and Regional Ministries of Education and Economic Planning are represented, as well as the Federal Ministry of Labour. One member is appointed to represent agricultural interests, and private employers and organized labour have two representatives each. University interests are represented by three members, one of them being the Secretary of the National Universities Commission. The Federal Economic Adviser is also a member of the Board. This gives a total membership of nineteen—twelve official and seven unofficial members, the latter being appointed for a term of two years, but subject so reappointment.

Regional Manpower Committees

In setting up the National Manpower Board, it was essential to take account of the Federal character of the Constitution. The agreement at the N.E.C. to establish a National Board was evidence of the growing desire among all the Governments for greater and more effective co-operation. Nevertheless each Government has important responsibilities for economic planning and development within its area of jurisdiction. If manpower planning was to be an integral part of general development planning, it was clear that each Government needed a body which would be concerned with the manpower aspects of its programmes. In examining the structure of the manpower planning organization, therefore, the National Economic Council decided that there should be Regional (including Federal) 'counterparts' to the National Manpower Board.

But the terms of reference of these counterparts were not defined. In view of the requirements that the Manpower Board must be inter-governmental in character and deal with the manpower problems of the Federation as a whole, it became necessary to reconsider the relationship between the Board and the Regional organizations. It was clear that if the Regional bodies were to have the same competence within their areas of jurisdiction as the Board had in respect of the Federation as a whole, there would be a wasteful duplication of staff and effort, and dissipation of financial resources. The attention of the Government was, therefore, invited to this and agreement was sought on a proper demarcation of functions. The Board subsequently discussed the matter at its first meeting and it was agreed that the Regional (including Federal) organs should be called Manpower Committees, with the following terms of reference:

(a) To assess the manpower requirements of the Regional Government, Regional Public Corporations and Boards and the Local and Native Authorities, and the Manpower implifications of their development schemes, and to supply necessary information to the Secretary to the National Manpower Board;

(b) to examine, from the point of view of the Regional Government, the implications of the results of the work of, and the recommendations of, the National Manpower Board;

(c) following from (a) and (b), to advise the Regional Government

on the implementation of decisions and recommendations of the
National Manpower Board; and

(d) to advise the National Manpower Board on matters referred to
the Committee by the Board.

The above terms of reference were subsequently considered and
approved by the National Economic Council. Accordingly, each of the
Regional and Federal Governments of the Federation has established
its own Manpower Committee. At the Regional levels the Committees
are located in the Ministries charged with responsibility for economic
planning. The Federal Manpower Committee is under the Federal
Ministry of Establishments.

The above demarcation of functions emphasizes the interdependence
of the Board and the Regional Committees. Each Government is free to
request its Manpower Committee to examine any particular aspect of
manpower problems within its jurisdiction in the light of the Committee's terms of reference. But the close inter-relationship of the manpower
problems of the various parts of the Federation is fully realized, and continuous liaison is maintained between the Committees and the Board. This
is ensured by the fact that the representatives of the Regions on the Board
are also members of the Committee, and the Secretary of the National
Manpower Board is an *ex-officio* member of the Regional Committees.

The National Manpower Secretariat

In accordance with the decision of the National Economic Council a
Manpower Secretariat is organized as a branch of the Federal Ministry
of Economic Development. By definition it renders Secretariat services
to the Board within the latter's terms of reference. But the Secretariat
is charged specifically with certain responsibilities as contained, for
example, in Sessional Paper No. 3 of 1961. Thus it is not only 'to
present business to the Board', but to 'handle manpower statistics,
promote the development of employed manpower, create employment
opportunities, expand training facilities, maintain a national register
of high-level manpower, and secure the optimum utilization of manpower resources.'[4] The functions of the Secretariat thus falls into four
broad headings:

(a) *Secretariat*—presenting business to the Board, keeping minutes,
disseminating manpower information and the decisions of the

[4] *Educational Development, 1961–70 (Sessional Paper, No. 3 of 1961)* (being a Federal
Government's Policy Statement on the Ashby Report), paragraph 59.

Board; and co-ordinating the manpower aspect of the work of various Regional and Federal Agencies.

(b) *Planning*—integrating manpower planning with general economic planning; evaluating the manpower implications of development projects; Nigerianization in public and private employment; and considering measures for dealing with specific manpower problems; e.g. unemployment.

(c) *Research*—with particular reference to evaluating Nigeria's Manpower situation and utilization; employment trends, and relevant influencing factors; etc.

(d) *Productivity*—promoting productivity movement in Nigeria, and rendering consultancy services to private and public organizations in respect to effective utilization of employed manpower with a view to raising labour productivity.

At the present stage of economic development in Nigeria, those are grave responsibilities; considering the constitutional, governmental and administrative set-up, they are complicated and difficult. Yet the extent to which they are effectively and faithfully discharged will determine to a large extent the success of the nation's economic efforts. It is clear that in carrying out the above functions, the Secretariat must among other things, organize continuous research into the various manpower problems, including particular questions such as unemployment, managerial techniques, distribution of available trained personnel, labour productivity, incentives, wage rates, etc.

It is intended to organize the Manpower Secretariat to cope with these duties. In acknowledgement of their importance the National Economic Council authorized that experts be recruited from overseas on various aspects of manpower problems, who will assist the Secretary and train Nigerian counterparts. Three such experts have been recruited in the fields of Employment Opportunities, Manpower Statistics, and Productivity. The Senior Staff at the time of writing consisted of the following:

The Secretary	(Economist)
Senior Assistant Secretary	(Economist)
Assistant Chief Statistician	(Statistician)
Principal (Education & Training)	(Educationist)
Principal (Productivity)	(Vacant)
Two Assistant Secretaries	(Economists)

Two Ford Foundation Consultants   (Employment & Productivity)
One I.L.O. Consultant   (Manpower Statistics).

It will be obvious that much of the basic material with which the Secretariat works, is statistical. Much of it has to be collected by surveys, inquiries, etc. Originally, it was expected that much of the field work that would be required by the Secretariat could be done by the Federal Office of Statistics, and that other basic information could be obtained from other agencies, such as the Census Office, the Ministries of Labour, Education, Commerce, Industry, Agriculture, etc. It is still hoped that this ideal situation will operate in the long run. For the time being, at any rate, most of the basic statistics and other information required from these other bodies are just not available, and there is no adequate machinery for collecting them. Accordingly, the urgent nature of the work of the Secretariat has necessitated its having to undertake surveys and inquiries direct. Nevertheless, the senior Nigerian in charge of statistics in the Secretariat is on the establishment of the Federal Office of Statistics. The Federal Chief Statistician, therefore, shares responsibility in manpower statistics and regularly advises and renders assistance to the Manpower Secretary. The analysis of the Secretariat's manpower survey in 1963 was, for example, machine-processed by the Federal Office of Statistics and by the Census Office.

The organization of the Manpower Secretariat is still, however, in a state of flux and after its initial experiences, consideration is being given to ways and means of making it sufficiently effective to deal with its peculiar functions. It will therefore be useful at this stage to examine some of the problems so far encountered and how it is considered that these might be overcome.

Some basic problems

It would be surprising if an organization such as the Manpower Board with its Secretariat, did not encounter initial difficulties. It is necessary, however, to record that the climate under which it was established was most favourable. The prestige of the Ashby Commission and Professor Harbison who recommended its establishment, remains very high; and indeed, their arguments for an effective national manpower planning organization becomes more forcefully potent with the passage of time. All things considered, the support which the Governments of the Federation have given to the Board is most commendable.

The co-operation of private employers and of most of Government Ministries has been readily available. The Universities for their part, have not only been most co-operative, but have, to a considerable extent, been willing to take the guidance of the Board in matters of planning curricula structure and student intake.

Yet some basic problems remain. While many people appear to have learned, at least, to talk of manpower, its full implications remain in their minds and thinking, rather obscure. Those who have in the past organized businesses, schools, training institutions, departments, etc., without much thought for manpower or without any special planning, naturally find it difficult to realize 'all the fuss' that is being made about it now. When it is suggested that each major Government department, agency or business organization should charge a responsible officer with specific duties for its manpower analysis and problems, and for the maintenance of manpower statistics, it sounds novel and is usually not to be taken seriously. Yet manpower planning and development must effectively start at the roots—in the minds of people: the employers and Government agencies, and in the workshops and in the training institutions which are the consumers and the suppliers of manpower.

Perhaps this is an inevitable initial difficulty which requires for its mitigation, effective propaganda on the part of the Manpower Board and its regional counterparts. But it cannot now be too strongly emphasized that if manpower planning and development are to be effective in Nigeria, it is vital to have the understanding and active co-operation of practically everybody—the general population as well as (but particularly) the government ministries, employers and educational institutions. They must be prepared to think, talk and plan in terms of manpower, take the Manpower Board into confidence and supply it with all the necessary information on their problems, etc. Only so can the Board be an effective instrument for economic and social change.

Nevertheless, perhaps the most pressing problems at present, in consideration of the future of manpower planning in Nigeria are the questions of staff and the status of the Manpower Board and its Secretariat, vis-à-vis the civil service structure. In the first place before the establishment of the Manpower Secretariat, there were practically no Nigerians with the required knowledge or training in manpower planning and development. This is not surprising. Even now, some of the posts in the secretariat still cannot be filled, and expansion is rendered difficult, for lack of suitable candidates. At present, the Secretariat staff are considered to be part of the general pool of administrative officers. They are, therefore, liable to be transferred or posted to other ministries and other duties. In the first two years of the Secretariat's existence, three such officers were so transferred, while one resigned. Yet the nature of the work of the Secretariat at the operational level, requires expertise and continuity. As things are, not only are the officers liable to transfers and new posting outside the Secretariat; they legitimately look forward to the normal benefits of the civil service, such as acting appointments, promotions, etc., irrespective of where the vacancies may be. What appears to be required is that the staff should be guaranteed reasonable continuity of service within the Secretariat, be allowed to specialize, and be assured of normal promotion prospects.

Another important experience has been that the operation of the normal civil service routine and regulations and the requirement to follow only special procedures, has at times, tended to delay the implementation of the directives of Government and of the Manpower Board, in spite of their urgency. It thus appears to need consideration whether the best solution does not lie in recognizing the Board, as such, not only in name, but in practice. This implies that, while bearing in mind the need to integrate manpower planning with general economic planning the Manpower Board and its Secretariat should be treated as an organizational entity, not entirely independent, but sufficiently so, to enable it to carry out its specialized functions. It appears that the National Economic Council had this question of semi-autonomy in mind when it approved that the Manpower Secretary should be in direct administrative charge of all officers of the Secretariat including any Advisers that are appointed, and went further to stipulate that the Secretary and the Advisers should be responsible for recruiting and training the officers of the Secretariat. Indeed, in Sessional Paper No. 3 of 1961, the Federal Government indicated that the Manpower Board would be established by law. So far this has not been done. The Manpower Secretariat continues, therefore, to function within rigid civil service structure and codes with all the inevitable problems to which reference has been made.

In India this very problem soon manifested itself, when manpower planning and the detailed research connected therewith, were (as in

Nigeria today) carried out by the Manpower Directorate in co-operation with the Ministry of Labour and the Perspective Planning Division
of the Planning Commission. While these agencies still have important
responsibilities in the process of manpower planning, it was soon
recognized that the pressures of day-to-day activities within the normal
administrative machinery were so heavy and cumbersome that the
kind of intensive, high quality manpower research which needed to be
undertaken, could not be assigned to the existing departmental
agencies. The Government of India, therefore, decided that the best
approach would be the establishment of 'a semi-autonomous body which
can undertake intensive studies of the more serious manpower problems now facing the Government'. The Government approached
the Ford Foundation with whose co-operation the relevant body,
namely, the Institute of Applied Manpower Research, was established
in 1962.

There appears to be much merit in this system, and it is one which
could, with advantage, be emulated in Nigeria. Such an Institute would
provide the mechanism for acquiring a more thorough understanding
of the nature of the increasingly urgent human resources problems of
the country as they relate to economic development, within the terms
of reference of the Manpower Board. To avoid being lost in a maze of
non-essential work the Institute would need to avoid long-term research
programmes which are more properly the functions of organizations
like the Nigerian Institute of Social and Economic Research and the
Economics Departments of the Universities. It would perhaps be
preferable for the Manpower Institute to have a working relation with
the N.I.S.E.R. or the University of Lagos. But its vital role, as emphasized by the word 'applied', must be to concentrate effort on current
pressing manpower problems in close collaboration with the Economic
Planning Ministries and ensure the continuous analysis and solving of
manpower problems in the basic industries, mining, transportation,
agriculture, etc., as well as with working out the manpower implications of development projects and proposed investments in private
industry with a view to maximizing employment opportunities in the
light of the unemployment problem.

These would not be new functions, as they are already contained
within the existing terms of reference of the Manpower Board and its
Secretariat. What requires emphasis is, as the Indian authorities found
out, that 'there are inherent difficulties in establishing an adequate

organization for manpower research in all its aspects within the governmental structure. As has been said, the pressure of day-to-day problems tends to upset research programmes within Government; and the urgency of immediate needs, and the influence of current policies, often deflect the course of investigation and influence its results.'

Furthermore the Manpower Board and its Secretariat are intended not only to concern themselves with the manpower problems of the public sector but also of private industries, agencies and employers. While it may be said here that the Nigeria Employers Consultative Association has so far co-operated magnificently with the Manpower Secretariat, it should equally be emphasized that there are inherent difficulties in ensuring satisfactory co-ordination and co-operation with private employers in matters of research carried out within the normal Government departmental organization. A semi-autonomous institution which is none the less closely allied to the Government, can deal with the whole manpower field in an integrated way, and ensure greater freedom for the utilization of its services by private employers. It may be significant, for example, that the private employers, in spite of their manifold manpower problems, have not yet, on their own initiative, requested any particular service from the Manpower Secretariat; yet it is essential that they should be free to do this without the fear that the agency involved will adopt a 'governmental' or 'inquisitorial' attitude to their problems.

Lastly, it may bear repetition that the continuity of research which is so vital to the success of the Manpower Board can be ensured, in the view of the writer, only through the specialization of officers of the Secretariat and the willingness to make provisions which will enable them to remain in continuous service of the Board. It is therefore, suggested that in setting up the proposed Institute, conditions of service should be worked out for the staff which are similar to those of other research organizations like the Nigerian Institute of Social and Economic Research. This will provide a promotion ladder for the staff and ensure their continuity of service as well as discourage the apparently normal tendency to look elsewhere for prospects.

If all this is agreed, the problem arises as to the financing of the Institute and also its constitution. Whatever the final form of the organization, it must be emphasized that it will continue to be the agency of the Manpower Board supplying it with facts upon which manpower policy and decisions can be taken. Accordingly, the

Manpower Board should continue to be the directing agency of the Institute, examining its proposals for research and field work.

The Federal Government will retain over-riding control through the Minister of Economic Development as at present; and to ensure continuity and effective liaison, the Secretary of the Manpower Board could continue for a time as head of the organization.

Ultimately, a different head could be appointed for the Institute. But as already hinted, the Manpower Board, in spite of its name, is not constituted by law. Such a legal base would be the most appropriate way to ensure the Board's effective functioning, on the lines outlined above, and it seems that the time has come to implement the Federal Government's intention in this report. The law may be called the Manpower Board Act. It would set out the constitution of the Board, the Institute being its agency in accordance with the above suggestions. In India, the Institute of Applied Manpower Research functions as a body registered under the India Societies Registration Act (XXI) of 1860, which is an Act for the Registration of Literary, Scientific and Charitable Societies.

As to finance, it is doubtful whether the proposed Institute working on the lines suggested, would be more expensive than it would cost the Federal Government to run the Manpower Secretariat, to fulfil its full functions. For it is clear that such cost is likely to rise as the Board's functions are progressively implemented. But there is the possibility that foreign organizations may be willing to provide funds to meet part of the cost for setting up and running the Institute, at least, during the initial period. The contribution of Government could, therefore, be limited to a grant to the Institute which is equivalent to the amount now voted for the staff and maintenance of the Manpower Secretariat. This means that the aid to be sought from outside would be equivalent to what is required to expand and reorganize the Secretariat into an efficient Manpower Institute on the lines suggested.[5]

Conclusion

It may, perhaps, need to be re-emphasized that no one is more aware today than the Nigerian Governments of the importance of the manpower factor in economic development. The growing problem of unemployment, at least, emphasizes the point continuously. It is

[5] It may be mentioned that the Ford Foundation of America has already made some substantial grant to the Board to foster its research programme.

because of this realization that this paper has been concerned with proposals for ensuring the most effective manpower machinery. Its tenet is that the value of the work of the Manpower Board is so important, with particular reference to future Development Plans and the growth of the economy, that nothing but the most effective machinery will suffice. It is in that light that this paper should be regarded.

8

Forecasting Nigeria's Manpower Needs, 1963–1968

A Note on Methodology

T. M. Yesufu

I. Introductory

In December 1962, the National Manpower Board at its first meeting directed that a comprehensive manpower survey should be carried out with a view to providing more accurate information on the manpower situation in Nigeria, and that the Manpower Secretary should, on the basis of the Survey, make a forecast of Nigeria's future manpower requirements. It had become clear that the success of Nigeria's current as well as future Development Plans, depended to a much greater extent than was hitherto realized, upon the availability of adequate numbers of high-level manpower with the requisite skills. The dire shortage of such staff made it imperative that programmes for their training should immediately be revaluated, and co-ordinated if possible, within the Six-Year Development Plan. The determination or forecasting of future needs for high-level manpower seemed, therefore, to be a first prerequisite to effective manpower planning and development.

The Survey was carried out from April to August 1963, and a forecast of requirements was made for the period up to 1968. The present paper is aimed primarily at explaining the method used in forecasting the manpower requirements, since the manpower budget so set can only be properly evaluated in the light of the method used, and the judgements upon which the method was based. Manpower forecasting savours in a sense of crystal-gazing.[1] But it is much more than that,

---

[1] This underlies Harbison's objection to the use of the term (see Chapter 6). In the context of this paper the word 'forecasting' is virtually synonymous with making an estimate for a future date.

especially as there are no incontrovertible methods of approach. The actual method or combination of methods adopted, therefore, becomes in itself, of great statistical and economic significance, because of the dangers in both over-estimation and under-estimation. An over-estimated manpower budget might mean that financial and other resources which could more profitably be invested in other fields of economic development, would be wasted in developing programmes of training and education. Moreover, it could lead, for a time at least, to an over-supply, and, therefore, unemployment of educated, highly skilled men, with all the serious economic, political and social consequences involved.

Serious under-estimation of manpower needs, on the other hand, leads to non-fulfilment of important development programmes. To the extent that it is possible to recruit expatriates to fill the gaps, the dangers of under-estimation may appear, in the short run, to be less serious than those of gross over-estimation. But the use of expatriates is relatively very expensive and may unduly inflate the cost of development. In any given situation, therefore, the method used in forecasting manpower requirements, must be critically examined, and if possible, different methods should be used to check and counter-check the results.

II. *General Methods of Forecasting Manpower Requirements*

As already indicated, there are many ways by which future manpower requirements can be estimated. The actual method or combination of methods adopted depends upon a number of circumstances. In the first place, an estimate of manpower requirements will be meaningful only in the context of the economic structure for which it is intended. Where a comprehensive Development Plan already exists this aspect of the problem is minimized since the resultant manpower budget must take into account the manpower components required to implement the Plan as well as the structure of the economy which is likely to materialize as a result of the implementation of the Plan itself. This is so because the proportions of different categories of manpower tend to differ in the light of that structure—for example, the relative importance of agriculture or manufacturing *vis-à-vis* the rest of the economy. Where no Plan exists, or where an existing Plan is not all-embracing, the manpower forecaster must himself envisage an economic structure. This structure, however, must be sufficiently realistic, and must bear in mind the recent economic history of the country, the current levels and pattern of employment, and the hopes and aspirations of the State, of the people in general, as well as of private employers.

Once this judgement is made, manpower forecasting becomes essentially a statistical exercise. But further human judgements are usually inevitable depending on the type, volume and completeness or otherwise of available statistics. Thus, one of the first duties of any organization, such as the National Manpower Board, which is charged with responsibility for manpower forecasting, is to assemble a large number of relevant statistics. Where the statistics are absent then machinery must be devised or improved to ensure their collection and collation on a continuing basis.

The type of statistics required are easily identified. A census of population provides generally the most accurate data, at a specific date, of the labour force and its composition by sex, age, levels of training and education and of its geographical, educational and occupational distribution. Where census of population figures are incomplete or out of date, they must be supplemented by an industrial census or labour force surveys. These provide information on labour force distribution by industry and related levels of production, employment, unemployment and underemployment, hours of work and earnings, etc. It is also important to obtain, regularly, full information about educational and training institutions and facilities, together with related costs.

These statistics are useful to the extent that they throw light on the past and current trends of manpower utilization as a function of the economic structure. If adequate, they should indicate a pattern or trend which could be projected into the future with some measure of accuracy. This, of course, presupposes that the future contains seeds of growth which are not remarkably different from those of the past, which is often not the case. But even where a conscious effort is being made to alter the pattern of growth, on the basis of a Development Plan, historical statistics may still reveal useful inter-relationships in particular cases—e.g. the number of Engineers relative to various levels of production in manufacturing or investment in the constructional trades.

Since the manpower in respect of which an estimate is being made is part of the labour force, a prior necessity is the estimation of the potential labour force itself for the forecast year. Its size will depend on a number factors—the rate of growth of the population and its age cohort, the male/female participation rate in the labour force, depending on custom, legal requirements as to working age, the availability and extent of utilization of educational and training facilities, etc. For an intelligent and reasonably reliable estimate to be made, it is also important to have available the current or recent pattern of employment, by economic activity, by industry and by occupation. This is essential because one of the major aims of a manpower forecast is to estimate, for a given date, the volume and type of employment by economic activity and, especially, by occupation, so as to provide a guide on the number of persons to be trained, the types of education and training to be given, the additional facilities to be provided, and what action, if any, should be taken to gear the economy into a given or desired line of development. The authorities of the country may alter or supplement this aim in the light of its particular circumstances. The forecaster must take this into consideration in determining the type of statistics to be used or collected.

Against the above background the method of forecasting resolves into a series of statistical steps which have been summarized as follows:

Step 1. Derive a rough first approximation of the future employment structure by economic activity, consistent with the anticipated increase in the labour force.

Step 2. Make a detailed analysis of each important economic activity, taking into account anticipated changes in demand for its products or services and in hours worked and productivity; thus arriving at an estimate of future employment.

Step 3. Modify the first approximations of future employment in accordance with the results of the detailed analysis of each important activity.

Step 4. Derive an occupational breakdown of employment in each economic activity in the future period by applying the best available occupational composition patterns, with particular attention to all occupations requiring specialized training or education. Sum the estimates of each occupation from the various economic activities.

Step 5. Estimate training requirements for each important occupation by analysis of the probable supply of qualified workers under existing training arrangements and facilities in comparison with the requirements as indicated by occupational estimates for the future period.[2]

[2] W. Willard Wirtz, *The Forecasting of Manpower Requirements* (U.S. Department of Labour, 1963) BLS Reports, No. 248, p. 11.

It is clear from the foregoing, that the process of manpower fore-casting will be complicated, relatively difficult or simple, depending upon the nature of statistics available and upon their completeness and reliability. There are accordingly three basic conditions as identified by Wirtz, under which a forecast can be made.[3] In the first case, the available statistics of economic activity may not be sufficiently compre-hensive. Secondly, statistics of employment may be available only for the base year from which a forecast is being made. Where they are not available the deficiency can be made good by a comprehensive man-power or labour force sample survey. Thirdly, employment statistics may be available, not only for the base year, but for some previous years.

III. *The Nature of Nigeria's Manpower Statistics, 1963*

At the time of the high-level manpower survey in 1963, some man-power statistics were already available in Nigeria. They were, however, notoriously incomplete and fragmentary. The first duty of the Manpower Secretariat should, therefore, have been to build up the relevant statistics. But the pressure for a manpower budget to guide the Governments, private employers, the universities, etc. in their educa-tional and training programmes was urgent. In the event, the absence of reliable statistics, could be but a poor excuse for not making a forecast. However inadequate the available statistics, they often pro-vide some useful information, and indicate, at least, the degree of deficiency which it is the task of a manpower planning organiza-tion to remedy. It may accordingly be useful to understand the nature of statistics available in Nigeria at the time of the Manpower Survey.

The last available census statistics were those for 1952–3. They in-dicated a breakdown of the population by age and sex, and by industry and occupation, and should, therefore, be of primary importance for manpower forecasting.

But the efflux of time and consequent constitutional, economic and social development which had since taken place, suggested that the statistics would be rather unreliable. Moreover, the age, industrial and occupational classifications in the census reports were themselves deficient. For example, persons engaged in Trading (on their own account) and in clerical occupations (mainly as employees) were classi-

---

[3] Ibid.

fied together. In using the statistics, therefore, indirect methods had to be employed to identify particular groups more accurately.

Employment and Earnings returns have been collected by the Federal Ministry of Labour since 1956. The returns are confined to establishments employing not less than ten persons. Such statistics are vital for manpower planning. They are useful, for example, in suggesting relations between various categories of manpower, such as the proportion of high-level manpower to total employment. But the classifications used in the reports have often changed and are, in many respects, inadequate. For example, skilled and semi-skilled workers were often grouped together. The returns also show serious and erratic fluctuations of the level of employment from year to year, globally as well as within industrial and occupational sectors, which suggest basic deficiencies in coverage and inaccuracies in analysis. Moreover, since 1961, the time of the returns has been changed from September to December of each year. Some of the difficulties in using the statistics may be illustrated by Tables 9(i) and 9(ii) based on the Report on Employment and Earnings Enquiry, for December 1961.

The Ministry of Labour itself has said of these statistics that 'the absence of a Social Security Scheme, which could have provided the bench mark figures for employment, makes it impossible to check the correctness and trend of the employment figures obtained as a result

TABLE 8(i)[4]   *Estimated Number of Persons Employed by Type of Employer, 1957–61*

Type of Employer	September 1957(a)	September 1958(a)	September 1959(a)	September 1960	December 1961
Federal Government	45,500	47,500	51,200	54,700	48,000(b)
Regional Government	70,600	73,400	77,400	83,900	80,000
Local Government	100,600	92,200	97,700	95,100	88,000
Public Corporation	93,300	96,600	84,900	73,800	80,000
Commercial Firm	}217,600	}206,300	197,200	212,200	182,000
Voluntary Agency			10,900	34,500	35,000
TOTAL	527,600	516,000	519,300	554,200	513,000

Note: (a) Southern Cameroon figures included.

(b) Drop from 1960 said to be due to possible over-estimation in September, 1960.

[4] *Report on Employment and Earnings Enquiry*, December 1961. Table B.

TABLE 8(ii)[5]   *Level of Employment Returned in Selected Industries*

Year	Manufac-turing	Construc-tion	Electricity and Gas	Transport & Communica-tions	Services
September 1958(a)	29,154	116,596	9,847	46,943	117,678
September 1959(a)	32,000	96,860	16,309	45,838	136,519
September 1960	32,821	112,719	8,340	39,272	183,604
December 1961	34,263	89,303	11,248	42,737	143,172

Note: (a) Figures for Southern Cameroons not included.

of the inquiry from year to year'.[6] So far as manpower planning and forecasting are concerned, therefore, these, the most comprehensive manpower statistics so far available in Nigeria, were of only limited utility.

Statistics of public expenditure are available for all the Governments in respect of both capital and current expenditure for a number of previous years as well as estimates for the period up to 1968. But in view of the erratic and yet unexplained nature of past manpower statistics, no intelligent relationships appear so far to be discernible either between public expenditure and employment in the public sector of the economy, or between the trend in public expenditure and the employment level in general. Similar statistics in respect of the private sector are extremely deficient.

There are a few other fragmentary historical statistics (e.g. of national income); but once more, these are as yet too meagre for full-scale manpower forecasting.

IV. *Manpower Requirements Based on Employers' Expectations*

The High-level Manpower Survey was planned to be as comprehensive as possible, to cover all institutions and establishments employing ten or more persons, and which are clearly the greatest consumers of high-level and skilled manpower. Ultimately the survey covered establishments and institutions which engaged 530,167 employees, of which 113,297 were teachers and research staff. This gave a coverage of about 90 per cent of the total numbers of persons which are estimated to have been engaged in the establishments within the scope of the Survey. One method for forecasting manpower requirements, where historical

---

[5] Ibid.—Table D.   [6] Ibid.—para. 12.

statistics are as deficient as they are in Nigeria, would be for the employers and institutions covered in a comprehensive survey to furnish information on future levels of employment, based upon expectations of market and other trends, and upon their current or proposed plans for expansion or contraction. Adjustment could then be made for wastage in the form of deaths, retirements, etc., and for further growth, on the basis of certain ascertainable factors—e.g. the rate of growth of the economy in the recent past, and the requirements of Development Plans. It was hoped that in rendering such returns under the Survey the manpower requirements of the Plan would be reflected as well as those of private employers.

In spite of the apparent deficiencies which would be inherent in the results, it was nevertheless decided that, as a means of providing a greater insight into employers' reactions in the process of building up a sound statistical base for future manpower forecasting, the employers should be required to furnish information on their expected future demand for high-level and skilled manpower. A request to this effect was accordingly included in the Survey forms. Many employers expressed inability or unwillingness to forecast manpower requirements because, according to them, there were too many variables to consider—for example, the rate of growth of external as well as internal competition, unpredictable fiscal policies of the Government, movements in the terms of trade, etc. Many establishments appeared to have no definite plans for the future, while those which made forecasts tended to be cautious. Some appeared to have put down just any figures, because they felt obliged to do so.

In analysing the returns, the level of employment in establishments which failed to attempt a forecast, was taken to be constant over the forecast period. It is possible to object to this on the ground that for the purpose of determining trends, it would be more realistic to take account only of the returns which included forecasts. This would be acceptable if the proportion of those who made forecasts is sufficiently large and adequately distributed by types of industry, etc., to be representative. In this Survey, however, this was not the case, and the number of employers who did not attempt a forecast was also large, widely diffused, and perhaps, therefore, equally 'representative'.

Taken together the returns showed an expectation on the part of employers of a downward trend in the employment of high-level and skilled manpower in the field of Commerce of between 8 and 20 per cent during the five-year period, 1963–8. Since the establishments covered were mainly the large commercial firms, it is possible that their outlook was affected by the trends in recent years when many of them had to reduce staff in deference to the policy of the Governments that retail trading and produce purchasing should be controlled mainly by Nigerians. Thus, the recorded trend would not necessarily mean an actual decline in total employment in Commerce: it might merely confirm a transfer of commercial activities to Nigerians organized in small-scale enterprises of the size not included in the Survey.

No overall decreases were, however, recorded in other industries, although a few cases of erratic movements were noted; for example, in the drop in the craftsmen grades, under Transport and Communications of about 20 per cent over the period 1963–8. On the whole, under-estimation of future requirements was greatest in respect of the crafts-men and junior supporting staff (referred to in the Survey as 'Other Category').

So far as a trend was discernible from the employers' expectations, it showed a general upward movement in the level of employment, which appears to indicate, to some extent, a healthy confidence on the part of employers in the future of the economy. The trends in the employers' forecasts also tended to indicate that the employment of high-level and skilled manpower in the public sector would expand much more rapidly (at about 6 per cent per annum) than in the private sector (about 2·5 per cent per annum), with an overall average of about 5 per cent per annum. There are no grounds to support this view especially as the rapid expansion of governmental administrative machinery to cope with the federalization of the Constitution, and with increased responsibility consequent upon political and social advance appears to have slowed down. It is probable, however, that the fore-cast in the public sector, so far as a comparison may be made, is more reliable, because of the definite guidance given to public authorities by the Six-Year Development Plan. If any reliability be placed on the public sector estimates, therefore, then the rate of growth of employ-ment of high-level and skilled manpower in the private sector, is likely to be greater than 6 per cent per annum. This question is referred to subsequently.

On the whole, however, the degree of non-response (which was higher in the private sector), the great differences in the pattern of the forecasts which were made, as between public authorities and private employers on the one hand, and on the other hand, between individual employers themselves within each sector, suggested that it would be clearly unrealistic to depend exclusively upon the figures as a basis for determining Nigeria's future manpower needs.

V. *Alternative Methods*

Even if an analysis of the estimates made by employers were considered sufficiently reliable, it would still have been necessary to revise them upwards to take account of new industries in order to arrive at the approximate needs of the future. In the absence of an all-embracing Development Plan,[7] this could be done on the basis of statistics indicating the rates of change in important sectors of the economy in the recent past—e.g. the rate of growth of manufacturing *vis-à-vis* primary production and other industries, in relation to manpower utilization—and further amended to take account of any impact which it is judged the public sector Development Plan would have on the private sector. In fact this procedure could not be used because of the inadequacies of historical statistics, to which reference has already been made.

Another method would be to analyse the manpower situation in one or more other countries where the relevant information is available, where the economic structure is similar to that of Nigeria, or where the economic structure is of a pattern which it is desired to attain in Nigeria. On the basis of such analysis, it is possible (with relevant adjustments for size of population, etc.) to make a forecast for Nigeria. It appears that this method was recently used in Puerto Rico, where it was assumed that the non-agricultural economy of that country in 1975 would have many of the characteristics such as the United States had in 1950. How realistic this assumption would prove to be, is a question of time; perhaps the very close link between the economy of Puerto Rico and that of the U.S.A. justified the approach. As a general rule, however, although the method may seem attractive, it is in practice, fraught with basic difficulties, because of the fundamental differences in the social, political and economic climate, and in the financial and other resources available to different countries. This does not mean that nothing of value can be learned from the experience of other countries. Very often, detailed analysis can, and do, reveal comparative conformity

---

[7] The Six-Year National Development Plan is basically a public sector plan, although it contains ingredients which are specifically designed to encourage the growth of private industry, for example, the Niger Dam and the iron and steel programmes.

of sectoral trends (e.g. of employment in agriculture *vis-à-vis* other sectors) in different countries, and thus provides useful lessons. The extent to which the forecast in Nigeria benefited in this way, is referred to subsequently. The main danger lies in identifying the totality of one country's situation with another.

In the circumstances the approach which seemed best applicable was to envisage an economic structure for the forecast year, which was realistic in the context of the conditions prevailing in Nigeria. At the time of the Survey, a major important element of consideration was the fact of rapidly growing unemployment in Nigeria. It has for some time been engaging the urgent attention of the National Manpower Board as well as of all the Governments of the Federation. It has accordingly been accepted as a major aim of policy that while the country is being industrialized and the economy modernized, full employment must nevertheless be maintained. Indeed while the manpower survey was in progress the National Manpower Board was called upon by the National Economic Council to examine the unemployment problem and to make recommendations for its solution as a matter of urgency. It seemed natural, therefore, that the impending forecast of Nigeria's high-level and skilled manpower requirements should bear this in view as perhaps the major objective of policy; that is to say, that the size of the high-level manpower forecast, should be of a level which would sustain a full employment economy as this appeared to be the objective of Government. The following assumptions were therefore made:

that there should be full employment in the forecast year, 1968;

that factors such as the terms of trade do not change in such manner as to affect the economy too adversely;

that there will be an adequate inflow of foreign capital to sustain the growth of the private sector of the economy as well as the Six-Year Development Plan;

that the political climate will remain stable;

that there will be no major social disasters, such as famine, pestilence, etc.

Simply stated the procedure ultimately adopted for forecasting was as follows:

(1) estimate what the employment level should be for the forecast year, assuming 'full' employment;

(2) determine the pattern of employment;

(3) determine the proportion of employees that would be in the high-level and skilled jobs; and

(4) finally, break down the proportion by type of occupation, in sufficient details, to permit their training and educational content to be ascertainable.

A number of important human judgements are inevitable in processes of this nature. But like the previous assumptions, the judgements must be reasonable in the light of the circumstance of the country and its history; and particularly, if no reliable information is available, then in the light of the experience of other countries. The judgements which were made by the writer in respect of the Nigerian forecast are explained in the details which now follow.

It should be noted that the forecast year chosen was 1968—i.e. only five years from the base year 1963, when the manpower survey was conducted. It is usual to make additional manpower forecasts for longer periods, for say ten, fifteen or twenty years. In this case, however, a Development Plan had already been adopted and it was considered best that any manpower plan should be for the same period. Moreover the errors in a forecast tended to be greater, the longer the period for which it is made. The deficiency of basic statistics, therefore, was such that it would be hazardous to make a forecast for too long a period ahead. It was also intended to supplement the preliminary forecast within a couple of years when details of the 1963 census (then in preparation) would be available and other more reliable statistics have been developed.

VI. *Projected Manpower Situation, 1968*

Population and labour force

What the level of employment should be at any given time depends on the total population, and what proportion of this can normally be engaged economically, in the light of prevailing customs, legal prescriptions, etc. The population of Nigeria during the 1952–3 census was a little over 31 million. At a growth rate of between 2 and 3 per cent per annum, it was estimated that the 1963 population of Nigeria was about 40 million. This was accordingly taken as the benchmark.

The Labour Code Act forbids the employment of children below 15 years of age. Owing to the low average life-span of the average Nigerian, the normal age of retirement (55–60 years) has very little overall employment significance. Therefore the potential labour force would include all persons 15 years of age and above. At the 1952–3 census persons aged 15 years and above constituted 56 per cent of the total population. Allowing for improved medical facilities in the last 10 years and, therefore, for a probable longer life-span, it appeared that the potential labour force was currently about 58 per cent of the total population.[8] On the above assumptions,

Nigeria's population for 1968 = 44 million[9]
Potential Labour Force, 1968 = 25,520,000

Major distribution by economic activity of employment

It was important to determine how many of the potential labour force would be engaged on their own account especially in primary production and trading. The 1952–3 census indicated that about 77·45 per cent of the occupied population was engaged in primary production. Economic development would normally result in a decrease in this ratio, as many people leave agriculture for employment in industry, while most of the educated new entrants into the labour force tend to look almost exclusively to new types of employment in urban areas. This is the trend in most developing countries which have not reached the stage (as India has, for example) of population explosion. Purely from the economic point of view the trend is not undesirable, particularly if the economic plan makes provision for schemes to increase productivity in agriculture.

That the downward trend is applicable in Nigeria is clear from the scanty statistics available. These show that in 1938, for example, about 99 per cent of the occupied population was then engaged in primary production. Between 1938 and 1953 (15 years) the proportionate

---

[8] A recent household occupational survey of some urban towns showed that persons over 14 years of age were about 61 per cent of the population. This would definitely be higher than the overall national average, because of better medical facilities in the towns, and the fact that many young persons at school or seeking employment tend to move to the urban areas.

[9] Subsequent to this paper the population of Nigeria, based on the 1963 census, has been given as 55·6 million. The calculations here have, however, not been amended because, following the report of the Seminar the full employment assumption which was basic to these calculations has been abandoned in setting future manpower targets for Nigeria (for the revised estimates and the method adopted see *Nigeria's High-Level Manpower 1963–70* published by the National Manpower Board). The main value of this chapter, therefore, is to indicate in some detail, but in as simple terms as possible, an example of the varying stages of determining a manpower target. The basic figures (such as those of the population) can easily be substituted without affecting the method.

decline was thus about 21·5 per cent or an average annual decline of between 1·3 and 1·5 per cent. Experience elsewhere indicates, however, that the rate of decline is usually not uniform, being steep at first particularly in a period of rapid economic development, and then gradually levelling out. In the early period from 1938, therefore, the rate of decline could have been higher than 1·4 per cent per annum, and possibly lower, in the few years up to 1953. In the period between 1953 and 1968 (another 15 years) the annual rate of decline should, therefore, on the average, be lower still. The overall situation appears to be that in that period the proportion of persons engaged in primary production (mainly agriculture) in Nigeria would be between the range 77·45 and 56 per cent assuming that the high rate of decline in the earlier period were continued. But in view of what has been said the exact position would be between the two points. In the absence of reliable historical statistics for locating the point, the best approach appeared to be to examine the relevant rate of decline in countries for which information is available at a point in time when this or allied sectors of the economy employed between 56 and 77 per cent of the active population. The following Table summarizes the position in such other countries:

TABLE 8(iii)* *Agricultural Employment as Percentage of Economically Active Population in Selected Countries*

| Country | Year | Percentage | Decline | |
			Total	Average p.a. (a)
Egypt	1937	70·7		
	1947	63·8	8·9	0·89
Brazil	1940	67·4		
	1950	60·6	6·8	0·68
Mexico	1940	65·4		
	1950	57·8	7·6	0·76
Philippines	1939	72·9		
	1948	65·7	7·2	0·8

Note: (a) Interpretations subject to remark already made that rate of decline is not uniform.

* Adapted from *The Forecasting of Manpower Requirements*, op. cit., Table 3.

The average rates of decline as indicated in the last column of the Table are strikingly close, ranging from approximately 0·7 per cent per annum (Brazil) to 0·9 per cent per annum (Egypt). It suggests that a rate of this order could reasonably apply to Nigeria, and the least rate of decline, 0·7 per cent was therefore used. In this way it was surmised that the proportion of the active population in Nigeria engaged in primary production would be about 68 per cent in 1968 as against 77·45 per cent in 1953.

The next major sector of economic activity in Nigeria, for those engaged on their own account, is trading (commerce). Allowing for some deficiency in the occupational classification to which reference has been made, the proportion of the occupied population so engaged on the basis of the 1952–3 Census, was about 12·3 per cent. The general trend in developing countries is that as an economy grows the ratio of those engaged in commerce increases. In Nigeria there are no historical statistics, as in agriculture, to suggest the rate of change of employment levels in commerce. But the Six-Year Development Plan is based on the assumption that the economy would grow at 4 per cent per annum. In Venezuela the economy was developing at about that rate in the 1950s. At the same time, considering the non-agricultural work-force, the ratio of those engaged in commerce increased from 16·7 per cent in 1950 to 17·7 per cent in 1955 and further to 18·2 per cent in 1959. In the first five years, 1950–5, the average rate of increase was about 0·2 per cent per annum. In the second, 1955–9, the average rate of increase slowed down to approximately 0·13 per cent per annum. The overall average for the nine-year period was approximately 0·17 per cent. Applying this in Nigeria, the proportion of the potential labour force that would be employed in trading, in 1968, would be 15 per cent approximately, as against 12·3 per cent in 1953. The bulk of the rest of the potential occupied labour force would be engaged as wage-earners or in crafts.

To summarize the projections so far, Nigeria's manpower situation in 1968 would be as follows:

(a) Total Population   = 44 million
(b) Potential Labour Force   = 25,520,000
(c) Total Occupied Population   = P
(d) No. in Primary Production on own account $= \dfrac{68}{100} \times P$

(e) No. in trading on own account $\qquad = \dfrac{15}{100} \times P$

(f) Wage-earners, etc. $\qquad = P - (d + e)$

$$= \dfrac{17}{100} \times P$$

To obtain P, it was assumed that for full employment, all males would normally be gainfully occupied, equivalent approximately to 50 per cent of potential labour force, i.e. 12,760,000.

As regards females the proportion which was occupied in 1953 was approximately 80·3 per cent. If this proportion remained constant, then in 1968 the occupied females would be approximately 10,246,280 giving a total potential occupied labour force of about 23 million. It should be noted that about 80 per cent of the women gainfully occupied were in Primary Production, and approximately 20 per cent in trading. Indications, however, were that the 1968 distribution of females among major industrial groups would alter somewhat, in view of established upward trend in the employment of females in the wage-earning sector. This is confirmed by the annual Employment and Earnings Enquiry of the Federal Ministry of Labour as follows:

TABLE 8(iv)   *Female Participation Rates in Wage-Earning Employment, Nigeria. 1956–61*

	Participation
Year	rate (%)
1956	2·1
1957	2·2
1958	2·6
1959	3·6
1960	5·1
1961	5·5

By projecting these figures, the female participation rate in wage-earning employment would be approximately 10 per cent in 1968 as against 2·1 per cent in 1956 and 5·5 per cent in 1961.

It is not so clear how the male/female participation ratios would have changed in the primary and trading sectors by 1968. But on the basis of what has been said so far, the potential employment distribution at full employment would be as follows:

M.P.D.N.—5*

TABLE 8(v)   *Forecast of Nigeria's Occupied Manpower in 1968, by Major Economic Activity*

Activity	Employment level
Primary Production (own account)	15,640,000
Trading (Commerce) (own account)	3,450,000
Wage-earning, etc.	3,910,000
ALL ACTIVTIIES	23,000,000

In Table 8(v), the sector which is most important from the point of view of high-level and skilled manpower forecasting is that on wage-earning, etc. It includes, generally, the senior officers, trainers and Government extension workers for the primary production and trading (commercial) sectors. Moreover, an allowance needed to be made in the residual figure of 3·9 million for students undergoing training and education in schools, colleges, etc., where students come within the age groups in the potential labour force, i.e., 15 years and above. This was estimated at about 433,000, giving the estimated number of persons engaged in wage-earning and crafts to be about 3,444,000 as against a corresponding figure for 1963 of 3,181,000.

In 1963 the demand for high-level and skilled manpower of all grades covered in the manpower survey was approximately 6 per cent of the total number of persons estimated to be employed in wage-earning. As the economy grows, however, the ratio of high-level and skilled manpower grows in relation to total employment. The rate of increase in the ratio differs according to the interplay of many social and economic factors—e.g. educational policies, the availability of training facilities, rate and direction of economic growth, etc. On the basis of observed trends in Nigeria and in some of the countries already mentioned, it was estimated that in 1968 the proportion of high-level and skilled manpower to total employment in the wage sector would be about 9·5 per cent. On this basis the number of high-level and skilled manpower required in 1968 would be about 335,000.

Employment distribution by manpower category

The next step was to determine the proportions of total employees that would be in the various high-level manpower categories and for this the ratios indicated by the Survey were, to some degree, used as a guide. The extent to which modifications were made will be referred to later.

The number of high-level manpower so obtained was then allocated as between public and private employment. The Manpower Survey showed that in 1963 the private sector accounted for 38 per cent of the high-level manpower employed. It seemed clear, however, that the growth potential of employment in private industry was now greater than in the public sector. This is because the rapid growth of employment in the public sector was slowing down considerably with the attainment of Independence and the settlement of the administrative and institutional structure required to sustain the new constitutional set-up, while a major aim of policy is to foster and encourage the growth of private industries. It was accordingly presumed on the basis of recent performance of the economy, that by the end of the forecast year in 1968, the overall utilization of high-level manpower in private industry should be about equal to that in the public sector.

The final step in the forecast was to allocate the high-level manpower budgets between the various categories and occupations. Here again certain important judgements had to be made. It had been observed from the Survey that the high-level and skilled manpower structure, i.e. the proportional relationships between the senior, intermediate and other categories was rather top heavy. In advanced countries the relationship was often of the nature of $1:5:20$ or $1:5:25$. The situation for private industry in Nigeria as revealed in the Manpower Survey was approximately $1:1\frac{2}{3}:3$, as follows:

Senior Category	5,916
Intermediate Category	10,040
Other (Skilled) Category	17,617

The proportions of the various categories actually used by employers appeared, however, to be explained mainly by their relative supply and not by preconceived ideas of an ideal or most economic skill-mix. In budgeting for the future, therefore, it appears desirable to allow for a gradual build-up of the Intermediate and other (skilled) categories to achieve a more rational relationship, within the realms of feasibility. It had to be accepted that the approach to the relative proportions of the more advanced countries could not be immediately realized. Even if the resources were available to turn out the large numbers of 'other (skilled) category' personnel, for example, in order to realize such ratios, it was unlikely that enough employment opportunities would be available in the short period of five years covered by the Survey, to absorb all of them; and the result would be to create an army of skilled unemployed persons. It was accordingly decided that a reasonable approach should be, during the forecast period, merely to improve on existing ratios.[10] The result of this approach is that in the private sector the 1968 skill-mix was taken as 1:2:4 as follows:

Senior Category	24,140
Intermediate Category	48,280
Other (Skilled) Category	96,570

In view of the peculiar nature of their structure, ratios of 1:4:2 were used for the Civil Service and the Local and Native Authorities. The ratios for Public Boards and Corporations were taken to be the same as for private industry, namely, 1:2:4. These give composite ratios for all Public Authorities of about 1:4:3 in 1968 as against 1:4:2 in 1963.

In classifying the manpower needs by occupation, provision was made for the necessity to allow for a build-up in the fields of acute shortages. For example, provision was made in the public sector for nuclei of chemical and metallurgical engineers and for physicists, none of which existed in 1963. The continued importance of primary production and the need for specialist staff and extension workers to increase agricultural productivity were acknowledged by allowing relatively large increases in agriculturists, veterinarians and their supporting staff.

Occupational needs were budgeted also with due regard for desirable inter-occupational ratios; e.g. engineers *vis-à-vis* engineering assistants and technicians; in 1963 the demand for engineers in the public sector (i.e. actual number employed *plus* vacancies) was 1,048 and the corresponding figure for engineering technicians and assistants was 4,043, giving a ratio of roughly 1:4. The 1968 forecast provided for 2,575 engineers and 11,000 engineering technicians and assistants, thus giving a ratio of 1:5.

Teaching and research staff

The future needs for teaching and research staff were calculated on the basis of the future high-level manpower needs in other fields, the

[10] It is suggested that Nigeria might attempt to attain the 'ideal' ratios of 1:5:25 over a period of four Development Plans as follows in the private Sector: 1963–8—1:2:4; 1968–73—1:3:9; 1973–8—1:4:16; 1978–83—1:5:25.

requirements for expansion in the educational and training institutions necessary to meet those needs, and assumed teacher-student ratios.

The needs for teachers in the Technical Institutes and Trade Centres were forecast respectively on the estimated enrolments which was considered necessary to meet the needs for the intermediate and other (skilled) categories. In the case of the Technical Institutes, account was taken only of such occupations in the intermediate category which could best be, or are traditionally, developed within the Institutes. For example, although the needs for junior managerial and administrative staff and for nurses and midwives were high, these do not need to be trained in the Technical Institutes. The same considerations were used in determining the enrolments in the Trade Centres. Thus a selection was made of the occupations for which training can be provided in the Trade Centres and similar institutions such as mechanics, plumbers, welders, carpenters; it was then assumed that the students would spend not more than three years in the Trade Centres, the rest of their training being carried out in industry.

Having decided on the numbers to be trained in the Technical Institutes and Trade Centres, an additional 10 per cent was allowed for student failures, drop-outs, etc. The levels of teaching staff required were then estimated on an assumed teacher/student ratio of $1:15$ in the Technical Institutes (the optimum now being used in Nigeria) and $1:30$ in Trade Centres. (The advisability of using these ratios is discussed subsequently.)

The teaching staff estimates for primary and secondary schools are based on their enrolment forecasts in the Six-Year Development Plan. The estimated enrolments in Teacher Training Colleges from which their teaching staff requirements were calculated, were based mainly on the figures of estimated teaching staff requirements in primary schools.

Table 8(vi) summarizes Nigeria's high-level manpower as forecast in this paper, compared with the Ashby Commission's target for 1970.

VII. *Appraisal of the Forecast*

It is clear that the utility of a manpower forecast must depend greatly upon the degree of reliability put on it. In a sense, there is nothing like a reliable manpower forecast. This is because, by its very nature, a forecast is an attempt not only to see the future, but to foretell what it

TABLE 8(vi)   *Comparative Estimates of Nigeria's High-Level Manpower Targets*

Manpower Category	Ashby Commission 1970 Target	1963 Actual	Full Employment Target
Senior Managerial and Professional	28,875	17,890(a)	48,264
Intermediate	37,275	48,767(a)	129,260
Graduate Teachers	7,000	3,571	
Non-Graduate Qualified Teachers	18,000	25,680	134,215
Other Teachers	—	78,727(b)	

Note: (a) Equivalent to total demand; i.e. allowing for non-response (10 per cent) and vacancies.
(b) Includes Grade III and other non-qualified Teachers.

holds in store. The problems of manpower forecasting are essentially human problems, and human problems and reactions are highly unpredictable. Nevertheless, development planning is predicated upon the realization that the course of human endeavour can be consciously affected and, if need be, significantly altered. Manpower forecasting is a prerequisite to ensuring that current and future economic development shall not be frustrated because of a failure to find the necessary trained manpower. It is therefore equally important not to use the unpredictability of future events as an excuse for not making a manpower forecast. As already mentioned in this paper, the important thing is to ensure that, local circumstances considered, the judgements upon which the forecast is made are reasonable, and that there are no inherent inconsistencies in the methods used and the results obtained. It is for critics to evaluate, and subsequent events to justify or modify, the judgements made. This section is an attempt to find some criteria for examining the reasonableness or validity of the forecasting method used in this paper, particularly from the point of view of feasibility.

An essential question appears to be whether it is reasonably possible for Nigeria, considering its resources of finance, etc., to achieve the targets set out by the forecast? A valid answer could be that it is not for the forecaster to determine questions of feasibility and means, but only ends. The position is that on the basis of the assumptions explained in this paper, it appears to be desirable that Nigeria should achieve the high-level and skilled manpower targets forecast, if she is to have a dynamic full-employment economy. Nevertheless it is for practical purposes necessary to examine the said needs in the light of available resources—particularly the educational and training facilities, and the rate of economic growth.

The following table indicates the estimated out-turn between 1963 and 1968 of persons in the various categories of manpower and the estimated additional needs arising from the forecast developed in this paper.

TABLE 8(vii)   *Estimated Needs and Out-turn of High-Level and Skilled Manpower 1963–8*

Category	Estimated Additional Needs	Estimated Out-turn (Existing Schemes)	Short Fall
Senior	35,133	7,285	27,848
Intermediate	94,851	14,141	80,710
Other (Skilled)	129,214	9,001	120,213

The table indicates that if the targets forecast are to be attained, current output of trained manpower has to be stepped up by nearly five times in the senior category, by over six times and by about 14 times, for intermediate and skilled manpower, respectively. Equally, in order to meet the needs for intermediate manpower on the basis of the forecast, the teaching staff in the Technical Institutes would need to be expanded tenfold, from 95 in 1963, to 990. But as already indicated, this is based on a teacher/student ratio of 1:15 which is the optimum currently used in Nigeria. In fact, the ratio in 1963 was, for the whole country, about 1:27. It varied from about 1:10 in Northern Nigeria to about 1:40 in the Federal Territory. The UNESCO Conference on the Development of Higher Education in Africa has, however, recommended that for this category of manpower the teacher/student ratio should be 1:20.[11] If this were applied to Nigeria then the teaching staff required would be only about four times instead of ten times its present strength. If on the other hand, the needs were regarded as an emergency, lower ratios of 1:30 or 1:40 could even be used, thus reducing still further the number of additional teachers required.

It does not seem that an expectation of about a threefold increase in the number of teachers in Technical Institutes is unreasonable, particu-

[11] *The Development of Higher Education in Africa* (UNESCO, 1963), p. 71, Recommendation 16.

larly bearing in mind the possibility of foreign technical assistance in this field and the current under-utilization of the student places in the Technical Institutes. The problems of equipping the Institutes to cope with the increased size of students is of course another problem.

The estimated needs would also mean that Nigeria should produce about 8,000 graduates and professional staff per annum. The current estimated output of 7,285 from all sources up to 1968 is about 1,500 per annum. The Ashby Commission recommended that in future, Nigeria's senior category personnel should normally be trained through the Universities. With five universities in Nigeria, the esti-mated needs would mean an average out-turn of 1,600 graduates per annum and a student population of about 4,800 per university (assum-ing three-year degree courses); and allowing for failures, drop-outs, etc., an enrolment of about 5,000 per university.

The UNESCO conference to which reference has been made, recom-mended a teacher/student ratio in the Universities of approximately 1:15. If this were applied to Nigeria, then the University enrolment in 1968 would be approximately 22,500. It appears, therefore, that only a little extra effort would be required to reach the target of 25,000 for the five universities which the estimated needs seemed to require. And it may be mentioned that this goal of an enrolment of 5,000 per University happens to be the optimum size recommended for African Universities by the UNESCO Conference.[12] From the point of view of existing University facilities, therefore, it does appear that the targets of manpower needs forecasts for 1968 are feasible, provided early effort is made to meet the staffing needs.

Because of the various means by which craftsmen are trained, it is not easy to evaluate the forecast in respect of the skilled (other) category on the above lines. On the assumption that most craftsmen will in future do at least part of their training in Trade Centres or equivalent institutions (a somewhat unreal assumption) the teaching staff required to meet the needs have been estimated at 1,244 or just over three times the 1963 strength of 357. This appears to be feasible.

The current educational and training targets in Nigeria are guided principally by the recommendations of the Ashby Commission as amended in the Federal Government Sessional Paper No. 3 of 1961.[13] The targets forecast above may now be examined in the light of those

12 Ibid., Recommendation 18, p. 71.
13 *Educational Development 1961–70* (Federal Printing Division, Lagos, 1961).

targets. The Sessional Paper set a target of total university enrolment at 10,000. This would produce about 3,000 graduates per annum. The current manpower forecast would therefore necessitate more than a doubling of current University targets as set by the Government. It is clear, however, from the current plans of the universities that their own targets would exceed those set by Government. The Government's target for technicians allows for an out-turn of 5,000 per annum from Technical Institutes as against about 12,000 which the forecast would require. Again, the Government set a target out-turn of agricultural assistants at 600 per annum. The current out-turn is a little over 100 per annum, while on the basis of the forecast, the annual out-turn should be about 1,550, the five-year additional needs having been estimated at 7,855. Since the targets already set by the Federal Government have not been attained, it may seem unrealistic to set new targets which exceed existing targets by such wide margins.

Finally the manpower forecasts may be examined in the light of the views of Professor W. Arthur Lewis.[14] On the basis of his own assumptions Professor Lewis estimated that Nigeria's requirements for persons with graduate or equivalent education should be of the order of 1,400 per annum. As in the method used in this paper, the acceptability of that depends on the assumptions upon which it was based. For example, using a predetermined formula, Professor Lewis 'guesses' that the number of graduates and persons with equivalent qualifications, required per annum in Nigeria should be 13·9 per cent of the *existing* number of graduates (or equivalent professions), and the figure which he used as a benchmark was a little over 10,000. In fact, however, the position of 'graduates (or equivalent professions)' in Nigeria in 1963 was as follows:

Senior Managerial and Professional Staff	13,780
Graduate Teachers and Research Staff	3,571
	17,351
10 per cent Under-estimation	1,735
	19,086

On this basis and using the formula of Professor Lewis, the out-turn of graduates (or equivalent professions) required in Nigeria, would be about 2,640 per annum, *not* 1,400. It is to be noted that Professor

[14] cf. W. A. Lewis, *Education and Economic Development*, Annex IV in the *Final Report of the Conference of African States on the Development of Education in Africa*, Addis Ababa, 15–25 May 1961 (UNESCO).

Lewis appears to ignore the fact that the actual number of graduates in a country at any particular time is a result of the interplay of many factors, and does not necessarily acquire any scientific merit. The fact that, as in Nigeria, the demand for graduates (or equivalent professions) may far outstrip the actual number available and that the latter may bear no necessary or immutable relationship to the former appears also to have escaped his attention.

On the above grounds alone, it appears that the estimate of Professor Lewis for graduates (or equivalent professions) in respect of Nigeria would be invalid, and provides no useful basis for appraising the forecast of approximately 8,000 graduates per annum that has been made. In any case it is to be noted that his estimate is already short of the existing rate of out-turn of graduates of over 2,000 per annum which, judging from the large number of vacancies, is far from adequate to meet current demand.

Merely to say this, however, is perhaps, to do some injustice to Professor Lewis. For he was probably more concerned with an aspect of manpower planning and development ignored by the method developed in this paper—namely, the question of the capacity of the economy to absorb high-level manpower. In the long run, as Professor Lewis points out, an economy can absorb any number of educated and trained manpower. In the short run, however, there is the danger of creating unemployment due to oversupply. This means that the feasibility approach (i.e. the output capacity of the educational system) which has been adopted above, in appraising the manpower forecast is perhaps inadequate. The question is, if it were possible for Nigeria to produce all the high-level manpower that has been forecast by 1968, will the economy be able to absorb them? If the judgement of employers is to be taken as any guide, then the answer is decidedly in the negative, especially bearing in mind that the effects of future development and plans were supposed to have been taken into consideration in the employers' estimates. On the other hand, the indirect employment effects of investments envisaged in the Development Plan and by the private employers who made a forecast do not appear to have been taken into consideration, and this again suggests that their estimates were doubly inadequate.

Nevertheless the gaps between the estimates of the employers and the forecasts made in this paper are so wide that there appears to be no doubt that even if it were possible to achieve these targets in the limited time for which the forecast was made, it might be unwise to accept them in full. While it is clear that the estimates of the employers are too conservative it is not so clear what margin of error there is in the present forecast, or by how much it should be revised downwards in the light of the principle of absorptive capacity. An essential consideration of the Seminar, therefore, was the examination of the possibilities of revising the estimates. Had the National Development Plan been more comprehensive, it might have been sufficient to anchor manpower estimates to it, although this might mean that the full-employment objective, upon which the forecast is based, would not be attained. Thus, it does seem that if the estimates now made have to be revised downwards, then Nigeria must for some time to come be content with some measure of unemployment. On the other hand, in revising the current estimates downwards, one must not lose sight of the fact that properly educated and trained manpower, if they are in the 'right' occupations tend, to some extent, to generate their own demand even if this means a revaluation of their economic status and aspirations.

In conclusion, therefore, the problem which this paper posed for the Seminar was by how much, in what direction, and on what basis, should the forecast of Nigeria's manpower needs for 1968, examined in this paper, be revised to take cognizance of the need for adequate manpower to sustain a desirable rate of economic growth without training so many that the economy is itself unable to absorb them.

9
Summary of Discussion and Conclusions (II)

1. The starting point for the consideration of manpower planning in Nigeria is the comprehensive National Development Plan for the period 1962–8. The objectives of the plan are the raising of general living standards and the achievement of a diversified and self-sustaining economy through accelerated industrial development and the improvement of agricultural production. It should be noted, however, that the Plan does not specifically establish employment objectives, and it is desirable, or indeed essential that this should be remedied during future planning.

2. The Seminar was in general agreement with Professor Harbison that the central objective of manpower planning is to construct a strategy of human resource development consistent with a country's broader aims of social, political and economic development. For giving a realistic shape to this objective it is necessary to assess Nigeria's present and future needs for high-level and skilled manpower, and to provide those responsible for planning education and training arrangements with targets both in terms of numbers and categories of disciplines and crafts. The setting of targets would require, on the one hand, working out the manpower supply and demand at the current period and, on the other, estimating these needs for the plan period. The task of manpower planning can indeed be conceived of in two stages, the short-term covering the period of the National Development Plan, and the long-term, a forecast of needs in ten or twenty years.

3. Certain salient aspects of the manpower situation in Nigeria require early emphasis. The country's economy is characterized by a small but growing modern sector with the majority of the population engaged in peasant agriculture. (It is agriculture which provides through the export crops the bulk of the country's foreign exchange earnings.) The latest available returns show that only about 550,000 persons are employed in establishments with ten or more workers—and this

includes all government establishments, schools and universities. The rate of growth of this labour force is critical on a number of counts. Firstly, as an indicator of the rate of growth of wage-earning employment and of the pace at which industrial diversification is being achieved; secondly, because it largely controls the rate at which high-level and skilled manpower will be utilized; and thirdly, and perhaps most important of all, it is an indicator of the extent to which young people entering the labour market for the first time can be absorbed into productive wage-earning employment. We shall refer again later to this last point, but it should be recognized at once that only a fraction of the young people who are leaving school and looking for work each year can at present be absorbed into wage-earning employment.

4. The numbers employed in establishments with ten or more workers have risen from 415,000 in 1956 to approximately 550,000 in 1963. The extent of the coverage of the relevant statistics was notably more complete in 1963 than was the case in the first year in which these returns were called for from employers (1956). To this extent the increase in numbers employed will tend to be on the optimistic side. But taking them at their face value the average annual rate at which new jobs have been created in Government employment and in industry has been approximately 20,000. A more detailed analysis of these figures should, however, be undertaken to identify, so far as possible, the sectors of employment in which these increases have taken place. It is apparent, for example, that the expansion of Government services and of the educational system accounts for a considerable proportion of the total increase in jobs since 1956, and that expansion in the field of industrial employment was less rapid.

5. Although the bulk of high-level and skilled manpower is to be found among this group, i.e., those employed in establishments with ten or more workers, it would be valuable if an examination could be made of the possibility of extending the coverage to employers having five or more workers, or alternatively to seek, by sampling methods or otherwise, to establish what proportion of wage earners are employed in establishments with less than ten workers. Experience elsewhere suggests that the proportion so employed may be as low as 5–20 per cent,[1] but in view of the large numbers of self-employed craftsmen and entrepreneurs in the Nigerian economy who employ one or two helpers

[1] Based on detailed surveys of high-level manpower conducted in Ghana, Tanganyika, Uganda, British Guiana from 1959–62.

for wages it is possible that the proportion in Nigeria may be substantially higher. At present there is little evidence to suggest that the rate of new job creation in wage-earning employment is likely, in the near future, to exceed the 20,000 each year which represents experience since 1956. This must be placed against the figure of about 400,000 additional school leavers who each year will be looking for work.

6. Turning from this broad review of the labour market, the valuable report placed before the Seminar by the National Manpower Board gives an insight into the high-level and skilled components of the labour force and a basis for estimating future needs. A serious bottleneck towards long range manpower planning in detail is the lack of requisite statistical data. Current statistics on economic and social characteristics of population, labour force participation rates, employment, unemployment and under-employment, output, productivity, rural-urban migration, replacement needs, capital-labour ratios, etc., are either still lacking or, if available, suffer from serious limitations. In view of this, the available data and their reliability are at present not sufficient for detailed manpower calculations. For these reasons, which are common to all countries in the early stages of development, attention should be concentrated on short-range manpower planning based on available firm data about the existing position regarding wage-employment in larger establishments (employing 10 or more persons), the likely needs in the immediate future, and matching these needs against the supply prospects.

7. It is recommended that high priority should be given to the identification of the statistical gaps and deficiencies and that steps should be taken to improve them progressively. This would be useful not only to the Manpower Board but also to other agencies engaged in planning. In this connection it should not be necessary for the Manpower Board to saddle itself with the responsibility for the collection of all manpower statistics—as much of these as possible should be entrusted to the statistical services of the Federal and Regional Governments which, in planning and executing these statistical projects, should work as appropriate within the framework of objectives established by, or agreed with the Manpower Board. A further advantage arises from co-ordinating these statistical projects with the over-all integrated programmes of statistics development being formulated and implemented under the guidance of the Standing Committee on Statistics of the Joint Planning Committee of the National Economic

Council. It is understandable, however, that for some time to come, certain types of statistics, particularly of a diagnostic type requiring investigations by specialists, will have to be collected by the Manpower Secretariat.

8. In the discussion of Dr. Yesufu's papers and the reports of the National Manpower Board, it was noted that estimates of future man-power needs were based on the desirability of the economy to achieve full employment. In the light of the arguments advanced earlier, it was agreed that having regard to the employment potential of the current Development Plan, and the current rate of economic growth, this objective was not likely to be attained by 1968. Thus assumptions about full employment embodied in the existing forecasts should, for the time being be modified. Moreover, where comparisons are made for planning purposes between, for example, the proportion of graduates and technicians in developed countries with the proportions found in Nigeria, such comparisons should only be made between the advanced economy as a whole and the 'modern' sector only of Nigeria's economy; preferably, however, the comparison should be between the appropriate sector of the more advanced economy and its counterpart in Nigeria.

9. It is strongly recommended that in estimating future needs the principal factor on which estimates should be based should be the rate of growth of wage-earning employment, employers' estimates of future needs being tested by the application of ratios of high-level manpower growth deriving from experience elsewhere in developing economies.[2] These rates convey broad orders of magnitude only and will clearly vary as between one sector of the economy and another; it is desirable, therefore, that at an early stage there should be undertaken an analysis of skill-mix in the separate sectors of the economy. The ratios thus established can then be used as guide in estimating future needs, sector by sector (or on the basis of physical stock), and providing a check on employers' estimates. As indicated in the report of the Manpower Board, an additional allowance should normally be made for wastage at the rate of 3 per cent per annum[3] on the existing employ-

[2] As a rough guide, the following multipliers may be useful. Where the annual growth rate of the national income is or is expected to be X per cent, total employment may, at the stage of Nigeria's economy, normally be expected to increase annually at about $\frac{1}{2}$X per cent, the need for technicians at 3X per cent and senior categories by 2X per cent.

[3] This is based on present experience but should be subject to periodical review.

ment level. Included in the 'stock' figure will be the number of expatriates at present employed. In the absence of reasonably accurate basis for estimating the rate at which these expatriates will be replaced it may be convenient to show a higher and lower target figure for manpower targets, the higher figure being based on the complete replacement of expatriates in the plan period; and the lower figure on the assumption that no change takes place in the number of expatriates in that period.

10. It is important to note, however, that as the administrative structure of Government becomes more settled, and schools and universities become better staffed, the rate of growth of the manpower requirements for the social services and public administration is likely to slow down, particularly in respect of qualified graduate manpower. It should be possible to establish with some measure of accuracy the rate at which any slowing down will take place, and to take cognizance of this in determining future manpower requirements.

11. Attention is drawn particularly to the special importance of high-level and skilled manpower in the agricultural sector, and it is recommended that urgent attention should be given to the relationship between existing vacancies in this sector and the anticipated outturn from universities and training establishments. Special attention should be paid in this connection to the supply of middle-level manpower particularly for agricultural extension work (recruited so far as possible in the rural areas). The relationship between current vacancies and scholarship policy and the extent to which the university faculties were being fully utilized, also require examination. In this connection it was noted that the National Manpower Board was already being consulted on scholarship policy.

12. In view of the importance to the work of the National Manpower Board of the rapid implementation of sample surveys, specific research projects, etc., and the value of building up the senior staff of the Board on a basis of experienced specialists, the administrative and financial arrangements for the National Manpower Board and its degree of autonomy, including the possibility of statutory status, should be such as to facilitate these objectives.

Part Three

Education and Training

10

Educational Philosophy and Structure for Economic Development

A. Babs Fafunwa

PROFESSOR OF EDUCATION, UNIVERSITY OF NIGERIA, NSUKKA

I. Philosophies of Education

Man, in his quest for certainty, turns to philosophy, the science that seeks to organize and systematize all fields of knowledge as a means of understanding and interpreting the totality of reality. Educational philosophy is any philosophy dealing with or applied to the process of education, and used as a basis for the general determination, interpretation and evaluation of educational objectives, practices, outcome, needs, and materials of study. Philosophy attempts to ask and to answer questions that are sometimes stubborn, often baffling and occasionally disturbing, but so long as human societies are confronted with perplexities, obstacles and choices, men must think as much as they are able and act in terms of their thinking. Sometimes, of course, some philosophers are far more skillful in questioning answers than in answering questions.

Education is the aggregate of all the processes by means of which a person develops ability, attitudes and other forms of behaviour of positive value in the society in which we live; education is, therefore, more than schooling. A system of education to be useful, must be based on certain philosophical or theoretical assumptions and should seek to justify its usefulness in terms of its practices and results. However, there is no such thing as the philosophy of education: indeed there are many philosophies of education. According to John Brabacher, the noted educational historian, Plato in his *Republic* produced the 'only notable philosophy of education' before the twentieth century. It would be recalled that the ancient philosopher proposed an ideal society in which the citizens were divided into three classes: the philosophers who governed the state; the warriors who defended the state; and the farmers and craftsmen who produced and distributed its material wealth. To implement these goals, three different institutions were created for the selection and training of each class. The twentieth century has, however, witnessed many conflicting theories of education and the main extremes are to be found in traditionalism, conservatism and essentialism—theories that represent or emphasize the importance of authority, order and control by fixed standards or more precisely, theories that uphold educational authoritarianism and educational *laissez faire* as opposed to progressive education, otherwise known as Educational Experimentalism, or Pragmatic Education.

No doubt each has its value and it is unlikely that both are mutually exclusive. But the question to be answered later in this paper is 'what, not which, will serve Nigeria better in the light of her present and future development?' Plato, Kant, Harris, Horne and Gentile were noted for their idealistic philosophy. Locke, Johann Herbart and Herbert Spencer were noted for the realistic philosophy of education. John Dewey and William Kilpatrick, two leading American philosophers believed in pragmatism and instrumentalism in education. Educational authoritarianism signifies external imposition and dictation. It is the attitude assumed by all those who think, plan and act as though education is a pre-determined process and that there is only one sure road to success and no other. This term is also applicable to those who defend and support theories that justify such external control and direction. After the Middle Ages and just before the industrial revolution, most of Europe was divided into two classes; the upper and the lower classes. The former controlled all sectors of the economic, social and political life and stoutly defended the *status quo*.

When charity schools for the poor were becoming popular in England in 1722, Bernard Mandeville clearly expressed the upper class attitude to the education of the lower class:

'There is no need for any learning at all for the meanest Ranks of mankind; Their Business is to Labour not to Think; Their Duty is to do what they are commanded, to fill up the most servile Posts, and to perform the lowest offices and Drudgeries of Life for the conveniency of their Superiors, and common Nature gives them knowledge enough for this purpose . . . The more a shepherd, a Ploughman, or any other peasant, knows of the world . . . the less fit will he be to go through fatigues and hardship of it with cheerfulness and content . . .'

The famous Dr. Samuel Johnson once said: 'Those born to poverty and drudgery should not be deprived by an improper education of the opiate of ignorance.' A familiar English folk rhyme goes:

'God bless the squire and his relations
And keep us in our proper stations.'

Educational *laissez faire*, on the other hand, assumes that education is determined by factors within the individual while *progressivism* or *experimentalism* regards education as cultural transition. This educational philosophy unlike the other two schools, recognizes the dynamism of any given culture; it is a transitional philosophy standing between the old and the new, the conservative or traditional and the progressive states of mind, men and matters. The philosophy of experimentalism is sometimes designated as pragmatism, instrumentalism or humanism. Pragmatism is built on the hypothesis that the truth of any judgement or idea is tested by and consists of its success when applied to practical life situations.

For many centuries, education relied almost solely on religious philosophers for its guiding principles, but within the last one hundred years and particularly during the present century, educational theories and principles have been greatly influenced by psychologists, sociologists, biologists, psychiatrists, physicians, pediatricians and many other professionals and specialists. Through the aid of research, experiments and observation, we now know more about muscular control and motor co-ordination; general and special mental abilities; emotional balance, imbalance and control; the learning process, etc. Through sociological and anthropological studies, we now know that a child's cultural background and socio-economic environment play an important part in his growth and development. For example, Darwin's theory of evolution, Mendel's work in genetics, Pavlov's experience in the conditioned reflex have influenced educational theories and practices and these in turn have stimulated many studies in theories of learning. We now know that the study of Latin and Greek neither sharpens the mind nor makes the individual a master of all trades. Thorndike and other eminent psychologists and educators who have studied individual differences, proved that it was the superior ability of the pupils tested that enabled them to master such difficult subjects as Latin, Algebra, Greek, etc., and that it was not the study of these subjects that made these pupils superior. John Dewey, the great American philosopher and psychologist of the twentieth century emphasized *Learning* through *Doing*. His philosophical approach to education, generally styled pragmatism, has almost completely revolutionized childhood education and formal education in the school.

II. *The Importance of Education for Under-developed Countries*

Nigeria, if it is to move rapidly from the eighteenth century into the late twentieth century, will have to place education into the mainstream of economic, social and cultural development, for it seems inescapable that no major industrial revolution can either take place or be sustained, no new society can be built or maintained, in a country where the masses are still held down largely by ignorance, disease and poverty. Traditional educational pattern, *à la* United Kingdom, has contributed in no small measure to the failure of social and economic progress in Nigeria. A complete reassessment of the present educational system in the light of our changing circumstances is a *sine qua non* and a pragmatic approach may be of immense help to us in this direction.

It cannot be over-emphasized that a good system of education is one which is realistically geared to the needs and aspirations of the people and the country it purports to serve. The classical concept of education for its own sake is frankly a luxury which no under-developed country such as Nigeria can afford in this twentieth century. Indeed, it would be a remarkable achievement if by A.D. 2000 the average Nigerian citizen could claim to have had at least an elementary education or its equivalent (we shall return to this point later). When we say that an educational system, if it is to be meaningful, must relate to the needs and circumstances of the people it serves, we mean that it must take into account the social, economic, cultural and political needs of the citizens. What, we may ask, is the good of basic or fundamental education if it does not help the individual who receives it to solve some of his immediate personal problems or worse still, if all it does is to make him worse off than if he had had no formal education at all. Surely the alternative path does not lie in the discontinuance of the system but in an agonizing reappraisal of the system with a view to making that system more potent and more dynamic in the hope that it can be remoulded to suit the changing needs of a changing society.

Some of the major problems of education in Africa are largely tied to the problems of illiteracy, poverty and disease; these three often go hand in hand. Africa's millions still suffer from these maladies; they were part of the colonial heritage, but by and large the problems still persist in varying degrees today, in spite of the tremendous effort that many African leaders are exerting in these directions. The cause for the slow process of change is partly due to the fact that many of the African leaders are attempting to solve these problems with an antiquated tool, which, in this case, is the old colonial system of education. But it is most unlikely that one can use yesterday's tool for today's job and expect to be in business tomorrow. There is indeed no greater force for social, economic and political advancement than a good educational system realistically organized and judiciously applied with skill and insight. Many economists and educators have come to appreciate the inescapable fact that education is a basic factor for economic development today, with particular reference to under-developed countries. New skills have to be developed, new attitudes to life and work have to be built into the personality of the average Nigerian youth through the instrumentality of education—formal or informal. Technical know-how, appropriate use of tools of all kinds, are related to the attitude of the users. 'Productivity, the measure of the *efficiency* with which a nation's resources are transformed into commodities and services, is not simply a function of the amount of manpower, raw materials, physical capital and equipment available and in use. Productivity also depends heavily on the attitudes, knowledge and skills of people, which in turn reflect the education, training and complex organisations which modern technology requires.'[1] It, however, takes a little longer to develop new attitudes than to construct multi-storey buildings, erect complex machinery, dam rivers or tar roads.

It is not a mere coincidence that certain countries, such as the United States and United Kingdom, are considered to be developed and certain others, like Nigeria, are under-developed. The following table summarizes some of the significant contrasts between the two categories of countries.

Each of the items listed relates to human factors such as attitudes, skills and tools, incentives or aspirations. There seems accordingly, to be a clearly defined relationship between under-development on the

[1] H. W. Peter, 'Guidelines in the Process of Change', *United Nations Conference Paper on application of Science and Technology*, Geneva, February 1963 (E/Conf. 39/J/81).

TABLE 10(i) *Contrasting Characteristics of Developed and Under-developed Countries*

Developed Countries	Under-developed Countries
1. High-level economy	1. Low-level economy
2. High percentage of literacy (80–98 per cent)	2. Low percentage of literacy (5–50 per cent)
3. Large percentage of technical labour force, specialists and highly industrialized community; efficiency	3. Peasant and agrarian economy, inefficiency and poor organization
4. High *per capita* income	4. Very low *per capita* income
5. Low mortality rate, preventive health programme	5. High mortality rate, disease, squalor
6. Independent for many years	6. Recently autonomous or still colonial
7. Well-organized and fairly stable political system	7. Transitional political stage
8. Citizenship rights and obligations recognized	8. Transitional stage
9. Education geared to the needs of the people and the country	9. Inherited system from the colonial era with little relevance to the needs of the people and the country or sheer imperviousness to changing times
10. Manufacturers	10. Consumers
11. Masses, by and large scientifically oriented, less superstitious and generally efficient	11. Masses largely superstitious, scientifically illiterate and have not acquired technical efficiency

one hand, and mass illiteracy, low level or peasant economy, low *per capita* income, shortage of technical and skilled labour, and high mortality rate, on the other hand. The common thread that runs through the eleven listed items in the table above is the presence or absence of poverty, disease and ignorance, depending on which side of the table we are concerned with.

Nigeria's natural and human resources remain largely untapped. Its greatest potential and most valuable asset is its human resources—men, women and children. Nigeria needs literate manpower to help develop her natural resources adequately, since it is clear that excellent programmes in the areas of agriculture, health, welfare, slum clearance, town planning, housing, maternity and child welfare centres, costing millions of pounds, may fail to mature if the people are not educated to use modern contrivances effectively. Even in advanced countries simple rules and laws of sanitation are kept constantly in the public mind by posters and notices such as 'Men', 'Women', 'Don't Spit', 'Out of Bounds', 'Danger', etc. Without constant visual aids and the written words, the educated or the so-called sophisticated man may even fall below the expected standard. What is more, teachers, research workers, other professional people in medicine, law, engineering, etc., lean heavily on the library and other collections as educational props. An illiterate individual is invariably a poor consumer of goods, a pawn in the hands of the unscrupulous politician, and a victim of superstition and magic. No nation can ever hope to develop to maximum capacity for as long as the majority of its people are illiterate.

III. *Towards Universal and Functional Literacy*

To reach the masses of the Nigerian non-literate population, that is to say, men, women and children, greater emphasis must be placed on Nursery, Elementary and Adult Education. A close analysis of the problems of the under-developed countries in terms of economic, social and political developments will show that every conceivable aspect of the people's lives needs some adjustment or further development. In fact, in any dynamic society, all areas of human activities are undergoing tremendous changes; consequently, new ways of doing things, new problems, emerge as old ones are resolved; new skills, new tools and new knowledge open new vistas and again create new problems and challenges. Highly skilled manpower calls for training at high levels, preferably at the secondary and higher education level; but high-level manpower cannot work in a vacuum and low-level manpower must, therefore, be trained, lest high-level manpower will have little or no supporting lower cadre of skills, and this in turn will have to be done at the elementary level; otherwise, the higher manpower will be forced to perform low-level manpower function, thus wasting valuable human assets. It is therefore essential that all under-developed countries should develop all levels of education, but greater emphasis or priority must be placed at one or two of these educational levels.

Irrespective of whatever level of education is chosen as the first priority, training and procurement of teachers must precede all other considerations; nevertheless, training of teachers is an integral part of educational planning for any level of education and, that being the case, the introduction of elementary education or the development of secondary or higher education will presuppose the availability of teachers in sufficient numbers to man the institutions. While there is a dire need for personnel of university calibre at the top level and a realistic need for personnel with secondary education training for intermediate level, perhaps the only levels that reach the grass roots in terms of the millions of any given population are the primary and adult education levels. These combined, are the ones that may do the greatest good for the greatest number, provided the curriculum is realistically planned and judiciously carried out.

Education, broadly defined, is all efforts, conscious and direct, incidental and indirect, made by a given society to accomplish certain objectives that are considered desirable in terms of the individual's own needs as well as the needs of the society where that education is based. As was mentioned earlier, an under-developed country must develop its various levels of education—primary, secondary, technical, teachers, higher education and other forms of education. But when the question of priority arises as it always does, in terms of what level gets the heaviest financial support and which gets the least, it seems that elementary-cum-adult education should be given this place of honour for the following reasons. It is democratic and is a great social leveller, in that all children irrespective of their geographical location, the economic limitations of their parents, the social status of their fathers, the religious beliefs of the parents, will have an opportunity for at least an elementary education. It will, if adequately planned, help to arrest superstition, ignorance and disease. Politically, it will help develop intelligent citizens. Economically, it will help produce, in the lower cadre of manpower, an intelligent working class, literate consumers and producers of goods, village craftsmen, artisans and the like. Culturally, it is through a universal system of education or the education that reaches every individual irrespective of age, sex, religion, tribe, language, or geographic, economic or social status that the culture of the people can be adequately transmitted and new challenges that characterize the twentieth century can be satisfactorily met. This also calls for the establishment of village nurseries all over the federation and government encouragement and leadership in research and new methods.

It is often argued that the content of the primary school syllabus or curriculum is such that all it can hope to achieve is a minimal education which does not equip the child for a specific skill or vocation and that it will be ridiculous to put children of eleven-year-old plus to work at such an early age. This theory is hardly acceptable as far as under-developed countries are concerned. It would be recalled that before primary education became universal in Europe during the early period of industrial revolution, young children were pressed into the factories as workers. 'As late as 1910, approximately 2,100,000 children—ten to fifteen years of age in the United States were gainfully employed. In some industries, they comprised as high as 25 per cent of the total labour force.'[2] There was at a later stage a reaction against the practice and, eventually, laws were passed declaring child labour under certain stipulated conditions illegal. This was indeed a very wise step.

In most parts of Africa today, that is to say Africa south of the Sahara and north of the Limpopo, the average African child does not attend a school, either due to lack of funds on the part of the parents or lack of educational facility or a combination of both. Even in the few coun-tries where education is now free (but not compulsory), such as Ghana and certain regions in Nigeria, at least 10 per cent or more of the children of school age are not in school either because the parents are too poor to release the children from farm work or because the nearest school is miles away or too small to accommodate all the children who want to attend.

It is perhaps true that the average African child of today reaches maturity earlier than his European or American counterpart. More than 50 per cent of the Nigerian children of school age are not in school (the percentage is even higher in many other African countries today). Over 80 per cent of Nigeria's population are in rural communities; so are the majority of the Nigerian children. What, we may ask, are these millions of non-school-going children doing?

If they are males, they help their parents with sowing and harvesting, cattle rearing, fishing, weaving, carpentry, carving, house construction and the like. By the time they are a little older, say fourteen or sixteen years of age, they may be given their own small plot to farm or net to fish. In the case of the girls, they assist the parents with sowing and harvesting, buying and selling, weaving and sewing, dyeing and design-ing as well as with general domestic duties in the household or com-pound. In addition to this side of the child's education, there are social

[2] F. J. Brown, *Educational Sociology* (New York: Prentice-Hall, Inc. 1947), pp. 177–8.

and cultural demands from the community that encourage early maturation of the child. A hundred years ago children in the advanced countries were living under conditions similar to those prevalent in Africa today. But as Europe and America prospered, children in these countries are now expected to stay within a free and compulsory school system until the age of fourteen or sixteen. In other words, Britain and the United States, for example, are able to extend the child's maturation period. This period of extended adolescence makes growing-up less painful and less demanding as compared with the lot of the average African child of today. As the African countries prosper, they are likely to be less austere and perhaps more generous with regard to the economic and social demands made on young persons. But to continue to copy blindly practices elsewhere without regard to local realities, is to stultify social growth and the creative genius of the people.

IV. *The Objectives of Elementary Education*

Due to financial limitations of most African countries, it is highly improbable that African countries will be in a position to afford the luxury of the Western type of educational structure and systems as they obtain today. However good these may be, the 'best' for Europe may be appallingly inadequate when transported to foreign soil. Each educational system must be realistically related to its environment. As pointed out earlier, certain problems are currently peculiar to the under-developed countries; marked ignorance, poverty and disease.

The curriculum in Africa south of the Sahara, at least before the advent of the European, consisted of the following essentials; moral instruction and civics, on-the-job training, trading, hunting, farming, fishing, etc. for boys, and domestic science for girls, and sanitation. These and other forms of informal but practical education were what the old Africans deemed the needs of their society. The ancient Persians also had a simple curriculum geared to the needs of their society; riding, shooting and speaking the truth. Both the ancient Persians and the pre-colonial Africans felt, and rightly too, that such educational experiences would make their children good members of their family, the clan, the ethnic group and the nation, where applicable. Indeed, most of our non-literate population in Nigeria today still follow the old African curriculum.

The pattern of development with regard to education in Africa within the past 200 years has been haphazard, partly because the African had no say about the type of education his child should have during the colonial era and partly because the African was faced with new challenges at a time when he was not in a position to do his own thinking— the imperial power knew all the answers and proceeded to meet the challenges as it thought fit with little or no consultation with the African who was supposedly to benefit by the scheme. But how has the picture changed today even with the attainment of Independence?

Before the beginning of the eighteenth century there was little difference between pre-industrial Western Europe and America on the one hand, and pre-colonial Africa and Asia on the other hand. Of course Europe's extensive and far-flung commercial empires enabled the people of that continent to accumulate substantial capital which was a necessary antecedent for industrial growth. The industrial revolution which took place in Europe and later in the United States was to my mind the most vital factor which helped the Europeans to forge ahead of the rest of the world, while Africa and Asia not only remained virtually static but also served as major areas from where raw materials were exported to Europe and where finished European goods were largely marketed. For almost two hundred and sixty years Africa remained a dark continent while Europe continued to be a continent of heat, light and electricity. While science and technology continued to change the face of Western civilization, magic and superstition continued to plague African civilization. There is no denying the fact that science in the twentieth century is a dominant cultural factor. It has become a necessary antecedent to good living, good citizenship, health, agriculture, home-making, vocation, leisure, etc.

The simple life of the old African has become more complicated as a result of the contact with the Western World. To be more precise, Western civilization has intermingled with African culture and the African who is so affected by both cultures is a man of both worlds; he is, therefore, called upon to operate on both levels with a juggler's dexterity. The African (as well as his Asian and Latin American counterpart) must, by force of circumstance, live under this ambivalent situation. Since it is most unlikely that the African will completely abandon his culture, and since he cannot survive without his newly acquired Western orientation, the African must seek a satisfactory synthesis between his cultural environment and Western skills and tools.

The last ten years has witnessed a tremendous change in the African.

He wrested political independence from his erstwhile colonial master and in the past few years enjoyed political self-determination. Under African rule, schools have multiplied, so have student population and educational expenditure. Industries of all sizes are springing up; these and other things call for special skills and special attitudes to life—work and leisure.

To meet the challenges of independence—citizenship, new skills, new attitudes to life and work in general—and at the same time cope with the demands of the African culture, the present educational systems operative in many parts of Africa, including Nigeria, need drastic change. British and French Africa inherited a curriculum designed by the colonial powers. Although some modifications and patch-work have taken place in some areas, this is not enough. A general review of our borrowed curriculum must take place because the curriculum was largely planned to suit the administering power—to train a cadre of clerks and junior functionaries within the colonial set-up. The curriculum does not, as a general rule, adequately meet the needs of African Society as presently constituted. If we are to close the gap between Africa and the Western world—indeed if Africa is to survive the atomic age—a radically different kind of curriculum structure should be introduced to supplant the current one.

Most of the Western countries whose curricula we copy have at least 80 to 90 per cent literacy. On the other hand, Africa has only about 10 to 20 per cent literacy. An illiterate individual is invariably a poor consumer of goods, a pawn in the hands of the unscrupulous politician, and a victim of superstition and magic. No nation can ever hope to develop to its maximum capacity for as long as the majority of its people are non-literates. Science education is less than thirty years old in most parts of Africa south of the Sahara. The scientific and technological skills necessary for industrial development are still scarce; consequently, development plans are often crippled partly for lack of skilled technicians and literate workers. Civic and citizenship roles in terms of national outlook and the nature of a democratic government need to be appreciated by the generality of the population if African governments are to survive.

V. *Wanted—a New Curriculum*

To meet the need for the African child and the nation in this age of rapid changes, it is evident from the foregoing that new measures and a new approach are called for. The following curriculum is recommended for all elementary and lower secondary schools.

Literary: Reading and writing in the child's mother tongue and English, French, etc. as applicable, are of primary importance. These would include indigenous literature, as well as the chosen cosmopolitan country's literature, and world literature, organized sequentially and progressively as the child's learning capacity develops within the educational ladder. This calls for proliferation of materials in the vernacular and in the second language. Effective communication is a fundamental skill.

Basic Science: This includes geography. Our lives are affected by scientific phenomena in terms of things above us, things below and things around us. Basic science in this sense would be a composite course that would embrace everyday science, simple phenomena, agriculture, health and sanitation, zoology, botany, physics, chemistry and the application of these to human growth and development. Because basic science promotes scientific thought, an area which is virtually new in Africa, it is recommended that a third to a half of the school time-table, from the first year of elementary to the first two years of secondary education, should be devoted to this subject. Since the majority of future African citizens would not be likely to have more than an elementary education for the next twenty-five years, it is a *sine qua non* that basic science should be taught from the first year of elementary education. Nature study and rural science, are not an effective substitute for basic science. It is suggested that basic principles on how the pulley and the lever work, simple phenomena such as echoes, rain, thunder and lightning would more likely be of lasting interest and possibly have vital meaning to the child of six and seven.

Above all, the child should and must be helped to understand natural phenomena in terms of cause and effect and thus disabuse his mind of the magical or supernatural explanation. The major problems facing the African schools today is the race between the magician and the teacher as to who gets the child first. The parents are almost always on the side of the magician (this will be discussed later). The African child unlike his European counterpart has many disadvantages. The home instead of being a help is mostly a hindrance due to the non-literate circumstances of many African homes. Educational toys, small or medium home libraries are non-existent; parents are in most cases unable to help their children with school problems. Pending the time the parents are sufficiently educated, it is imperative that African schools be provided with more educational toys, scientific equipment and a good library at the elementary school level. It is also essential that more advanced work in science be carried on at the lower levels of elementary education, as compared with what is presently offered by more advanced countries, if we are to make up for the deficiencies that exist in African homes. Simple scientific books should of course be translated into the vernacular and simple scientific gadgets should be manufactured locally.

Science is of great interest to children particularly in this supersonic age and it provides a natural opportunity to develop at a very early age the ability to solve problems. Indeed we need to do all that lies in our power to build into the African child's background a scientific attitude if science is to make a major impact in Africa.

Civics and social studies: This of course should also be taught from the first year of school and should include duties towards the family, the neighbour, the community and the state: this is a basic essential in most newly independent African States. The modern democratic concept, with particular reference to representative government, is new to many countries. To be specific, it is less than thirty years old even in many countries of Europe. What is more, democracy (whatever brand) is not a mere political jingoism to be proclaimed and championed once every four or five years by political office seekers for the purpose of getting elected; it is a way of life that must be practised daily, not only in parliamentary, but also in social, economic and cultural affairs. It must be taught. The course should, therefore, be a comprehensive and well integrated one embracing history, archaeology, government, economics religion, music and art.

Vocational education: For education at the elementary level to take on new and dynamic significance, it must make concerted effort to train the child for some specific skills. Education for its own sake, is a glorious ideal in countries where the period of adolescence has been extended, i.e. in countries where free secondary, technical and university education are available to virtually all students who are intellectually able to cope and profit by such opportunities. In that situation, training for specific or general but useful skills can be postponed to the next stage of education. But in Africa, for the next generation at least, over 80 per cent or more of the elementary school leavers may never see the inside of a higher institution, due to lack of finance or opportunity or both. It is very essential therefore, that one solid year of the six or seven-year primary education be devoted to a practical skill, viz., practical agriculture, carpentry, masonry, auto-mechanics and bicycle repairing, smithery or carving, weaving or sewing, shoe-making and shoe-repairing, commercial or business training, etc.

Physical education: This will include physical exercises, hygiene and sanitation. It should be more practical and less theoretical and should be demonstrable in terms of daily activities. It should not be a course to be taught but a life to be led; both the child, the teacher and the school environment should be harmoniously integrated and the three should combine to present a healthy community school. A good school environment in a small community or village generally serves as a stimulus for improvement, a rallying point for many community projects, meetings, adult education centres, religious services, and the like. The over-riding philosophy of elementary education should be to build into the personality of the young, self-reliance, creativity, imagination and resourcefulness.

The Elementary School Curriculum as presented above is based on the following calculations: of every 1,000 children who enter into elementary schools in an area where there is free primary education, about 800 may complete their six-year education. Of the 800, not more than 20 per cent or 160 pupils gain admission to secondary schools and other institutions; and of the 160 who enter a secondary school less than 2 per cent or about four pupils gain admission into a university. Elementary education will, therefore, continue to be the main contact point with the masses of the Nigerian, or indeed other African, children as far as formal education is concerned. It is therefore mandatory on the part of educational planners to construct a curriculum that will be largely terminal and, therefore, practical. It is unrealistic to plan a curriculum that leads to University entrance for 160 students when only 3 or 4 of them will get to the University anyway.

The idea that elementary education does not fit a child for anything is of European origin and there is no conceivable reason why Nigeria or any other under-developed country should accept it. With new methods and techniques in teaching and learning, coupled with the fact that the average African child by tradition is called upon to perform

M.P.E.D.N.—6*

adult roles earlier than his European counterpart, the new trend in education in Nigeria should be to develop a curriculum that will make the elementary school leaver fit for something. To do the opposite is to slow down our economic and social progress and to re-embrace the old classical type of education which Europe itself is struggling to abandon. At least half of our economic and social future rests with the masses of the young illiterates we neglect in our social and economic planning today.

VI. *Adult Education*

One of the most neglected national resources in under-developed countries is the adult. His need for education is second only to that of the school-age child. We have mentioned earlier on, that it is not a mere coincidence that illiteracy and under-development go hand in hand, and today, over 70 per cent of Nigeria's adult population is non-literate. It was also mentioned earlier that illiteracy impedes progress and that a country with a high percentage of illiteracy cannot hope to develop to maximum capacity for as long as the situation remains relatively unchanged. It is erroneous thinking to assume that illiterate adults will die away within a generation or two. The truth of the matter is that the size of the illiterate adult population is increasing while the pace of social and technological change is accelerating phenomenally. There is in Nigeria today millions of twelve-year-olds who may never see the inside of a school.

An economic case can be made for the education of the adult. With education, the adult is most likely to be a better producer or a better consumer of goods; he is more likely to be prone to changes; and to become an intelligent user of public facilities and amenities. A literate farmer, fisherman or trader is more likely to seek and find better methods of farming, fishing or trading. Indeed, he is more exposed to the various channels of education for personal and further professional or occupational growth. Of course, the adult needs more than mere literacy; he must be functionally literate. The adult must acquire the ability to read, write, perform simple but meaningful arithmetical processes, acquire civic sophistication, and be exposed to scientific thought if he is to become less superstitious. A child's school experience is often negated by the illiterate parents' own superstitious beliefs and habits.

The eradication of illiteracy is a matter of national urgency and should be recognized and treated as such. The objectives of adult literacy education should be:

(a) to help the illiterate adult attain functional literacy with a view to enabling him to acquire the art of reading, writing and numeration;

(b) to help him appreciate his economic, cultural and political role within his own society;

(c) to enable him understand his physical and biological environment;

(d) to help him improve his skills as a worker, thereby improving his own living standards and thus contributing to the economic development of his country;

(e) and above all, to help him play his own role as a good citizen of his nation and the world.

Literacy education should be carried out both at the formal and informal levels and the use of the various media of education such as evening classes, radio, television, mobile cinema and posters should be fully explored. Literacy education should not be restricted to the self-employed only. All non-literate workers in public and private industries should be drawn into the picture. Indeed, industry itself should play a major role in helping their own employees in this direction.

To meet the urgency of the situation in Nigeria, the Federal and the Regional Governments should set up a National Committee for the Eradication of Illiteracy. This Committee should be as representative as possible, to include government, civic, religious, educational and youth interests. It would be the primary function of the Committee:

(a) to co-ordinate the existing adult education programmes in the country, expand the programme extensively and provide the over-all leadership that is needed in this direction;

(b) to set up regional and local committees throughout the federation;

(c) to prepare new reading materials and improve old but good ones: the committees will work with health and agricultural authorities, primary, secondary, technical schools and universities, and the regional ministries of education with a view to adapting appropriate reading materials on health, agriculture, general science, commerce, etc.;

(d) to recruit in large towns and villages, clerks, army personnel, professionals, technicians, teachers, clergy, lay-readers, community workers and others for short in-service teacher training courses in adult education;

(e) to establish evening classes.

VII. *Compulsory National Service*

The cost of providing compulsory adult literacy is likely to be enormous. Within this limitation, it is recommended that in order to achieve functional national literacy as quickly as possible Nigeria should establish *Compulsory National Service for National Mobilization* which will have the following features:

(a) All adults (men and women) from 16 to 30 years old should be required to serve for a year or two either instalmentally or at a stretch.

(b) All literates—teachers, clergy, clerks, business and professional persons, etc., would after a 6 to 8 weeks' intensive teacher training course teach all non-literates. This same group would also serve as evening class instructors for non-literate adults who are between the ages of 36 and 50 years.

(c) The curriculum should comprise reading, writing, arithmetic (for non-literates), and physical fitness, civics, basic science and one or two vocational skills (agriculture, mechanics, carpentry, welding, fitting, cooking, sewing, weaving etc.), for literates and non-literates.

(d) All adults who are over 30 years of age but below 51 years, must attend *compulsory* evening literacy classes, five days a week for two years.

(e) The functional literacy syllabus for item (d) above, would include, reading, writing, arithmetic, civics and basic science and a vocational skill—all in the vernacular.

(f) Proliferation of materials should be undertaken, preparation of new materials, improvement of old but good ones, adaptation of texts, etc., to meet the needs of the functional literacy programme.

Those on the Compulsory National Service programme would also be required to work on road and bridge building, farms, workshops, and engage in community development and in other programmes that are part of the local, regional or national development schemes.

It may be argued that the personnel, fund and material sorely needed for development will be partly tied up with the scheme. In the very short-run this is most likely to be true; but in the long run the resources committed to this scheme would be more than justified. At any rate, sooner or later, Nigeria, like many countries, may think of introducing compulsory military service which is generally an expensive scheme, much more costly in fact, than the proposed plan. Some countries may forge ahead with this type of scheme, cost not-withstanding. But if a proposal of this type is available as a better investment, these states would probably follow the less costly but more beneficial course.

The advantages of a well-integrated plan for compulsory National Service for National Mobilization will be the following:

(a) the percentage of illiteracy will be reduced considerably;

(b) the corps of skill and literate persons so sorely needed for development will be available within a short period of time;

(c) citizenship, responsibility and loyalty to the nation will become the norm for these citizens who will in turn influence others;

(d) a new breed of potential self-employed individuals, literate and resourceful, ready to engage in farming, petty trading, repairing, small scale manufacturing, etc., will emerge, and,

(e) superstition and magic will be at a discount.

VIII. *Conclusion*

We have tried to show in this paper that the quickest way to increase productivity in an under-developed country, such as Nigeria, is to invest as much as possible in the education of the young and old, men and women. The cumulative effect of such an investment over a period of years is immeasurable. 'Development—authentic development as opposed to mere economic growth—is a process carried out by and for man. . . . Nor should it be forgotten that man himself is the object of development. If it were possible—which must be doubted—to achieve a high level of technological and economic growth, while at the same time neglecting man's legitimate desire for adequate food and housing, for health and education, for security and happiness, such development would be a hollow and insubstantial thing.'[3] If, indeed, our legitimate aspiration is to do the greatest good for the greatest number (and it is assumed that this is the case), economic development must not be planned for the benefit of the few at the expense of the many. To do so, is to court national disaster. Nigeria needs to be more pragmatic in its approach to educational philosophy and structure as well as in our attitude toward what constitute economic progress by desisting from erecting extravagant school buildings and £20,000 science blocks, and ultra-modern, multi-million-pound hotels that are out of tune with our economy and circumstances. It is only then that the masses of the population can be convinced that our plans, be they economic or social, are primarily and significantly in their own interest.

[3] *Report of the Secretary-General on Human Resources*: United Nations Conference on the application of Science and Technology for the Benefit of the Less Developed Areas. Geneva, February 1963 (E/Con. 39/Gr2B).

II

The Structure and Development of Nigerian Education

Stephen O. Awokoya

FEDERAL CHIEF ADVISER AND PERMANENT SECRETARY,
FEDERAL MINISTRY OF EDUCATION, LAGOS

I. Introduction

This paper is an attempt to present a picture of the present educational situation in Nigeria. It describes the basic philosophy behind Nigeria's educational endeavours, the institutions which have been established to formulate the necessary policies, and also the structure of the educational machinery, and the major educational objectives of the Government of the Federation. Many changes have taken place, especially since 1952 when Nigeria began to enjoy a certain measure of self-government. Most of these changes occurred under the pressure of necessity, and naturally, many problems have had to be identified and tackled. Finally, this paper attempts to take a look into the shape of things to come, if the manpower targets now being fixed and scientific and technological plans now being formulated do come to fruition.

II. Education During the Pre-Independence Period

A description of education in Nigeria during the pre-Independence period remains a fruitful field for research. A certain amount, however, is known about the educational objectives of the country as defined by the colonial power. In the first place, Nigeria was expected to occupy the periphery of British economic enterprise. As such, it was a valuable market and a territory for the production of agricultural and mineral products. As long as the labourers to be employed in the mines were available and a few literate people could assist in the administration of the mines and plantations as well as in the transportation of produce to the ports, the economic objectives appeared to have been satisfied. The few Nigerians that were anxious to advance themselves economically were satisfied to play the role of middlemen. No far-reaching economic plans were formulated either by Nigerians or Great Britain. Shortly before World War II, however, efforts were made to create the Marketing Boards in order to stabilize the prices of such commodities like cocoa and palm produce. Even then, the creation of the Marketing Boards did not lead to any fundamental change in the economic perspectives nor in the concomitant educational development. Further, Nigerians themselves were not in such a position as to influence, in any dramatic way, the economic and educational objectives of the country because they did not exercise any political power. However, a few Nigerians, knowledgeable in law, medicine and journalism, became political agitators, preaching a new educational philosophy, fighting legal and constitutional battles and stimulating the masses to a desire for Independence. At different times, leaders of thought and opinion spoke about rejuvenating national art and music, adopting African costumes, going back to the land, and liberating the minds of youth from the dead weight of conservatism and paganism. In southern Nigeria, for instance, where missionary bodies have been active since before the middle of the last century, many primary schools attached to the churches were opened and a few secondary schools were also started; but higher education was obtainable only from the United Kingdom and Fourah Bay College in Sierra Leone. This period may be regarded as one of introspection. Leaders groped in the dark in search of economic, political, social and cultural objectives. Such enthusiasm as they had was devoted to criticizing the cosmopolitan powers and little preparatory work was done beyond what was within the competence of individuals or little groups and what the government was prepared to offer.

The professions that were highly favoured were law, medicine and divinity. All three constituted the top echelons in society and those who failed to distinguish themselves became clerical assistants to the commercial firms. Only during the early 1930s did Nigerians begin to specialize in the engineering disciplines. The first few engineers had sorry tales to tell. After facing difficult situations overseas with inadequate scientific and mathematical background, they succeeded in coming back home to find no employment for themselves. This kind of situation continued for a long time, and many Nigerians returning home after specializing in some narrow fields found employment difficult to obtain in an economic and political situation which they were powerless to change. Those with limited education readily found employment in Government service, in the customs and commercial houses, in railways and even in the banks. In the course of years, competence increased through in-service training as the establishments grew.

The total number of people with any pretensions to education was extremely low, partly because there was no considerable response to education, for it was with difficulty that the early missionaries succeeded in inviting children to schools. Those who were prepared to adopt the Christian religion had a measure of primary education thrown into the bargain. The best became clergymen, and the sons of the well-to-do middlemen became lawyers and doctors, while those of poor parentage became workers in the trading firms. As a result of the economic advantage which those who had education nonetheless enjoyed, parents began to desire more and more education for their children and primary education in southern Nigeria began to grow. During this period of educational growth, Northern Nigeria was hardly touched. Education which was at first free became so valuable that parents had to pay for it and the cost continued to rise until 1955, when universal primary education was introduced first in the Western Region and later in the Eastern Region and the Federal Territory of Lagos. Meanwhile, secondary education also began to expand as a result of the pressure of demand from the government, commercial houses and educational institutions themselves. In fact the needs of the government were so acute that government had to open a number of primary and secondary schools in order to increase the output of educational institutions and so meet its requirements.

Since government's entry into the field of education, interest in the development of educational institutions has grown at a phenomenal rate. In 1931, when Nigeria was facing the problems of economic depression, the then Director of Education, Mr. Hussey, formulated the Higher College plan which was then the crowning glory of educational development in Nigeria. The plan envisaged the training of assistant science masters, assistant engineers, assistant medical officers and assistant agricultural officers. Brilliant students were recruited from the secondary schools in the country and the new government high schools which included science and mathematics in their curriculum were able to provide the students for the old Yaba Higher College. No sooner had government shown its interest in the development of higher education than the Nigerian leaders of opinion commenced to wage a vigorous war against the government, on the view that the government wanted to release on the people, half-baked doctors, engineers and agricultural officers. The intentions of the Government were seriously doubted. The leaders wanted nothing lower than what was available from the colleges of Oxford, Cambridge and London. This public outcry was valuable in many ways: firstly, it led the national leaders to think seriously of higher education; secondly, it compelled government to prove that its intentions were honourable and that there was no desire to make the Higher College an institution for producing half-baked specialists.

The standard of work at the old Yaba Higher College was acknow-ledged as high by all those who had contact with the institution and its graduates. Since the students were not allowed to present themselves for overseas examinations, government action was misinterpreted as a device for preventing Africans from acquiring qualifications comparable with those which were obtainable in England. In actual fact, the syllabus followed at the Yaba Higher College was modelled in such a manner as to make doctors and engineers trained there more appropriate for the needs of Nigeria than those trained overseas. Most of the hospitals, engineering establishments and educational institutions in Nigeria were manned to a large extent by the Yaba Higher College graduates. The College was already influencing the growth and development of scienti-fic education in the secondary schools of the country when the second world war broke out. Although the work of the Yaba graduates was widely appreciated, public confidence in the intentions of the Colonial Government was only restored at the end of the last war when the Eliot Commission was appointed to consider the development of higher education in the West African territories.

The report of the Eliot Commission on Higher Education went a long way in setting the pattern of educational development in the former British West African colonies. For the first time the public of Nigeria realized that the British Government had good intentions in the promotion of higher education in British West Africa. When the University College at Ibadan was founded, students from the Yaba College formed its foundation students. Today it is a University in its own right awarding its own degrees. The old Fourah Bay College has also become the University College of Sierra Leone with all the mak-ings of an independent university. The University of Ghana is also a consequence of the Eliot Commission's Report. Four colleges of science and technology were also founded, three of them in Nigeria and one at Kumasi. It can be stated that the Colonial Government as well as West African educational leaders realized that the stage had been reached when higher education in every field of human endeavour must be properly institutionalized in West Africa.

The University of Ibadan was in special relationship with the University of London, although the curriculum was, to some extent, adapted to the needs of Nigeria. By this arrangement London University awarded the degrees in order to ensure that high standards were maintained. It has also enabled the public of Nigeria to have faith in this institution, promoted by the metropolitan power. The distrust which attended the Yaba Higher College was thus completely eliminated. It is probably no exaggeration to say that apart from our law and Constitution and the gift of democracy, the greatest legacy that Great Britain left to Nigeria, was the University of Ibadan. Furthermore, the needs of science and technology were not only recognized but provided for by the establishment of the colleges of arts, science and technology; and it is remarkable that this far-reaching innovation in the development of higher education in Nigeria probably owed its origin to the terrible demands of World War II for scientists and technicians.

The post-war educational awakening in Nigeria is difficult to assess because it is still growing and we are too close to the events. Throughout the country, the number of primary schools began to increase and secondary educational institutions were also opened in response to public demands. As a result of this general awakening, the political parties that controlled both the Regional and Federal Governments since 1952 found themselves faced with a situation in which they had to respond to public demand by expanding the facilities for education at the primary, secondary and higher levels. This phenomenal expansion continued until the eve of independence. In the West, universal primary education was introduced and was widely supported by people in every walk of life. Similarly, in the Federal Territory of Lagos and in the Eastern Region, phenomenal development of every level of education began, enrolment increased threefold and universality in primary education was virtually attained. Although the rate of educational development in Northern Nigeria has not been as phenomenal as in the south, the percentage increase has been no less spectacular and within the last few years, the Northern Regional Government has faced the situation with firm resolve.

III. *The Problems of Transition, 1952–1960*

For three years before 1952, there was a great deal of political activity in Nigeria, all directed towards the framing of a new Constitution. The Government of Nigeria which was hitherto unitary, became federal. Three regions were created—the North, East and West. Although at first the capital city of Lagos was included in the Western Region, it was later excised from it and became the Federal Territory of Lagos, separate and distinct from the Western Region. As from 1952, a certain degree of independence was enjoyed throughout the Federation. Education became very largely a regional matter. Although a Federal Department of Education existed, it was only part of the Ministry of Social Services which included the Medical Department. It was during this transitional period that Nigerian leaders became directly involved in the formulation of political, economic, social and cultural policies. No programmes could thereafter be undertaken without consideration of their political and economic implications. In the field of education, no less than any other field, these problems were intense. It was difficult, at first, to know where federal responsibility ended and where regional began. But although British officials continued to exercise a considerable amount of financial control at the centre, the Regional Governments began to assume major powers in the field of educational development. For instance, they formulated far-reaching policies without any reference to the centre: they planned their development, built their schools, awarded their scholarships, conducted their examinations, visited overseas territories, drew up their curriculum, inspected their schools, sometimes going to the extent of barring certain federal inspectors from appearing in Regional schools, altered the structure of their education, extended their training, formulated higher education policies; all without reference to the central government. The immediate effect of this was to create an intense form of rivalry between the regions. Primary schools and secondary schools expanded at unprecedented rates. A large number of scholarships was awarded by the governments and a considerable proportion of the government revenues went into the recurrent cost of education.

The economic implications of the various programmes of educational development became apparent right from the very initial stages. To start with, a programme of such huge dimension as universal primary education could not be implemented without a substantial amount of money. In one region, in particular, the constitutional review of 1953 provided the occasion not only for the regionalization of the Central Marketing Board but also for canalizing its accumulated funds into education. Nevertheless the Federal Government remained in control of major economic projects which required a lot of money. These undertakings brought vividly to the minds of the leaders that their activities might come to grief if they did not have an adequate number of trained manpower at the highest, intermediate and other levels. The University College at Ibadan which was established in 1947 could provide only a small range of subjects for study. The colleges of science and technology were still a subject of acrimonious debate in the House of Representatives. The only levels of education which did not provoke too much dispute were the primary and secondary. Many of the scholarships awarded by the Federal and Regional Governments, were only tenable in higher institutions overseas owing to the fact that many of the courses were not available at the University College, Ibadan.

The Colleges of Science and Technology could not start as originally scheduled because the programme proposed in 1952 could not receive the assent of the House of Representatives. Later, when the assent was given, the legislature expected the Nigerian colleges of arts, science and technology to give post-secondary courses in science and technology. It was, however, impossible for these courses to commence because qualified students were not available. The colleges were therefore obliged to promote courses leading to the Advanced Level of the General Certificate of Education and a number of other courses that could hardly be described as post-secondary. The failure of the colleges of science and technology to meet public demand led eventually to their dissolution and absorption into the regional university system. It would appear that even during this inchoate stage there was a public recognition of the fact that high-level manpower in a wide spectrum of disciplines must be trained, that intermediate manpower must be produced, and that the base of education must be broadened. The translation of this public desire into concrete realities was left to the governments. It may be stated that the creation of broadly based primary education has been achieved in the south, that the expansion of the secondary school system is going apace, and that the development of high-level manpower on a systematic and progressive basis responsive to the needs of the national economy has now begun. The problems of manpower development remains most acute in the Northern Region owing to the relatively lower enrolments in the schools.

The following table indicates the student population at various levels of education in Nigeria during 1962.

TABLE 11(i)   *Nigeria's School Population by Level of Education and by Region, 1962*

Type of Institution	Regions			
	North	East	West	Lagos
Primary school enrolment	359,934	1,266,566	1,108,999	98,511
Secondary school enrolment	10,603	34,283	145,798*	12,056
Teacher training	6,320	11,160	12,954	736
University	426	1,148	1,932	100

Source: *Statistics of Education in Nigeria, 1963*
* Includes Secondary Modern Schools, none of which existed in the North and East.

Many other problems of transition also became apparent shortly after 1952. Educational planning was undertaken without adequate statistical data. The need for trained teachers was acute; consequently Teacher Training Colleges were opened in large numbers. Both in the East and the West, the standard and quality of teacher training dropped for some years. Today, standards are beginning to rise and Grade III teachers are no longer being trained. The period of expansion has, however, only just begun in the North.

Perhaps the most difficult problem of all was that of finding funds to meet the capital and recurrent costs of education. This problem has not yet been solved. In the East, West and North, 40, 42 and 20 per cent respectively, of the Government revenue is spent annually to maintain the school system. Only in Lagos is the percentage as low as 5 per cent. Even now the capital cost of developing the universities and the secondary schools system is proving difficult to find. Quite recently, the governments of the Federation applied to the World Bank for assistance in meeting the capital cost of the expanding educational system. In Lagos alone a recent costing has shown that the capital cost of expanding the secondary educational system, between now and 1970, will be of the order of £12 million, £7 million of which will be devoted to the provision of hostel accommodation for students, and quarters for residential staff. The actual cost of school buildings will be about £3 million while that of equipment will be £2 million. The requirements of the North in the field of secondary education today will probably be of that order. Both in the Western and Eastern Regions, much larger sums will be required to meet the demand for secondary educational expansion. It is expected that the capital cost will be met somehow by raising bonds, by borrowing and by appropriation from the public revenue. The recurrent cost will become more and more staggering unless some re-orientation of fiscal policy is done so as to ensure that the general economic development is able to stand the strain.

During this transitional period from 1952 to 1960, the administrative machinery for education was taxed to the utmost, because that machinery which was primarily designed to handle a few hundred schools was now expected to take in its stride 15,743 primary schools and 997 secondary schools. In many cases the administrative machinery had to be reconstructed at a time when few Nigerians were available to man them, while expatriates were departing in large numbers. One consequence was that most of the men had to be over-worked, but the situation is improving year by year.

In most under-developed countries of the world, the problem of facing educational development in its initial stages is primarily that of leadership against conservatism and inertia. Happily, these no longer exist in Nigeria today. Even in the remote villages, there is an impelling urge to promote education. Young men and women are anxious to receive education and rise to positions of leadership in their community, for education has been identified with leadership in the new Nigeria.

Many other problems are still present. For instance, constitutional problems, which assumed importance in the immediate pre-independence period, have not yet completely disappeared in educational affairs. As Nigeria proceeds to develop her universities, technical colleges and secondary schools, more and more external aid becomes necessary. The external relations of Nigeria are, however, under the control of the Federal Government. The control is exercised primarily by the Ministry of External Affairs and secondarily by the Ministries of Economic Development and Education. It is not easy to decide when external aid is to be accepted, what machinery should be used for its distribution, and how the utilization of foreign assistance can be promoted without causing constitutional misunderstanding. The situation is, however, becoming better clarified with the establishment of the Bureau for External Aid and the Co-ordinating Committee for External

Aid for Education, a committee with representation from all the Ministries of Education in the Federation.

The most important problems of the transitional period stem from the fact that Nigeria is facing far too many problems at the same time and the amount of planning necessary had to be rushed in the face of public demands. What is important is the fact that there is a progressive review of plans and an honest endeavour to make them harmonize with the economic, social and political objectives of the nation.

There is also the problem of employment of the school leavers which will continue to occupy the minds of the governments. The Nigerian situation appears critical because the rate of educational development seems to have out-stripped the rate of economic development. Employment opportunities are not being created fast enough. Many primary and secondary school leavers have wrong notions of the fields in which they can be employed and migrate into the towns. The governments of the Federation are faced with the problems of finding them employment and training them to be useful to the economy at the same time. There is danger that the whole educational machinery might go into disrepute owing to the fact that the products of the schools are not being adequately absorbed into employment.

Perhaps the problem which worries the governments most, is that of finding the finances to maintain the educational machinery in a state of continuous growth and development. For it is clear that the financial commitment of governments in the field of education must continue to rise during the remaining years of this century. The expansion cannot be stopped. It is necessary, therefore, constantly to see these problems in their full dimension so that the magnitude of the tasks facing educational administrators and planners may be fully recognized and appreciated.

IV. *The Situation Since Independence*

The complex of problems which has been described led to the recognition of the importance of comprehensive educational planning on the eve of Independence. It had to be linked with the economic objectives of the nation, satisfy the political aspirations of the masses, to respond to our finest ideals of social service, and harmonize with our cultural heritage. It is against this background that in 1959, shortly before the attainment of Independence, government took the momentous decision to appoint a Commission on Post-Secondary and Higher Education in Nigeria. The terms of reference specifically stated that the Commission was to conduct an investigation into Nigeria's needs in the field of post-secondary and higher education over the next 20 years. It is to the eternal credit of that Commission that they examined not only the problems of post-secondary and higher education in Nigeria but also the effect of other levels and forms of education on national development. The famous Ashby Commission published its report entitled 'Investment in Education' in 1960, and since then, the Nigerian educational scene has been the consequential development of the recommendations of the Commission.

The recommendations of the Ashby Report were wide, and ranged through the whole field of primary and secondary education, sixth-form development, teacher training, technical education, commercial education, agricultural and veterinary education, university institutions, national universities commission, inter-regional manpower development and international aid. Of particular significance was the importance which the report attached to manpower budgeting, sixth form education, teacher training, technical and commercial education below university level and agricultural education. For the first time in the history of educational thought in Nigeria, the concept of manpower planning, budgeting and development was introduced by Professor Frederick Harbison in the section of the Ashby Report on 'High Level Manpower for Nigeria's Future'. His recommendations have led to the establishment of the National Manpower Board and the programme of activities with which the Manpower Secretariat has been engaged during the last two years. In outlining some of the developments which have been necessitated by the report of the Ashby Commission the following are significant:

(i) The National Manpower Board;

(ii) The National Universities Commission;

(iii) The National Committee for the Co-ordination of External Aid for Education;

(iv) The rapid development of sixth form work;

(v) The registry of high-level manpower and registry of students in higher institutions both in Nigeria and overseas;

(vi) The Establishment of the National Council for Science and Technology;

(vii) The expansion of primary education and teacher training in the North;

(viii) The opening of advanced teacher training colleges for secondary schools throughout the Federation;

(ix) The establishment of three more universities bringing the Nigerian total to five;

(x) The development of educational statistics on a national basis; and

(xi) A number of various other developmental schemes still in their formative stages.

In the field of higher education, which was the major concern of the Ashby Commission, planning and development in the national interest have been institutionalized with the establishment of the National Manpower Board and the National Universities Commission. The one maps out fields of studies and quantitative manpower requirements, the other regulates the growth of the institutions by the supply of funds for their development. Both these organs are served by their own secretariat. The Manpower Board is compiling a register of high-level manpower in employment while the Federal Ministry of Education is compiling a register of students in higher institutions both in Nigeria and overseas so that the pattern of growth during the next four to five years may be accurately assessed. As a result of the national survey of manpower situation already undertaken and the targets being fixed, a scientific basis has been laid for programmes of institutional expansion and development. The possible increase during the next four or five years is already determined by the number of those already in institutions. Thereafter, however, a great deal can be effected through the administration of scholarship programmes, through the counselling and guidance of students and through the expansion of schools and colleges.

Owing to the extent to which it will become increasingly necessary to train high-level manpower in a wide spectrum of disciplines, the secondary level of education will have to grow more and more and become increasingly diversified; otherwise, the development of higher education in Nigeria will face increasing crisis. The need to diversify the forms of secondary education available, especially in the scientific and technological fields, is already universally recognized and comprehensive plans are already being made in this direction.

The Ashby Commission devoted a considerable amount of space to the subject of Form VI work in the secondary schools of Nigeria since university students are generally recruited from this class of students in the British Commonwealth. Besides, if the Nigerian Universities are to attain standards comparable to internationally famous institutions with which they have been associated, the standard of entry must be high. Since the Commission wrote its report, form six work has continued to expand. The number of candidates presenting themselves for the Higher School Certificate Examination between 1961 and 1963 has increased from 500 to between 800 and 1,200. The number of candidates presenting themselves for examination for the General Certificate of Education (Advanced Level) has been equally phenomenal.

Of particular significance in the development of secondary education is the dearth of facilities for the teaching of scientific and technological subjects. This situation is general throughout the Federation. In Lagos alone, out of 3,383 students entering into secondary schools in 1962, only 58 were admitted into technical high schools. The total enrolment in technical and vocational institutions for the whole Federation in 1962 was 13,003, out of a total of secondary school enrolments of 208,502. In short, less than 7 per cent of the total enrolments in Nigerian secondary schools are pursuing technical and vocational courses. The imbalance in this regard must be rectified without delay before Nigeria's investment in education can begin to yield adequate dividends.

This consideration has led to a programme of reform in the curriculum of schools both at the primary and secondary levels, a necessity which was emphasized in no uncertain terms by the Ashby Commission. Already all the ministries of education throughout the Federation are anxious to reform their scientific mathematical and technical curricula. Various workshops have been organized with the assistance of philanthropic organizations and foreign agencies. The Ford Foundation has given considerable assistance to the Educational Services Incorporated to stimulate the reform of the mathematics curriculum in the primary schools. The University of Nigeria, Nsukka, has conducted a study on primary school science. Various in-service training schemes have been organized at Ibadan to increase the competence of teachers in the teaching of science and mathematics. The College of Technology, Yaba, is reconsidering its curriculum. A new teacher training College that will inject technical teachers into our secondary schools is in construction with the assistance of the World Bank. The University of Lagos commenced an engineering faculty in October 1964. A chain reaction has been started which may well generate a scientific and technological revolution.

The reform of the curriculum has also extended to the introduction of modern languages in the secondary schools. The demand for teachers of French continues to increase, owing to the increasing role which Nigeria has to play in the international scene and the necessity of communicating with the neighbouring countries of Africa. Various international tours are being arranged by the secondary schools, students exchanges are also being organized, language teaching aids are being utilized to increase the capacity of the coming generation to communicate with the rest of the continent and the outside world. The teaching of history and of geography has also undergone considerable improvement. There is a long-standing criticism about the teaching of the metropolitan powers in Africa. Increasingly, however, African history is finding its way into university and secondary school curricula.

The form and content of secondary education in Nigeria is characterized by a considerable diversity. In different parts of the Federation, one can find grammar schools, modern schools, technical schools, trade centres, secondary teacher training colleges, commercial schools, all giving one form or other of secondary education. Agricultural, arts and crafts schools also exist. This diversification of the form of secondary education is a measure of the extent to which it is intended to make the content of secondary education respond to public demand.

Perhaps the greatest difficulty in the expansion of secondary education along the lines outlined in the Ashby Report is the difficulty of recruiting the right kind of teachers. The importance of science and technology is no longer arguable but an economic breakthrough may be difficult to attain until an adequate number of trained teachers have been produced. It is for this reason that efforts have been made to train a higher cadre of teachers specifically to man this diversified system of secondary education. With the aid of UNESCO, United States Agency for International Development, Ford Foundation and the United Kingdom, advanced teacher training colleges have been founded in Lagos and all the regions of the Federation to train teachers for the growing net-work of secondary schools. Courses of three years duration are being given. It is hoped that these advanced colleges will ultimately develop into colleges of education attached to the various universities, or become universities in their own right. Teachers have also been requested from various external agencies in the fields of science, mathematics and modern languages. The number of Peace Corps teachers in Nigeria has increased from 100 to 500. Many of them are teachers of science and mathematics. It is generally recognized, as a result of the report of the Ashby Commission, that teacher training and the supply of teachers occupy a strategic place in the whole development of education in Nigeria. It does look as if the external aid required to promote teacher training for science and technology may influence Nigeria's international relations in the coming years.

Indeed, external aid in education has been most useful for Nigeria's development since Independence. It is for this reason that a Bureau for External Aid for Education has been created and a co-ordinating committee for the distribution and channelling of external aid was established. Various forms of external aid have been offered to Nigeria and have been accepted. In fact, it is true to say that, so far as the field of education is concerned, more aid has been offered than the country has been able to absorb. Scholarships totalling nearly 1,000 have been offered and accepted. Nigerian students can be found in India and Pakistan, Cairo and Jerusalem, Athens and Rome, Cologne and Frankfurt, New York and California, London and Toronto, Ethiopia and Congo, Dakar and Ghana, Moscow and Washington. Financial assistance has also been given to assist in the building of institutions and in their equipment. The University College Hospital in Ibadan, the Engineering Faculty in Lagos, the University of Nigeria in Nsukka, the Advanced Teachers Training Colleges in Zaria and Lagos, all have received substantial external aid to enable the colleges to be constructed.

It is difficult to imagine Nigeria receiving aid from so many countries of the world without doing her utmost to preserve amicable relationship with them. It can be seen from this that a nation in dire need of educational development to ensure her survival in the scientific and technological age, can have no room for participating in the cold war. The extent to which we are involved today in international education can be measured not only by the part we play at such international assemblies as UNESCO and the International Bureau of Education, but also in the regional conferences organized by the Organization of African Unity and in the various bilateral cultural agreements that Nigeria has entered into with various countries of the world. Indeed, the necessity for undertaking a comparative study of educational system with a view to collecting and utilizing the best available from many countries has been so apparent that the Federal Ministry of Education has taken steps to set up a unit in the International Education Division to collect data on comparative education.

No description of the situation since independence will be complete without dealing with the amount of reorganization which the various ministries of education have had to undertake. It is clear that progressive development cannot take place without the establishment of a viable statistical unit in each ministry of education, and such units now exist in all the ministries of education throughout the Federation and that a publication, entitled *An Annual Digest of Educational Statistics* is now available. It has been seen how, during the transitional period (1952–60), education was regionalized and how the situation led to rivalry throughout the Federation and to a phenomenal expansion in every area of educational development. Since independence and the publication of the Ashby Report, there has arisen a new spirit of co-operation between the Regions and the Federal Government. Various national committees have been established to study common problems. Among these are the Joint Consultative Committee, the National Advisory Council on Technical Education, the Co-ordinating Committee for External Aid, the National Committee of the West African Examination Council, the National UNESCO Commission, the National Antiquities Commission, the National Archives Commission, and the Committee for the Co-ordination of Educational Statistics.

V. *Educational Problems of Today*

Many of the educational problems of today are not different in kind from those of the transitional period (1952–60), only they are seen in greater relief. It is necessary, however, to recognize these problems because only a proper identification of a problem eventually leads to its effective solution. The most important problem is the rapid population growth which is facing practically all under-developed countries. Health measures have not only reduced infant mortality but also lengthened the life of adults. The 1963 census gave Nigeria's population as 55·6 millions. If this figure is compared with the 1953 census figure of 31 million, then the current rate of population growth must be seen to have frightening implications for the future.

This growing population has to be fed, housed, clothed, maintained in health, transported about, entertained in a manner befitting twentieth-century civilization. The government administrative machinery will have to be expanded and reconstructed. The pattern of foreign trade will have to change and the number of industries increased to meet the economic, social and cultural desires of the people. In view of this long catalogue of requirements, steps must be taken to reduce the rate of growth of the Nigerian population by advising young married couples not to have more children than is socially desirable for the nation as a whole.

This apparent population explosion makes continuous manpower budgeting important. In the first place, the National Manpower Board will have to determine what percentage of the population must work in order to maintain those who cannot work. Secondly, those that have to work will have to be distributed into levels—the highest, the intermediate, the skilled and the unskilled. It would appear from the survey just concluded that the ratio which obtains between these levels in the more advanced countries are far from being approached in Nigeria today. It is not unusual to find people talk about a ratio of $1:5:25$ or $1:10:50$ because each high-level manpower has got to work with 5, 6 or 7 intermediate people and each intermediate person has to work with a determined number of skilled and unskilled workers. The survey already completed appears to indicate that there is a great shortage at the intermediate level. For this reason, it may be useful to tackle manpower development in such stages that will progressively approach an optimum ratio. The first phase may be such in which a a ratio of $1:2:4$ is reached; the second $1:3:9$; the fourth $1:4:16$; and the fifth $1:5:25$. The distribution of these various levels of manpower according to the types of occupation will also continue to be the task of the Manpower Board. Here a great deal of research must be undertaken on a continuing basis so that the whole spectrum of occupation and employment may be adequately manned. The whole educational and training programme will have to conform to the targets fixed by the Manpower Board on the basis of researches, types and volume of national needs. The objectives of manpower development must be seen in terms of the need to promote the economic growth and development of the country, as well as its social and cultural advancement.

Of particular importance in an examination of the problems of manpower development today is the place of science and technology in our national development. The economy cannot grow without scientists and technicians. Our agricultural development cannot make giant strides without trained agriculturalists, veterinarians, soil chemists and silviculturists. Transport, communication and industrialization cannot develop without engineers, managers, technicians, and economists. The more advanced countries are developing faster and thereby increasing the distance between the heights they are reaching and the depth where we are. Against this challenge, a technological revolution will have to take place before success can be achieved. As already mentioned the Federal Government has recently decided to set up a National Advisory Council for Scientific and Technological Research. Important as research is, it is hoped that the Council will be renamed simply as a National Council for Science and Technology so that it may take under its wing not only the proposal of national policies for scientific and technological research but also manpower and natural resource policies. The Nigerian UNESCO National Commission which first met in November 1963 made a number of recommendations on the formation of the National Council for Science and Technology. It was the hope of those who attended the conference that the Council would break down resistance to scientific and technological change, start off the chain reaction that would gather momentum and eventually become a scientific and technological revolution without which the survival of the under-developed countries during the decades of this century will be problematic. The planning of scientific and technological policy will have to be as comprehensive as possible and must be integrated with general economic planning. Collaboration with other countries in Africa is important. Common problems must be tackled collectively. The nation must borrow from the methodology of planning adopted by the Western democracies and of the socialist countries in the East.

The importance of foreign aid in education has been discussed. In all other fields of development, external aid is equally vital and is welcome. Up till now, national policy in the utilization of external aid has been most diverse, but a considerable amount of co-ordination is at the moment being effected at the Ministry of Economic Development and the Ministry of External Affairs. A special study of the effective utilization of external assistance will be most rewarding. In mobilizing national effort for manpower development, the Governments of the Federation are faced with the task of finding both the capital and recurrent costs of educational institutions. External aid that will give relief in the capital cost of education will be most highly welcomed, especially if the burden of amortization can be spread over many years.

The greatest problem of today is that of employment. Trained manpower must be suitably employed. Many people feel that five universities in Nigeria are too many for Nigeria and that thousands of people trained overseas will return to Nigeria to find no jobs. They are pessimists. Employment opportunities in Nigeria have only started to grow. What is important is a machinery for deploying trained manpower into those employment opportunities that exist while creating more. It is believed that with the growth of industries many more employment opportunities will occur, although the adoption of the latest time-saving scientific devices may not enable the country to provide adequate employment for all. Plans will, however, have to be made so as to rationalize both capital intensive and labour intensive development in industry. It is for this reason that the institutionalization of planning in Nigeria, at this juncture, is most welcome as it will enable the various factors concerned to be properly examined and co-ordinated.

VI. *The National Education Plan*

Although the Nigerian Constitution does not place responsibility for education in Nigeria solely in the hands of the Federal Government, yet it is possible to talk of a national education plan. The Sessional Paper No. 3 of 1961 on Educational Development (1961–70) outlined the main aspects of the national educational development plan. It was based on the proposals of the Ashby Report and departed from them only in fixing targets that are larger than those suggested by Harbison. It was felt that educational activities required the stimulation of higher targets. They were, however, not based on any survey or any statistical appraisal. The paper summarized the principal findings of the Ashby Commission and proceeded to state the modified recommendations accepted by the Federal Government. Since then, Federal Government policy has been dictated very much by the proposals embodied in the Sessional Paper. Today, when one speaks of a national education plan, one must imagine on the one hand a synthesis of the regional plans and, on the other, the lines of development embodied in Sessional Paper No. 3, of 1961. Since then, however, the need for a more comprehensive national educational plan has become much more apparent. The economic development plan of the Governments embracing, as it does, proposals on primary production, on trade and industries, on electricity development, on transportation and communication, on urban water supplies, on town and country planning, on broadcasting and television, and on national security, makes it imperative that the Central Government must do something substantial on the manpower component of the Six-Year Development Plan. Projects such as iron and steel, petroleum, geological and water surveys, Niger Dam and hydro-electric power have been embarked upon by government since the policy paper was written. The high-level manpower implications of these economic projects are so vast and the demand for technicians so staggering that not much success can be achieved until manpower training on an unprecedented scale has become fully operative. The national educational plan must, therefore, be complementary to the Federal Government development programme, and the educational effort of the Regional and Federal Governments must be harmonized so that comprehensive economic development can be achieved. The Federal Ministry of Education has, therefore, assumed the responsibility of bringing together the Regional Ministries of Education in order to harmonize educational plans within the framework of national requirements. But the over-riding responsibility for education as laid down in the Constitution remains with the Regional Governments.

As stated earlier, primary education has practically reached universality in the Eastern, Western, Mid-Western Regions and the Federal Territory of Lagos. Only in the North is there still a long way to go. The position of the Federal Government was stated quite clearly in the Sessional Paper No. 3 of 1961 as follows:

'The Federal Government should do everything possible to intensify the rate of educational development in the Northern Region so that by 1970 there will be in the whole country a single educational system broadly based and broadly proportioned. The objective in the North should be to approach parity with the other Regions of the Federation and, in any event, development must be so planned as to give by 1970 a total enrolment in the Northern Region of not less than 50 per cent of children of primary school age. The Federal Government is resolved to assist the Northern Regional Government financially and otherwise to achieve this result. In negotiating for external aid and assistance this need of the North will be taken into full consideration.'

The Federal Government has fulfilled her promise in this regard. A contribution of £200,000 per annum has been made towards the expansion of primary education in the North. Scholarship funds worth

£177,000 per annum have also been given to assist in the training of high-level manpower so that educational development in the North may be further developed. It has now become increasingly clear, however, that the proposal of the Ashby Commission about the development of education in the North is perhaps the wisest of all. The Commission suggested that the pyramid in the North must be proportionate at every stage of its development, in other words, funds must not be canalized too much into primary education to the exclusion of secondary and higher education. By expanding all the three levels at the same time, a balanced development will take place and a complete pyramid, proportionate in every respect, will be achieved not too long after this has been achieved in the other regions of the Federation which have started with a broader primary base and are now surging up towards the creation of a broader secondary level and a bigger higher education apex.

The development of secondary education throughout the Federation is the most important aspect of the national plan. In the 1961 Policy Paper, the Federal Government undertook to develop inter-regional secondary schools. Three of these are to be built in the regions at a cost of £1·8 million. The sites of these three institutions have been chosen, building operations have commenced and the first intakes were admitted in 1965. The enrolment in secondary schools throughout the Federation as indicated in Table 11(i) gives an idea of the relative development by Regions. A casual glance will reveal that the enrolment in the North is still low although the rate of increase in recent years has been very significant. The Western figure of 145,798 includes the secondary modern school element which is 110,283. Throughout the Federation, it will be found that there is a disproportionate emphasis on grammar school education to the exclusion of commercial and technical training. A detailed analysis of the position in Lagos has revealed that out of 3,383 student intake into secondary schools in 1962, only 58 were enrolled in secondary technical schools while 1,712 enrolled in grammar schools, 1,028 in commercial, 432 in modern schools, and 153 in trade centres. The rectification of the imbalance in the field of secondary education is the cardinal element of the national educational policy.

As far as higher education is concerned there is yet a long way to go even though five universities are now in operation. The development of these universities is very rigidly controlled by the output of the secondary schools. For a long time to come, the universities will continue to depend on the students that have taken only the School Certificate while an increasing number with the Higher School Certificate or the G.C.E. Advanced Level will enter directly to the universities. The total number of entry for the school certificate examination in 1963 was 10,000. Many of these candidates will seek employment, others will go overseas and a large number will be unsuitable for university education. During the past few years, the number of candidates passing the higher school certificate examination from form six classes increased as follows:

1961	384
1962	568
1963	760

Apart from those who qualified for direct entry into the universities through passing the higher school certificate examination, a large number qualified by passing the General Certificate of Education at the Advanced level. Three-fourths of the candidates who took the Higher School Certificate examination usually passed, but the percentage of passes at the G.C.E. (Advanced) is generally low, being only 14·4 per cent.

The national plan as regards technical and vocational education remains unchanged although it has increased in emphasis year by year as the challenge of existence and the pragmatic interests of industries begin to show themselves. In three or four years' time progress will become more noticeable.

In view of the manpower targets and objectives already presented by the Manpower Board, it seems fairly certain that the educational plan in the remaining years of this century will have to be divided into three cycles of 15 years duration because a cycle of educational development takes at least 15 years to cover primary, secondary and higher education. The first cycle may be regarded as starting from 1955 and ending in 1970; the second cycle will begin around 1970 and end in 1985; the third cycle will cover the last 15 years of this century. It is hardly possible to attain the national target in the training of technicians between now and 1970. More modest targets will therefore have to be assumed. A ratio of 1:2:4 will probably be more reasonable as between high, intermediate and other categories of trained manpower. The target for the North will have to be separate from the target from the South if the national total is to have realism. During the second cycle, a ratio of 1 : 3 : 9 may be attempted. It is possible that during this period the South may be able to reach a ratio of 1 : 4 : 16 which, in any case, should be the ratio for the whole Federation before the year A.D. 2000. A better ratio, however, would probably be 1 : 5 : 25.

In order to approach a situation such as has been described, the growth of our population must be carefully watched, the percentage that will produce the goods for the rest must be carefully controlled and progressively increased and the ratio of high-level, intermediate and other categories of manpower must also be carefully regulated. It is for this reason, that the studies and researches of the National Manpower Board will continue to be the major factor in the formulation of educational policy not only during the present 15 years' cycle but also in the other two cycles that must follow during the remaining years of the century.

This broad generalization in the national educational plan may appear visionary or academic, but the various Ministries of Education have already started on a detailed programme of planning, the major segments of which may be stated as follows:

> Educational Statistics;
> Teacher Training;
> School Buildings;
> Curriculum Development;
> Education Law and Regulation;
> Education Finance;
> Education Publicity;
> External Aid for Education;
> Employment of School Graduates;
> Inter-relationship of different levels
>   and types of education.

At the June 1963 meeting of the Joint Consultative Committee, these 10 aspects of educational planning constituted the subject of study. Future meetings of the Committee would be devoted exclusively to the examination of educational statistics, teacher training and school buildings throughout the Federation in order to achieve a great measure of uniformity in the government programmes. Already, the standardization of educational statistics throughout the Federation which has led to the publishing of the Digest of Educational Statistics now enables the various Ministries of Education to plan realistically.

Teacher Training standards throughout the Federation are becoming increasingly uniform. Expansion has reached such a stage in the South that the training of Grade III teachers has been discontinued and these teachers are being upgraded to Grade II by sending them back to colleges. In Lagos, for instance, the Grade III teachers who finished their training in 1963 could not have been absorbed into Lagos schools if the same number of Grade III teachers had not been readmitted into colleges to train as Grade II teachers. Secondly, schools are also being increasingly supplied with teachers specially trained for them through grants-in-aid.

Owing to the high cost of building throughout Nigeria, it has been suggested that some research should be undertaken to introduce standardization in school building designs in order to effect savings. In the United Kingdom, after the war, a sum of £30 million was saved through standardization in design. The same applied to Western Germany. With the heavy building programme in the field of primary, secondary and higher education, it is hoped that substantial savings may be effected if building designs are standardized.

The national education plan also involves a complete reform in the curriculum of all our schools. The primary schools are to be introduced to elementary science, of things above us, around us and below us. The pupils are to be stimulated so that they can acquire the spirit of inquiry. This reform of our primary school curriculum in order to stir up a spirit of scientific inquiry is long overdue. A reform in the secondary school curriculum is also taking place not only in mathematics and the sciences but also in modern languages and social studies. One notes with pleasure that the reconstitution of the mathematics and science curricula in the United States has started to receive echoes on our own shores.

A national plan of the magnitude thus described must have the backing of a national law if it should succeed. It has been suggested that the challenge facing under-developed countries of the world is of such a description that their educational problems must be approached with the totality with which a nation faces military emergencies. For this reason, it may be necessary to enact something like a Defence Education Law which will make it imperative for all our schools to teach not only science and mathematics but also the modern technology on which our future economy depends. Nigeria cannot stand aloof and watch the vast economic growth of the advanced nations of the world, the prodigious programmes of space research, the technological advancement in food production and chemicals, the stupendous strides in the field of communication and transport, while national development takes place at pedestrian speed. A national law, in keeping with the impatience of the masses to progress is, therefore, obligatory.

It has been stated earlier that the greatest problem in the national educational plan is to find adequate funds for capital investment. In fact, it will be a valuable exercise to analyse the manpower component of our development plan so that an adequate investment in manpower may be undertaken. The educational sector of the development plan was planned as a unit separate and distinct from the rest. That sector obviously needs a revision in the light of the economic proposals in the other parts of the plan. The cost will undoubtedly be heavy but there is no reason why the total cost must be met by the present generation alone. Loans, capable of spreading to 40 or 50 years are, therefore, imperative and the Governments of the Federation must leave no stone unturned in securing such loans. In implementing a programme of such importance as the national educational plan, universal support must be obtained. A great deal of publicity must also be given to every aspect of the plan so that the people as a whole may make the necessary sacrifice and participate.

VII. *The Shape of Things to Come*

An examination of all the plans already in operation throughout the country would probably make one feel that everything was in order. One must realize, however, that a setback may be experienced if there should be a world war and if internal security in the country were to be in danger. While, therefore, the national educational plan is of great importance, the security of the nation must be regarded as paramount. Nigeria's international and national affairs will have to be conducted in such a manner as not to endanger the great economic scheme on which the country has embarked and also the manpower development without which it cannot come to fruition.

Confidence in the future is, however, assured by the fact that every plan that has been made for the development of higher education, science and technology, technical and vocational education, primary and secondary education, has been institutionalized in organs that have perpetual succession and existence. In the case of higher education, the Manpower Board and the National Universities Commission will continue to look after its fortunes. Again, in the case of scientific and technological development, the National Advisory Council on Technical Education, the National Council of Science and Technology and the National Manpower Board will jointly direct the progressive development of science and technology and their applications for the benefit of the country. Further, the development of primary and secondary education as well as teacher training throughout the country is in the hands of the Regional and Federal Governments as well as boards of education that have been established by law to advise the Ministers charged with responsibility for education. It is this institutionalization of machineries for manpower development at every level that gives the guarantee for systematic future development.

One can therefore look forward to a future in which Nigeria can hold her own among the advanced nations of the world. If these plans come to fruition, and there is every assurance that they will, the end of this century will find the country contributing to the peace of the world and the progressive development of mankind.

12

Educational Problems in Economic Development

Charles L. Shaffer

ASSOCIATE PROFESSOR, FACULTY OF BUSINESS AND SOCIAL STUDIES
UNIVERSITY OF LAGOS

I. Introduction

Anyone who attempts to evaluate the Nigerian educational system cannot help but be overwhelmed by the progress that has been made in this past decade. In 1952 there were 519,944 students enrolled in formal education programmes in Nigeria. (F—6)[1] In 1961 that number had increased to 2,803,836.[2] This is an increase of 500 per cent over a ten-year period. Sixteen years ago there was no university in Nigeria. Today there are five with a student body of approximately 4,000. The progress has been tremendous and at no small expense to the people of Nigeria.

In looking at the problems confronting higher education, one becomes immediately aware that educators in Nigeria are already very cognizant of the problems that exist. If awareness of a problem is a great step forward in meeting that problem, Nigeria has made that step. For the person studying education in Nigeria three classical documents are available. They are, first of all the 'Investment in Education,' commonly called the Ashby Report; The Federation of Nigeria White Paper on 'Educational Development 1961 to 1970'; and the 'Report of the Commission Appointed to Review the Educational System of Western Nigeria', commonly referred to as the Banjo Report. It was with great vision that the writers of the Ashby Report recommended the setting up of a National Universities Commission as well as a

[1] Letters refer to references in the bibliography annexed hereto. Numbers refer to the page number of the reference.
[2] The figures quoted here are those of the preliminary report submitted to the seminar. The final figures are contained in *Nigeria's High-Level Manpower, 1963–70*, National Manpower Board, Lagos (Manpower Study No. 2).

National Manpower Board. It augurs well for Nigeria that both of these recommendations have been followed and such boards now exist.

About forty years ago in the United States a labour leader was asked specifically what his union wanted. His answer was 'more'. It is apparent from looking over the educational needs in Nigeria that the thing that is needed is 'more'—teachers, money, and facilities. It is, however, only by examining the National Manpower Board's report on the need for high-level manpower during the next five years that one becomes aware of the dimensions of the problems.

According to the Manpower Board survey,[2] a need for high-level senior-category manpower is much greater and more critical than even Harbison suggested. This is understandable since Harbison was presenting only minimum requirements for appropriate economic growth. According to the Manpower Board survey there are now 15,679 high-level senior-category manpower employed in Nigeria. Of these, at the present time, 33 per cent are held by expatriates and 15 per cent are vacant. The projected needs, as indicated by the Manpower Board's survey for 1968 are for 35,133 senior-category top-level people. This means a 500 per cent increase in the number of high-level manpower needed. The Manpower Report itself envisions, even with present plans, a shortage of 28,000 in this category.

We can suggest that at least 70 per cent of these individuals should have had a university education. This means a minimum of 25,000. University graduates including both those studying in Nigerian universities and abroad are probably not over 1,000 a year. An optimistic figure would put an average of 1,500 a year for the next five years or a total of 7,500. To put it quite bluntly, from the standpoint of advanced planning and facilities, Nigeria, unless radical measures are taken, will have only about 25 per cent (at a maximum) of the top-level manpower that it requires. This paper will concern itself with the most critical areas, as this writer evaluates them, in developing this top-level Manpower.

II. *The Problem of Balance in the Hierarchy of the Educational System*
In Nigeria, of the students enrolled in formal educational programmes, 95 per cent are in primary education and only 5 per cent in all others. This contrasts with the United States where approximately 55 per cent are in primary education and 45 per cent are in all others. To a certain extent this contrast is understandable. Nigeria is a young nation made

[2] Ibid.

up of young people and free primary education is of recent origin. Looking at the primary schools alone, registered in the first year are 700,000 students (D—22), but in the fifth year only 311,105.

While the universities are geared to take in over 3,300 students a year by 1970, there are less than 1,000 students in formal sixth form education, although there are probably another 5,000 studying outside of formal institutions to take the sixth form examinations which are entrance requirements for most of the universities in Nigeria. In other words, although the universities may be equipped to take 3,300 students a year, it is doubtful if the secondary educational facilities are equipped to turn out over 1,000 a year of potentially qualified university applicants.

The question of balance of educational facilities is raised in the first report in manpower studies put out by the National Manpower Board recently. They say, 'in 1961 the estimated number of persons graduating from primary schools was approximately 261,000. Further education and training facilities were available to about 50,000. This left about 211,000 primary school leavers to be put into gainful employment. (M—9).

Father James O'Connell states, 'due to the lack of science streams and teachers in the secondary schools Ahamadu Bello College in 1962–3 has not been able to fill its engineering student quota—just as the University of Ibadan has not been able to fill its medical quota. The temptation for the universities is to expand in a liberal arts direction where students are equally available, but soon there will be over-production of these students even as skills are still lacking in many other vital areas of higher education' (R—65).

The Ashby Committee was also aware of the need for increasing the number of secondary institutions especially of the sixth form type that lead to university studies. They report, 'therefore Nigeria's objective for the years 1960–70 should be to have the equivalent of 150 streams of sixth form pupils. Over the next ten years another 110 sixth form streams will be needed and at least 350 additional highly qualified teachers' (B—12).

In response to the Ashby Report, the Federal Government went even further in recommending sixth form education. The White Paper on 'Educational Development 1961–70' stated 'of critical significance is the increase in the number of pupils undertaking sixth form work, for this is a controlling factor in the number of students proceeding to university institutions. An all-out endeavour to raise the sixth form streams to a total of 350 must therefore be made in order to bring the number of students preparing for higher school certificate or the "general certificate" of education to over 10,000' (C—5). Later on in the Ashby Report, we read 'to meet Nigeria's need for high-level manpower the first step is to create places for some 18,000 more entrants to secondary schools' (B—9).

Whether or not the universities indicated by the Ashby Report will be sufficient is subject to question. In a memorandum to the Ashby Commission, the Eastern Nigeria Science Association states, 'we suggest that Nigeria should aim at a total of about fifteen universities in twenty years from now' (O—66). As far as the actual enrolment in sixth form education in Nigeria in 1960 is concerned there were 553 students in twenty-two schools. It is true that at the same time there were probably at least a few thousand students studying on their own to pass the sixth form. It is possible, however, that the 'bottleneck' to developing high-level manpower will lie not so much in the university facilities as in the facilities provided for sixth form education.

Accepting that a problem does exist with regard to the relative amount of facilities for secondary and primary education, the following suggestions are made to help alleviate the problem:

(a) Wherever possible increase the sixth form streams by adding to secondary grammar school facilities and at the same time developing, wherever possible, comprehensive secondary schools out of existing institutions.

(b) Although the Ashby Report does not recommend that universities attempt four-year programmes of education, this writer suggests that universities be allowed to develop both three and four-year programmes to enable them to take in ordinary school as well as higher form graduates. Evidence gathered at this time seems to indicate that students entering the four-year programme do as well during their third year of study as do those students who enter the three-year programme during their second year of study.

(c) While free universal primary education is popular with all, it can be a tremendous drain on developing countries where the birth rate is extremely high. Consideration should be given to establishing nominal fees for the first three years of primary school. A fee of £2 per year per student would make available to the government over £2,000,000 to put into secondary and higher education.

(d) A method of sixth form education should be developed which would combine the use of television courses with correspondence work. The writer believes that this programme would not only stimulate the general population's knowledge regarding the need for higher education, but would also increase the supply of sixth-form graduates in a most expedient and financially efficient manner.

III. *Relating Formal Education to National Needs*

If there is a desire to Nigerianize top-level positions at the earliest possible moment there must be a demand that education in Nigeria be Nigerianized without delay. It has become very obvious that the needs for Nigeria as an independent nation are quite in variance with her needs as a colony. Firstly, Nigeria cannot afford the luxury of the 'gentleman's education'. Secondly, it is no longer sufficient merely to develop people who can carry out orders efficiently. More important, is the development of leaders who can solve the problems of Nigeria and direct the implementations of their solutions. Thirdly, it will be through the development of the agricultural and technological sectors that Nigeria will grow. Yet, because of past educational practices, these are the sectors that have been most neglected and discouraged.

The editors of the 'West African Journal of Education' have these comments to make on education in Africa.

'As in Africa, education elsewhere is in flux. A commonly accepted stereotype of American, British, French, and Russian education are demonstrably false. America is concerned with quality as well as quantity; Britain is *not* content merely to live on the legacy of its educational history; France is moved by social justice as well as by reverence for élitism; USSR is *not* prepared to sacrifice all scholarships on the altar of totalitarianism. If there is one single lesson to be learned from considering these articles it is simply that African educational planning should not be motivated, positively or negatively, by ideas about the education of other peoples which are themselves perhaps twenty years out of date' (S—127).

Mr. Solarin, Principal of the Mayflower School, says, 'an education if given for its own sake or as generally held by civilized countries like Britain and France, as a personal possession by the person being educated is not the education needed in present day Africa. The secondary education that the African needs today is one that would be directly useful to the commonwealth' (R—77). In another article, Dr. S. O. Biobaku states, 'The African universities cannot afford to imitate Oxbridge in their organization; they must set their sights differently and so take into their purview day students as well as residential ones, evening classes, and arrangements for external degrees, where appropriate. The task before them is so urgent that they must eschew any kind of snobbery and the only students they must turn away from their doors are the incompetent, not the under-privileged' (R—62).

In a speech before the Nigeria Employers Consultative Association, Dr. Yesufu had this to say, 'Nigeria is turning out annually more than one-third of a million primary school graduates who, nevertheless, remain functional illiterates' (P—3). The Banjo report states, 'The last aim, that of the acquisition of skill of hand and the recognition of the value of manual work, is the least achieved. It was hoped that the literate primary school leavers would go back to be better farmers, carpenters, bricklayers, and so on, but all the pupils themselves want to be are junior clerks in offices' (E—4).

What then are some of the specific need areas to Nigerianize education? Dr. Fafunwa indicates the following need areas. 'Reading and writing in the child's mother tongue and English, French, and so on as applicable. This calls for proliferation of materials in the vernacular and in the second language. Effective communication is a fundamental skill.' 'Arithmetical and Mathematical process; these will enable the African child to develop precision, problem solving and effective thinking to mention only a few skills.' 'Because basic science promotes scientific thought, an area which is virtually new in Africa, it is recommended that a third to a half of the school timetable for the first year of elementary to the first two years of secondary education should be devoted to this subject' (R—67).

Based upon the author's own experience in university work in Nigeria, it is believed that two of the major weaknesses of students are that they lack skills in mathematics as well as skills in problem solving. These can be improved not only by the introduction of appropriate subject matter, mathematics and science, into the curriculum but also by the method of teaching used. A method of teaching and an educational system which puts great emphasis on rote learning, memorizing is not likely to foster creative thinking ability. On the other hand, educational methods which stimulate thought through the introduction of problem solving, scientific reasoning, and greater awareness of one's surroundings and the role of cause and effect is needed. To achieve these changes requires not only introduction of new teaching methods but also possibly the utilization of new types of achievement tests.

With the above problems in mind, the following recommendations are made:

(a) That all course offerings from primary through university education be evaluated to determine their appropriateness in the curriculum in relationship to Nigeria's high-level manpower needs. Specifically, courses of a practical, vocational, scientific, and commercial nature should be introduced into the curriculum at appropriate levels to satisfy the needs of not only those continuing on in higher education, but those who will be school leavers at that particular point in their education careers.

(b) Specifically, science and agriculture, both of which should be applicable to the tropical scene and further emphasis on mathematics and English should be introduced into the curriculum.

(c) Teaching methods should be evaluated and modified to encourage the use of critical reasoning, greater awareness of the surroundings, and problem solving rather than memory.

(d) Effort should be made to develop tests of reasoning skills and problem solving rather than those emphasizing only the retention of materials.

(e) The author recognizes that the changes in the curriculum as well as teaching methods require a great deal of time and money expenditure on the training of teachers themselves. Obviously, a teacher is likely to be content to teach the courses that he has been exposed to and in a way in which he was exposed to them. However, re-training of existing teachers as well as the training of new teachers should help to alleviate the problems indicated.

IV. Role of Government in Restoring a Proper Balance of Education

At the time of Independence, the Government of the Federation was spending something like twenty million pounds a year on all types of education and the annual budget was a higher percentage of the country's entire annual expenditure than in most other countries of the world (I—24). The Government recognizes that if it is to increase education output to meet the needs of manpower it will be required to put an increasing financial amount into education. The Government policy paper on education states, 'In short, Nigeria must aim to make and sustain education effort more than three times as great as is already being made now. The Federal Government will endeavour to play its full part in the implementation of these proposals. It is confident that regional governments will be willing to shoulder their share of the financial burden of implementing the proposals' (C—9). In education, as with the other areas of the development plan, the need of outside assistance in terms of personnel and financing is recognized.

The governments contribute financially to education in two ways. Firstly but least in amount, are the scholarships and moneys made available to individual students for study at home and abroad. Secondly, is the financial support given to schools and universities. The careful allocation of funds by the Government in both of these categories can substantially effect the progress in meeting balanced high-level manpower requirements. With regards to support through scholarships, a number of variables are important. First, is the basis of selection for granting a scholarship. Second, the length of the scholarship. Third, the amount of the scholarship, and fourth, the types of scholarships. In a country in which the need for top-level superior manpower is so great and financial resources for meeting this need so limited, it is imperative that moneys available go to aid the best qualified individuals. While recognizing that the need for financial assistance varies from student to student, any scholarships which are given on a basis other than merit are a disservice to the country.

A part of the problem here is having adequate predictors of the potential abilities of a given individual. This problem will be discussed in the next section. This writer believes that not only should the initial scholarship be granted on merit, but a continuation of it into the second and third years of a student's course of study should be based upon his performance at the university. While it is good to underwrite the full course of study of a student this should not be guaranteed, but be subject to the performance of a student during his course of work.

Another question that arises is the amount of scholarship aid given to any one student. Here, one has the choice of supporting relatively few with ample amounts or supporting many with limited funds. The number of qualified students available for further work requires that everything possible be done to broaden the base. It has been stated that at the University of Ibadan it has been necessary in the past to send down students for non-payment of fees which total £45,000. Assuming that these students were all qualified to go on, this is a waste not only of the manpower talent of these students, but of the existing facilities of the university. Every student capable of university work should be capable in some measure of supporting the cost of his work.

Scholarships that cover the cost of tuition and of room and board should be sufficient. Provisions can be made for an adequate supply of books in libraries that could be utilized by all students. Placement services should be set up in the different universities to help the student in finding summer employment. Loan funds, repayable after graduation, should be made available to aid in the financing of education for all well-qualified students.

The judicious use of scholarship funds can effectively balance the high-level manpower needs for a country. According to Mr. Solarin, 'In 1956–7 session there were, according to the Action Group Research Bureau of Information, 986 Nigerian students in the U.K. Of these, 343 were doing engineering; 196 B.Sc. Economics and 447 in law. The line-out of these studies points out so glaringly the disparity between the cockeyed education and education to work a primitive country like Nigeria' (R—77). In the recent Manpower Board report it is stated, 'The University of Nigeria, Nsukka, the University of Lagos and the University of Ife have each opened a faculty of law. It was recently reported that "there are 1,213 Nigerian lawyers, and half of them underemployed"' (M—15). The report goes on to add that at this time facilities for training in agriculture, engineering, science and education are not being fully utilized (N—15).

The second means the Government has of financing higher education is its direct support of the schools and universities themselves. To a certain extent this question hinges around the size of the university, whether you are going to have ten universities of 1,000 students each or five universities of 2,000 students each. There is something to be said for small as well as large universities. However, universities of the magnitude of 2,000 students cannot be considered as excessively large in any way.

One should, of course, ensure the proper dispersal of universities so that they will provide educational facilities for all areas of the country. However, it is questionable at this time, with the limited funds available, if the duplications of faculties and areas of study should be encouraged. There is a point to be made that with the duplication of faculties each faculty in a given field will seek to outdo the other one in performance and therefore increase the quality of education. However, the need for qualified university teachers is so great that it is questionable if this type of competition can be financially sound at this time.

The Universities Commission has been charged with disbursal of funds to the various universities. Through such disbursals a balancing of Nigerian manpower needs can be arranged. For example, in an unpublished report it is indicated that at the present time approximately 25 per cent of the students are in the field of arts, 16 per cent in science, 7 per cent in technology, 8 per cent in medicine and another 25 per cent in social studies. Thus, the science and technology fields account for approximately 22 per cent of the universities' students at the present time. If Nigeria is to balance its manpower resources with needs for study in the areas of science and technology, this should be increased probably to about 50 per cent of the student population.

At the present time it is financially more efficient to educate graduate students and students enrolled in highly technical studies overseas. Already, some work has been done in exchanging students and scholarships moneys with other countries in Africa. Encouragement of such exchanges between countries in addition to insuring the maximum use of facilities available in Africa will acquaint students with the cultures of other African countries and will lead to the African solidarity that is desired.

In short, the proper utilization of Government financing in the areas of scholarships and direct support of universities can insure that a quality and balance of high-level manpower relating to the needs of the country are achieved. There is plenty of evidence, based on experiences in other countries, that the Government's financial support of scholars and institutions does not have to lead to any type of infringement of the academic freedom of universities.

V. *Appraisal and Development of 'Meritocracy'*

In a recent New Year's address to the nation, His Excellency, the President of the Republic, Dr. Nnamdi Azikiwe, appealed to the people of Nigeria to strive for meritocracy as a way of overcoming mediocrity. All the financing and facilities in the world will be of no avail unless there is a desire on the part of every individual to excel.

Too often we equate excellence with high-level positions or high-level learning. Excellence may be displayed in the work of the most menial of labourers and may be absent from the performance of the highest level executives and administrators. Unless the development of additional top-level manpower is coupled with increased productivity in all levels and sectors of society the cost of 'investment in education' can be excessive.

All development in the long run must be self-development and the desire to excel is remitted to attitudes which the individual has about himself and his society-attitudes which are both hard to define and difficult to change. Attitudes which the author finds quite often in his students, and these impressions have been backed up by other educators and leaders in Nigeria, are that 'since the university student is of high calibre, society therefore needs to support him'. Accompanying this is a complete rejection of certain types of occupations requiring manual work, namely agriculture and technology. Administrative, 'pen-pushing', positions are highly sought after. Paper credentials, including degrees, are expected to insure additional money and security. In almost all cases these paper credentials are expected to be a natural result of collecting large bodies of facts. In every case, these attitudes are contrary to the needs of society in terms of the types of manpower required and in terms of the excellence that should be encouraged in every individual.

Attitudes are acquired unconsciously and over long periods of time. Awareness of Nigeria's long history as a colony makes many of these attitudes understandable. In most cases, under colonization, the road to advancement was in government service. However, in this, there was always someone higher up to do the thinking. The inequitable salary distribution between people working for the government and holding similar jobs outside of the government often encouraged these attitudes. Under the colonial system, educational methods and examinations encouraged the efforts to accumulate facts, in many cases in irrelevant study areas, to achieve a diploma. Too often hiring practices were based on the level of educational achievement that a man could document. This may not be directly related to his potential and his ability to understand and apply his knowledge. Certainly any system that wishes to encourage excellence must realize the existence of these attitudes and do everything possible to change them. Leadership must be encouraged and opportunities given. Salary and fringe differentials between governments, industry, and teaching have to a certain extent been decreased. With the introduction of new methods of teaching and new types of courses, a change can be expected in the method of approaching the problems.

Everything should be done to improve the selection and promotion process not only within the hierarchy of education but also throughout government and private industry. Within the education system, stressing of reasoning and critical thinking ability should be emphasized. Aptitude tests, which not only give some idea of a man's achievement, but the extent to which he can apply his knowledge and will apply it, are necessary. All selection and advancement should be made without prejudice and this includes the prejudice that we sometimes harbour towards a man who can do the job but does not have the necessary paper qualifications. With improvements in aptitude testing much more emphasis should be given to the guidance of students into appropriate fields of education which best match their talents and interests. The development of comprehensive secondary schools which will permit a student to decide his eventual career pattern at a later date will be helpful.

If the goals of high-level manpower are to be met, it is necessary to be able to identify and encourage each individual's potential. Also, the need for manpower in the intermediate category is even greater than that for the senior category. Individuals whose potential is such that they can accomplish these jobs should be encouraged to go into these intermediate-level positions.

V. *The Role and Responsibilities of the Private Sector*

Developing nations have a need for training as well as education. In fact, it is desirable they arrange a fine blend of both. There is a need for people who are trained, that is people who know how to do practical things. There is also a need for educated people who can question past practices in terms of their adequacy and efficiency and suggest newer methods. People often feel that it is up to formal education institutions to educate and to industries to train. In actual practice, education must be involved in some training, but industry should also recognize that it has the facilities and has also some educational role.

Studies have been recently completed that indicate that the usual variables we try to use to account for economic growth, only in part explain the magnitude of growth that takes place. Usually an attempt is made to combine man-hours of work with financial resources. However, this has been found only in part to account for economic development that takes place. Dr. Yesufu explains some of these findings in the following way, 'for example, studies made of economic growth in developed countries have shown that the total inputs in tangible capital and labour per annum account for only about one-third of the growth of real income. For the United Kingdom it has been shown that capital and labour inputs account for a quarter of the increased production in output per head in manufacturing industry between 1948 and 1954. The residual factors account for as much as two thirds and three fourths of the increased output: and among these education and basic science appear to have played a dominant role' (P—13). Dr. Yesufu further goes on to note that it is the employers, either public or private, who constitute the consumers of manpower. He further correctly observes that even in the developed countries (so-called developed countries since even the most advanced countries have a need for continuous development—their alternative being retrogression), have found their educational systems deficient in producing certain categories of high-level manpower (T—3).

That the Manpower Board's indications of high-level manpower need in the private sector is probably an underestimate of true needs is indicated by the following finds. In a recent study on the development of small industry in Eastern Nigeria conclusions were reached that, 'small industry, although it has received very little attention or government assistance, occupies a significant place in Eastern Nigeria's developing industrial economy. It provides employment for approximately triple the number engaged in large-scale manufacturing' (L—5). Later on in the same report, the author says, 'the managerial input is a prime limiting factor in the growth of the small firm' (L—15). This is not to suggest that every small firm can have university graduates to head it, but it is to recommend that there is a need for high-level manpower talent utilized on a co-operative basis by the small firms of the country. Specific skills needed according to the author are those in accounting, financing, marketing and business systems.

Education is needed not only for the future manpower requirements of the country, but also to reduce unemployment at the present time. According to a recent survey of industry, of persons unemployed 91·3 per cent had primary education and below while only 8·7 per cent had secondary education and above. Of the total unemployed only 2·2 per cent were in the professional, technical, and administrative categories (K—iii). The value of education as an immediate stimulant to reduce unemployment is indicated by Dr. Yesufu in this statement, 'for example, at a time when the Ministry of Labour had in its registers about 14,000 unemployed persons in March 1961, there were at the same time, 16,276 vacancies reported by employers through a sample employment market survey. About 10,000 of these vacancies required special qualifications in training which the registered unemployed persons did not possess' (T—9).

Industry can and has an obligation to contribute to the development of high-level manpower not only through the support of formal education institutions, but also in its obligations to its own employees. With regards to support for formal education, industry can, while not in a stage of development where it can give *carte blanche* to formal education, provide special chairs in universities. Thus, oil industries might wish to provide a Chair of Petroleum Engineering. Industries having a great need for marketing specialists might provide a Chair of Marketing. Scholarships could be provided in specific areas where the industry finds itself short of talent. These same scholarship holders might be invited for summer employment into the industries providing the scholarships, thereby giving the scholarship holder practical experience as well as developing a link between himself and the industry. Industries could also provide educational information to formal educational institutions regarding what they are doing, how they benefit society, and their organizational structure. In this latter connection, visits to various industries should be encouraged by the industries so that students will have a greater understanding of the role of industry in the development of the country.

Industry, of course, has the obligation to develop within its own ranks highly skilled manpower. Most industries are relatively small in Nigeria and do not have the facilities for adequate training programmes of their employees. This, however, should not prevent industries from joining together in co-operative training ventures and the financing of co-operative training facilities.

All of the personnel practices of private industries in areas of recruiting, selection, training, appraisal, and motivation will affect the development of high-level manpower. Unfortunately, not much is known about the personnel practices of industries throughout Nigeria. However, evidence that is available indicates that good personnel practices lead to individual productivity as great as can be found in any other country in the world. Universities, through their extramural programmes, can help industries to develop their manpower. I would suggest that the universities' appropriate role is in helping industries to train their own workers rather than doing the training for them.

A brief mention is appropriate here of the role of professional societies: accountants, lawyers and secretaries, in the up-grading of high-level manpower. These societies, at this stage of their development, have the responsibility not only to up-grade the existing profession but to encourage and help in the development of would-be members of a profession. In summary then, private industry as well as professional associations have a distinct obligation to assist formal educational institutions in the development and up-grading of high-level manpower.

VI. *Conclusion*

In summary, great progress has been made in the realm of education during the past decade by the people of Nigeria and at no small cost in terms of sacrifice to the people. According to the report of the Manpower Board, in terms of requirements for high-level manpower within the next five years, Nigeria has only started to meet its needs. Of course, the development of high-level manpower is but one of the vital ingredients in the development of the economy.

In developing countries, financial and physical resources are of necessity limited. This means that the greatest use possible must be made not only of internal resources, but also those supplied from the outside. A developing economy must insure that individuals with potential will be properly selected, educated, and motivated. This will make the most of their abilities and in turn make the greatest use of facilities available. Too often, one thinks of a semi-planned economy as one in which the government does the major portion of the work. Concentrated effort is required on the part of every individual— management, labour organization and professional society, as well as the government to develop the needed high-level manpower. In this paper an attempt has been made to suggest some of the most critical problems in the areas of high-level manpower development.

The author admits to laying himself open to the charge that he has put economic development as one of the major goals of education. There are certain people who will say that what we wish to do is to emphasize our arts and culture. To some people this is synonymous with maintaining the *status quo* or even retrogressing. Obviously, no outsider can tell the people of a country what they should want. This is a decision that must be up to them. I do not believe, however, that economic progress has to be at the expense of maintenance of heritage including art and culture. Indeed, to ensure that these are maintained and developed a concomitant in technology and industry is necessary. Plans can be made, facilities provided and financing arranged for development. The extent to which development takes place depends upon the desires of the peoples, their attitudes and their willingness to accept change.

In the introduction of change there is always the risk factor. Unevaluated and unplanned change presents the greatest risk of all. Nigerian leaders who have seen the inevitability of change, with great foresight, have set up plans for change as well as appropriate institutions to direct this change in a most productive manner. To a great extent, the problems facing Nigeria in its attempt to develop high-level manpower are the same problems other developing nations are attempting to solve. In every country it requires concerted efforts in all quarters and at all levels. In Mexico the campaign 'Each One Teach One' was very effective in reducing the amount of illiteracy in the country, inexpensively. Prefabricated school rooms that could be constructed by the people of a village in a single day appeared everywhere.

Fundamental to all growth must be the recognition on the part of all the people that education is not only a basis of economic growth, but also a way to enlightened and constructive citizenship. No plans, however well thought out or executed, can succeed unless all are aware of the need and willing to share the burden of meeting that need. One never invests in education as an end in itself. Rather, education itself is a sound investment in people—the future of their country. As Alhaji Sir Abubakar Tafawa Balewa, late Prime Minister of the Federal Republic of Nigeria, so aptly noted at the laying of the foundation stone of the new University of Lagos, investment in education is one of the best investments Nigerians are making today.

Reference Bibliography

A   Manpower Board Survey, *Nigerian High-Level and Skilled Man-power Needs 1963–68.*

B   *Investment in Education*, the report of The Commission on Post-School Certificate and Higher Education in Nigeria. (Federal Ministry of Education, Nigeria, 1960.)

C   *Educational Development 1961–70*, Federation of Nigeria, Sessional Paper No. 3 of 1961, Federal Government Printer, Lagos, 1961.

D   *Annual Digest of Educational Statistics 1961*, Federal Ministry of Education, Series No. 1, Vol. I.

E   *Report of the Commission Appointed to Review the Educational System of Western Nigeria*, Government of Western Nigeria, 1961.

F   *Education Graphs and Statistics 1952–59*, Extracts from the Ministry of Education Annual Report, 1959.

G   *White Paper on Education Development in Northern Nigeria*, Northern Nigeria Government, Government Printer, Kaduna, 1961.

H   Olumbummo, A., and Ferguson, J., *The Emergent University*, Longmans, Great Britain, 1960.

I   *Nigeria: Twelve Months of Independence*, Federal Ministry of Information, Lagos, 1961.

J   McHoney, Christopher, *A Survey-Study of Existing Secondary-Grammar School Education in Nigeria in Comparison with the U.S. System, 1961.*

K   *Industrial Labour*, Federal Ministry of Commerce and Industry, Lagos, 1962.

L   Kilby, Peter, *The Development of Small Industry in Eastern Nigeria*, Ministry of Commerce—U.S. Agency for International Development, 1963.

M   National Manpower Board, *Manpower Situation in Nigeria* (Preliminary Report) Federal Ministry of Information, Printing Division, Lagos, 1963.

N   The Nigerian Economic Society, *The Nigerian Journal of Economic and Social Studies*, Vol. 5, No. 2, July 1963.

O   Eastern Nigerian Science Association, *The Nigerian Scientist*, Vol. 1, November 1961.

P   University College, *Ibadan*, No. 15, March 1963.

Q   University College, *Ibadan*, No. 16, June 1963.

R   Institute of Education, University of Ibadan, *West African Journal of Education*, Vol. 7, No. 2, October 1963.

S   Institute of Education, University of Ibadan, *West African Journal of Education*, Vol. 7, No. 3, October 1963.

T   Yesufu, T. M., *Education and Training Problems in Economic Development*, lecture delivered before Training Officers Group, Nigerian Employers Consultative Association, 19 September 1963.

13

Manpower Training for Economic Development: Professional and Managerial Staff

K. Onwuka Dike

VICE-CHANCELLOR, UNIVERSITY OF IBADAN

The subject of this paper is a rather large one. A full treatment of it would include training of professional and managerial staff inside and outside university institutions, as well as training on the job in Government or private establishments; and it would have to take into account training opportunities abroad as well as at home. While I shall refer to these various aspects of the subject in this paper, my emphasis would be largely on training in university institutions within Nigeria, which I believe to be the core of the problem and which is also the area with which I am familiar.

I. *Some Basic Issues*

It is not surprising that the subject emphasizes economic development as the end objective of manpower training. As one of the most pressing problems of our time, economic development is now frequently used as the yardstick of progress or failure in many fields of human endeavour. If the educationist were to accept this limited aim of education, his task, as regards the planning of higher education, would be simple and straightforward. He would rely on the economists and the statisticians to furnish him with the manpower needs of the nation over a decade or so and would concern himself largely with designing an educational programme which would ensure that no more and no less than the specified manpower requirements are provided. At this level of the discussion, then, there would be two major problems: (1) that of the economist and statistician making the right forecast of manpower needs, and (2) that of the educationist ensuring that the educational system trains enough and only just enough men of the right skills for the jobs in hand. As we shall find, however, even these are not simple tasks and there are conflicting opinions as to how they should be approached. But the problems are necessarily more complex since the job of manpower training is certainly more than one of fulfilling the supply side of a man-power budget for economic development. In spite of the heightened interest in economic development, it is still not generally accepted that manpower training for economic development should be the over-riding aim of educational policy. Indeed, the literature on this subject abounds with controversies as to the proper role of education in a progressive society. The contrast is frequently drawn—though I think rather imperfectly—between education which serves the end of the individual and that which serves the goal of society; between education as consumption and education as investment; and between the 'man-power requirements' and the 'cultural' approaches to educational development.[1] These distinctions are, of course, familiar. All that need be noted here is that the whole question is largely one of emphasis. Each country would have to decide, in the light of her own circum-stances, which approach to emphasize in her educational programme. The Tananarive Conference on the Development of Higher Education in Africa took a very wide view of the role of education in the African context. It notes that,[2] 'In addition to its traditional functions and obligations to teach and to advance knowledge through research, the role of higher education in the social, cultural and economic develop-ment of Africa must be:

1. to maintain adherence and loyalty to world academic standards;
2. to ensure the unification of Africa;
3. to encourage elucidation of and appreciation for African culture and heritage and to dispel misconceptions of Africa, through research and teaching of African studies;
4. to develop completely the human resources for meeting man-power needs;

[1] See, for example, John Vaizey, *The Economics of Education*, Chapter II (Faber and Faber, 1962).
[2] UNESCO, *The Development of Higher Education in Africa* (Report of the Con-ference on the Development of Higher Education in Africa, Tananarive, 3–12 September 1962). A statement in the same terms is to be found in the paper by Joseph Ki-Zerbo, 'The Content of Education in Africa' included in the *Final Report* of the Conference of African States on the Development of Education in Africa, Addis Ababa, 15–25 May 1961 (published jointly by UNESCO and the United Nations Economic Commission for Africa).

5. to train the "whole man" for nation building;
6. to evolve over the years a truly African pattern of higher learning dedicated to Africa and its people yet promoting a bond of kinship to the larger human society.'

While this statement would be heartily endorsed by many educationists, the fact would still have to be faced that in the case of poor countries the choice of policy is necessarily circumscribed, particularly by limited financial resources. In such countries, in spite of the advantages of a broad approach, a more utilitarian approach to educational development may simply be unavoidable. This is even more so for higher education than for education at lower levels. While it is conceivable that primary education may be provided for its own sake—that is, for the mere purpose of developing the individual rather than training him for a job—this principle may not seem so plausible in the case of higher education. Not only does higher education usually involve considerably more expenditure than education at lower levels, but it is also likely that shortage or surplus of high-level manpower will create far more serious problems than shortage or surplus of manpower at lower levels. Although it will be argued later in this paper that a surplus of high-level manpower is to be preferred to a shortage, it can be said that, because of limited financial resources, higher education in poor countries must be planned and that it must stress the 'manpower requirement' rather than the 'cultural' approach.

A correct forecast of manpower requirements is thus the first and perhaps the most important aspect of the planning of higher education in under-developed areas. A second aspect is the quality of education to be given or the standards to be aimed at in the different fields. This second aspect is frequently not independent of the first. Given a limited financial provision, quality may have to be sacrificed for quantity or vice versa. The third aspect of educational planning is the content of the curricula. An educational programme can go wrong on any of these grounds. The size of it may be too large or too small; the quality of education may be too low for the jobs which have to be done or perhaps too high to enable a larger number of people to be reached; and finally the content of the curricula may be out of line with local needs and conditions. These, then, are some of the basic issues which we need to bear in mind both in reviewing Nigerian experience in the post-war period and in charting the course of policy for the coming years.

II. *Summary of Nigerian Experience*

Nigerian experience in the field of higher education can be delimited into three periods. The first period, which coincided with the existence of the Higher College, ended with the putting into effect of the recommendations of the Eliot Commission.[3] The second period, from about 1949 to about 1960, coincided with the first ten years of the University College, Ibadan. The third period began in about 1960 with the attempts to implement the Ashby Commission Report.

Little need be said about the first period. The Higher College, which was the only institution of higher education in this period, was concerned with the training of intermediate grade rather than higher-level manpower. What was envisaged was the training of engineering assistants rather than engineers, of medical assistants rather than fully qualified doctors, of teachers rather than education officers, and so on. The College did not prepare students to full degree standards, nor was it concerned about securing international recognition for its certificates and diplomas. Student enrolment was never much above a hundred throughout the fifteen years of the College's existence.

The second period began in the wake of tremendous economic and political changes. With the high commodity prices of the immediate post-war years, the economy of the country was more buoyant; government revenues were higher than ever before; the first attempt at development planning had been inaugurated; and a new programme of colonial aid, under the Colonial Development and Welfare Act, had been launched. Politically, the country had been initiated along the road of responsible government, and Nigerians had started to play a substantial part in the running of their country's affairs. The University College, Ibadan, thus came into existence in somewhat favourable circumstances. Nevertheless there were initial difficulties. Student enrolment rose steadily in the early years, but it was still well under a thousand by 1958; and it was not until 1959 that the annual out-turn of graduates rose to about a hundred.

By 1960, many of the initial difficulties of the College had been overcome, and the forces making for expansion had gathered considerable momentum. The development plans which had been inaugurated in 1955 were accelerated during 1960–2; expatriate staff were leaving the Governments in large numbers; and the coming of Independence

[3] *Report of the Commission on Higher Education in West Africa*, June 1945, Cmd. 6655.

created an almost insatiable demand for trained Nigerians. The availability of more facilities—particularly the completion of the University College Hospital and new halls of residence, enabled the College to increase its student enrolment more rapidly. Between 1958 and 1963, the number of students increased from just over a thousand to over two thousand and the annual output of graduates from about a hundred to almost three hundred. After fifteen years of special relationship with the University of London, the College became a full University in 1963.

It is not to be thought that the training of professional and managerial staff within Nigeria during this period was confined to the University College, Ibadan. The three branches of the Nigerian College of Arts, Science and Technology played a significant role in this regard, both in feeding the University of Ibadan with students of sixth-form level and in providing full training in certain professional lines such as pharmacy and accountancy.

The third period of Nigerian experience began with the implementation of the Ashby Commission Report, which brought four new universities into existence, in addition to the older University of Ibadan. One of the new Universities, the University of Nigeria, Nsukka, conferred degrees for the first time in 1962. The total student enrolment in all five universities in the academic year 1963–4 was 5,200.

The Ashby Report is significant particularly as the first attempt in Nigeria to base the planning of higher education on a projection of manpower requirements. Unfortunately, the Report was issued before the most ambitious development plan for Nigeria—the National Development Plan 1962 to 1968—was completed. And furthermore, the Plan itself contained no indication as to manpower requirements, nor any explicit statement as to the validity of the manpower projections on which the Ashby Report was based. This important task of ensuring the consistency of manpower training with the needs of economic development has now been passed to the National Manpower Board. But it is a task which involves as well the development planners and the educationists. The development planner, the manpower statistician and the educationist must work together to build up a consistent system of manpower budgeting. The educationist cannot accept the assumptions of the planner and the statistician without question; nor can the planner leave the content of education to the educationist alone. It is in this light that I would like to feel free in what follows to criticize the planner and the statistician whenever I find that their assumptions and their methods leave something to be desired.

In most of what follows, I shall attempt to analyze the problems of the future in the light of past and current experience, and I shall organize most of the discussion under the three main heads which I previously distinguished, namely the quantity of education, the quality of education and the content of the curricula.

III. *The Quantity of Education*

The factors which can limit the number of professional and managerial staff in training are many, but it is convenient to discuss them according to whether they arise on the side of supply or on the side of demand. The difficulties on the supply side are well known. They arise partly from the inadequacy of facilities and partly from the shortage of qualified entrants. While the size of facilities depends essentially on the size of finance, the number of qualified entrants available depends on the quantity and quality of education at lower levels of the educational pyramid.

On the demand side, if one accepts economic development as the main objective of educational planning, then the most important factor at work would be the rate of growth of the national economy. In that event, an educational programme based on an underestimation of the rate of growth of the national economy would give rise ultimately to an acute shortage of manpower. On the other hand, an educational programme based on an over-estimation of the rate of growth of the national economy would be likely to generate in time a surplus of trained manpower. An ideal educational programme or what one might call a policy of balanced educational development would, of course, try not to err, whether on the side of surplus or on the side of shortage. But even economists would concede that the margin of error involved in estimating the rate of growth of the national economy can be very wide and that consequently their forecast of manpower requirements cannot be precise. If err we must in our forecast of manpower needs, on what side is it more plausible to err? This question may seem more appropriate for policy makers to answer, but I would say that it is one on which all of us—economists, sociologists, educationists, etc. —should form an opinion. I venture to say that my own preference is for erring on the side of surplus. In the Ashby Report which I helped to prepare, we were of this mind. While we recognized that it was part of the duty of the educational system to meet the nation's 'manpower requirements' in the economic sense, we were emphatic in our opinion that, 'It would be a short-sighted policy to allow the educational system of a country to be controlled solely by "consumer needs" for manpower.'[4] We based our opinion on one fundamental tenet which I still hold as firmly today as I did at that time. This is that 'The upsurge of African education is so dramatic and so powerful that proposals which today appear to be reasonable and sensible will in a very few years appear to be short-sighted and timid.'[5] In this connection, I would like to draw support from the following statement on the subject by the well-known economist, W. A. Lewis:[6]

> 'The question how much education is needed implies that there are limits to the capacity of a country to absorb even the kind of education which adds to productive capacity. It implies that the need even for investment types of education springs from the level of development of the community, rather than that the level of development will depend upon the supply of education. For if the latter were true, the community would be capable of absorbing any quantity of education, however large, on the ground that the more educated it is, the faster it will develop.'

Lewis went on to distinguish between the short run and the long, indicating that 'in the long run the community can absorb any quantity of education'.[6] While over-supply can exist in the short run, in the long run, 'a surplus of educated persons tends to be self-adjusting through the reactions it sets up':[7]

(a) Some of the educated may emigrate;

(b) Some may use their education in new ways, thus increasing productive capacity;

(c) Some may lower their sights and move into less remunerative employments than they had expected;

(d) The educational requirements for some occupations may be raised.

At this stage one may question which of these reactions are likely to be most important in Nigeria. I believe that all of them are likely to be

---

[4] *Investment in Education* (The Report of the Commission on Post-School Certificate and Higher Education in Nigeria), Federal Ministry of Education, Nigeria, 1960, p. 7.
[5] Ibid., p. 3.
[6] W. A. Lewis, 'Education and Economic Development' in *Final Report of the Conference of African States on the Development of Education in Africa*, op. cit., Annex. IV, p. 71.
[7] Ibid., p. 72.

important. As regards the first, I believe that educated Nigerians are going to play a larger role in meeting the needs of other areas of Africa, where educational opportunities are not developing as fast as in our own country. This is going on already and the tempo of it is going to increase as the few remaining colonies in Africa become independent and as the machinery for African co-operation become more effective. Also, provided that we pay sufficient attention to the content of our curricula the second reaction is likely to be important. I shall have something to say about curricula in the latter part of this paper. Let me now say that the more we build creative ability into our educational system, the more important this second reaction is likely to be.

The third reaction is, in fact, already being experienced. For example as the administrative structure of the country has become more or less settled, and as the number of expatriates to be replaced has become less and less, so the opportunity for employment in the civil service has gradually diminished. Nowadays, unlike some years ago, a graduate cannot be sure of almost automatic employment in the civil service. At least one Region in Nigeria has introduced a competitive examination for graduate applicants. Furthermore, the extra facilities (basic car allowance, overseas leave, etc.) previously enjoyed by new graduate civil servants are gradually drying up, and I would like to predict that the present margin of advantage which the graduate civil servant enjoys over the graduate teacher will, in time, disappear.

The fourth reaction is similar to the third. Already school certificate holders are accepting jobs (such as primary school teachers) which they previously considered to be 'below their dignity'. Perhaps it may not be too long before the minimum qualification for secondary school teachers becomes a university degree. It is of course undesirable that those who have received expensive education should be employed in jobs for which less expensive training should have been adequate; and we must always be watchful that the returns to particular grades of education do not fall substantially below their costs to the community. However, provided that the situation does not get so much out of hand that a graduate is forced to join the job queue for clerical assistants I think we should be prepared to find graduates in less remunerative jobs than at present. In the light of all this, the fear of graduate unemployment which is already lurking in some quarters may be entirely without foundation.

Nothing that has been said so far should be taken as meaning that

M.P.D.N.—8

educational development should not be planned on the basis of man-power needs. What it is intended to emphasize is that since, because of human and statistical imperfections, plans must err, it is better that they should err on the side of over-estimation. While I do not intend to underrate the economists and the statisticians, I must say that the techniques of manpower forecasting still leave much room for improve-ment. For example, the report before us on 'Nigeria's High-Level and Skilled Manpower 1963–8' prepared by the Secretariat of the Manpower Board, has two sets of figures (based on two methods of estimation) indicating the country's demand for high-level manpower in 1968, and these figures differ substantially from those projected by F. Harbison for the year 1970. This is not surprising, considering the immense con-ceptual and statistical problems involved and the wide variety of assumptions (level of employment, rate of growth of national income, size and rate of increase of population, structural changes in the economy, etc.) on which estimates have to be based. However, the possibility of error should be clearly recognized in using any of the estimates as a basis for educational policy.

On the assumption that the number of graduates should increase by 20,000 from 1960 to 1970, the Ashby Commission recommended an output of 2,000 graduates per year. In 1963, the figure attained was still less than 500 per year (including the first graduates from University of Nigeria, Nsukka). This, of course, does not take into account graduates returning from overseas, an accurate figure of which is still not available. On the other hand, the report of the Manpower Secretariat now before us suggests that 'the estimated out-turn of trained persons required, so as reasonably to satisfy the 1968 needs for graduates and senior professional staff, is of the order of 8,000 per annum'.[8] Assuming that 64 per cent[9] of this number will be graduates, then annual output of just over 5,000 graduates will be necessary. One may go further and compare the two figures of the Ashby Commission and the Manpower Secretariat with an estimate of 1,400 graduates reached by W. Arthur Lewis through yet a different kind of calcula-tion.[10]

The upshot of the argument is that the educationist needs more guidance from the economists and the statisticians, even when it is

[8] This was based on a forecast of high-level manpower needs for full employment—an assumption which has been abandoned. See chapter 7.
[9] The percentage assumed by F. Harbison.
[10] W. A. Lewis, op. cit., p. 75.

agreed that the policy should be one of erring on the side of surplus rather than on the side of shortage. I am aware that the Manpower Secretariat has an ambitious programme of work for the coming year, the outcome of which should provide us with a comprehensive manpower inventory as well as greater knowledge of future needs. Until such definitive guidance can be given, there would seem to be no better alternative than to continue more or less along the lines laid down by the Ashby Commission.

So far Nigerian educational policy has been based essentially on a forecast of Nigerian needs. One cannot exclude the possibility that Nigeria's policy in the future will be influenced by overall African needs and prospects. We are well aware of the attempts which have been made in recent years to formulate an educational programme for African countries as a whole. These are very bold attempts, considering the immense problems which such a continental plan must encounter. If it is so difficult to project the educational needs of a single country, how much more difficult would it be to formulate educational plans for a group of countries, each with its own peculiar economic and social circumstances? In spite of the difficulties, the major conclusions and recommendations which have emerged from these attempts are not to be ignored. A full discussion of these will be out of place in this paper, but it is necessary to recall one of the most important recommendations, namely, that the needs of Middle Africa[11] in the matter of university institutions should be covered by those already in existence (including the five Nigerian Universities).[12] This would imply no further increase in the number of universities in Nigeria up to 1980. Whether we should work within this limitation or not will depend in part on a clearer assessment of our own needs and in part on the degree of co-ordination which can be achieved by African countries on this subject—perhaps through the Organization of African Unity.

Before leaving this question of quantity, I would like to refer briefly to the problem of finance. Finance may affect both the supply and the demand side of the manpower budget. As I mentioned before, the availability of facilities for higher education depends essentially on how much the nation is prepared to spend in this direction. But, on the demand side, the number of students coming forward depends in

[11] Middle Africa comprises all African countries south of the Sahara with the exception of South Africa.
[12] *The Development of Higher Education in Africa*, op. cit., p. 40.

part on the ability of private individuals to finance the education of their children and relatives. If there were a universal scholarship or loan scheme which guaranteed finance to every student qualified for university education, the question would not arise. But there is no such scheme at the moment and as the number of students pursuing university education has increased, so the proportion of those enjoying scholarship awards has diminished. This problem came into sharper focus about a year ago, when some students (many in their final year) were asked to withdraw from the University of Ibadan for non-payment of fees. I believe that the problem will become even more acute in the future as the number of students increases.

We thus have two problems connected with finance which we must attempt to resolve if our education targets over the next few years are to be fulfilled. As regards finance for the expansion of facilities, we have been fortunate to secure a good deal of foreign assistance to supplement our domestic resources, and we hope that more assistance will be forthcoming in the years ahead. However, this should not prevent attempts to find a fundamental solution to the problem at home. The total amount of governmental grants for higher education is, of course, a matter of national policy, to be settled by the Nigerian Governments and the National Universities Commission. What the Universities themselves can do is to make vigorous efforts to reduce the average cost per student enrolment. It is well known that the average cost per student in African universities is much higher than in Europe or the United States. Some of the causes are inevitable and there is no doubt that as the number of students expands the average cost per student will tend to fall.

For some time, the fall in the average cost per student will not necessarily cause the fee payable per student to fall, since the present level of fees already implies a substantial amount of subsidy. Rather, any savings in cost will be used to further increase the number of students. How then are we going to ensure that the educational programme is not slowed down through the inability of students to meet their fees? A universal scholarship scheme is not yet possible owing partly to the complexities of our Regional politics and partly to the present levels of government revenues. Already, the Government have reduced the cost of their scholarships per student with the object of increasing the number of awards. Also, some of the Nigerian Universities have established loan schemes to help needy students. One Regional

Government has recently made some financial contribution to these schemes.

So far, however, the scope of the arrangement is not broad enough to cope even with the existing problems. This matter will certainly demand more attention than has recently been given to it, although the solution is not going to be simple. My own approach would be a massive extension of loan schemes—if necessary with the participation of commercial banks and other finance houses. If articles of durable consumer goods like cars, radiograms and refrigerators can be financed on hire purchase, there is more reason to expect that higher education can be so financed. Although returns to education are hard to measure, there is no doubt that in the long run, investment in this direction is one of the most profitable for the individual as well as for the community.

IV. *The Quality of Education*

In education, as in many fields, it is inevitable that a colonial territory should borrow its standards from the metropolitan country. From the establishment of the University College, Ibadan, in 1948 until 1963, the College conducted all its teaching and examining in accordance with the scheme of Special Relation with the University of London, and in one Faculty, that of Medicine, made all its academic appointments subject to the approval of the University. It is not to be thought, however, that the scheme of Special Relation was merely a by-product of Nigeria's colonial status at that time. The arrangement conferred immense advantages on the University College in its early years. The high academic standards maintained at the College and the solid reputation it has achieved as a centre of higher education and research are attributable, in large measure, to the Special Relation scheme. The principal academic advantages of Special Relation may be summarized as follows:

(a) It guaranteed standards of achievement equivalent to those required in a leading English university, and provided a universally acceptable first degree, the degree, in a modified form, of the University of London.

(b) It provided arrangements whereby any member of the Ibadan academic staff could be a candidate for a higher degree of London University, without residence in London.

(c) It allowed certain professional qualifications (for example, medical qualifications) obtainable at Ibadan to be registrable for practice not only in Nigeria, but also in the United Kingdom and in all other countries where United Kingdom qualifications are recognized.

From these specifically academic advantages, other advantages, semi-academic in character and of great importance, naturally followed. They include: greater opportunities for attracting competent staff; and the retention in Nigeria of numbers of able students who would otherwise insist on seeking higher education abroad.

The high academic standards which the scheme of Special Relation ensured, was, however, not without its disadvantages. It was certainly one of the factors limiting the number of entrants in the early years of the College. Indeed, in one cheerless instance, more than 27 students were expelled from the College for not making the grade, and that at a time that total enrolment was a bare 190.

The Special Relation scheme was always intended as a temporary service, to be employed in the formative years of the College. It is clearly desirable, in order to ensure healthy growth, that a University institution should assert its autonomy, academic and administrative alike, as it can confidently do so, and should assume full responsibility for its own decisions. Once the College was sure that it had found its feet and could take its place among the rank of reputable institutions in the world of learning, the way was open for it to end the temporary arrangement under which it had been nurtured. We were conscious of the fact that substantial changes had to be made in the content of the curricula if Ibadan with its high academic reputation was to satisfy the needs and aspirations of the people of Nigeria. I shall say a good deal about this in the next section. But as far as standards were concerned, we were intent on maintaining the high level already attained in the full consciousness of the fact that, apart from helping to turn the wheel of African economic progress, African education must serve to project the African personality and promote 'a bond of kinship to the larger human society'. Although the maintenance of a high standard imposed a limitation on numbers in the early years, the rapid extension of secondary and sixth form education in recent years has largely removed this disadvantage. Indeed, the University has gradually shifted from relying predominantly on special entrance examination for school certificate holders in recruiting new entrants, to relying predominantly on direct entry by students possessing the Higher School Certificate or equivalent qualification. For example, in the session beginning in 1954, 152 of the 158 new entrants were School Certificate holders admitted through special entrance examinations, whereas of the 819 new entrants in the 1963–4 academic year, 742 came in by direct entry and only 77 by special entrance examination.

V. *The Content of Education*

I would like to open my remarks on the content of education by recalling one brief statement from the Ashby Report. A country, it says, can stay on the intellectual gold standard without, as it were, having to adopt the imprint of another coinage. In other words, the maintenance of high academic standards should not prevent us from adapting the curricula to our own needs and conditions. As Joseph Ki-Zerbo has aptly put it, 'The type of man who will govern Africa tomorrow is potentially contained in the curricula of education today.'[13]

The problem of the curricula has two aspects: the first has to do with the emphasis given to the various disciplines—arts, natural science, agriculture, etc., and the second has to do with the content of the syllabus in each discipline—i.e. the extent that it is founded on local materials, history and problems. In these respects, the criticisms of the curricula in the formative years of university education in Nigeria are well known. There was too much emphasis on literary subjects, too little on the natural sciences and too little on agricultural studies. And, as regards the content of the syllabus in each discipline, there was too much on subjects which were not strictly relevant to local conditions.

The situation is much better now than it was in the early years. Today, teaching and research in African universities emphasize African subjects much more than was the case some ten years ago; and it was expected that the Institutes of African Studies, which have now been established in three Nigerian Universities following the recommendations of the Ashby Commission, would hasten the speed of Africanization of the curricula.

The basic problem, however, is one of lack of balance between the humanities and the sciences; and this problem remains largely unsolved. Indeed we seem to be caught in a vicious circle. The high proportion of admissions for liberal arts rather than the sciences in our universities reflects the high proportion of students taking non-science subjects in the secondary schools. And partly because the universities are not

[13] 'The Content of Education in Africa', op. cit., p. 55.

producing enough science teachers, the secondary schools cannot expand their facilities for science teaching as rapidly as the situation demands. Another element in the problem is the availability of laboratory equipment. Because of the high cost of equipment, many of our secondary schools—especially those established by private agencies—simply cannot afford the expense of building and equipping laboratories. I believe that something like a crash programme may be needed here if the vicious circle is to be broken. I would say that the rapid expansion of laboratory facilities in our schools and universities ought to occupy a higher place on our scale of priorities than is the case at the present time. With the help of UNESCO, our education ministries could together examine the possibility of purchasing laboratory equipment on a larger scale than hitherto with a view to reducing their costs substantially. It is largely by expanding the facilities for science teaching in secondary schools that the present emphasis on the humanities can be reversed.

VI. *The Machinery of Co-ordination*

The planning of higher education implies the planning of numbers as well as the planning of quality and content. Where there is more than one institution of higher learning working towards the same national targets, close co-operation among them is an essential basis for effective planning. In Nigeria, the increase in the number of universities is only a recent development and the instruments of co-ordination are consequently still in their infancy. All the three instruments now in existence—the National Universities Commission, the National Manpower Board and the Committee of Vice-Chancellors were established in 1962. The National Universities Commission administers block grants, effects some co-ordination of courses and makes recommendations generally about university development in the country. The National Manpower Board attempts to co-ordinate the supply of manpower with the needs of development; and the Committee of Vice-Chancellors keeps constantly under review matters which are of common interest to the universities. The membership of the Manpower Board includes the Secretary of the National Universities Commission and two representatives of the Universities. Following the tradition established elsewhere, Vice-Chancellors are not represented on the National Universities Commission, but since both bodies deal with matters of common interest, they necessarily keep in close touch with each other. On occasions, the Committee of Vice-Chancellors invites the Secretary of the National Universities Commission to address it on the plans and projects of the Commission. Matters now being examined both by the National Universities Commission and the Committee of Vice-Chancellors include the establishment of common entrance qualification for Nigerian Universities and a Central Council on Admissions. The advisability of establishing an all-Nigeria Academic Council is also being considered.

Some collaboration between universities has indeed been going on outside the formal machinery of co-ordination. For example, Ahmadu Bello University and the University of Ibadan now collaborate on the preparation of students for the Bachelor's Degree in Veterinary Science. The first two years of the course leading to the degree will be undertaken in Ibadan and the remaining two years at Ahmadu Bello. The importance of such joint arrangements, as well as some degree of specialization of courses among universities can hardly be exaggerated, and more efforts in this direction can be expected as the machinery of co-ordination is fully developed.

It is expected that when the present assignments of the Manpower Board are completed, it would be possible to know just what the manpower situation is in any current period. Forecasting future demand and supply is a difficult exercise, but ascertaining the existing level of demand and supply should not be quite as difficult. It is suggested, therefore, that the Ministry of Labour and the Manpower Secretariat should consider the advisability of maintaining a register of current vacancies for high-level manpower based on regular returns from employers. This information would be made available to the Universities so that prospective applicants can be kept fully informed of the opportunities available. In turn, information from the Universities and other institutions on the numbers of trained manpower likely to be available at the end of the current session should be made available to prospective employers, so that they themselves can be kept fully informed of the trained personnel which would be available at the close of the academic year. Both returns should be as detailed as possible so that prospective employers as well as prospective applicants could have a clear idea of the current market situation for particular skills. Indeed, it may be necessary to appoint a Careers Adviser—maybe in the Federal Ministry of Labour—who will visit all Nigerian Universities before the close of the academic year for the purpose of advising students on the opportunities available in various lines of employment. This will, in fact, be putting on a more general and systematic basis what is already being practised by some of the larger employers.

VII. *Conclusion*

Although I would not like to conclude this paper on a note of pessimism, I am nevertheless impelled to draw attention once again to the possible limitation on our educational programme by limited financial resources. It is this which I believe will be the crucial problem of the immediate future. Even the execution of the present programme based on the Ashby Commission Report is likely to encounter increasing financial difficulties in the coming years. If the higher targets now proposed by the Manpower Secretariat are confirmed by further research, it is obvious that the difficulties will be further increased. Perhaps the financial situation of the country will improve sufficiently in the coming years to make possible the allocation of more funds to educational development.

14
Summary of Discussion and Conclusions (III)

Under the Nigerian Constitution, each Regional Government has wide responsibilities for the administration of its own system of education. Great strides have been taken by all the Regions since the Ashby Committee recommendations but, as is evident from the report of the National Manpower Board, there is still a considerable lack of balance in the facilities available at the different educational levels. The application of the following conclusions and recommendations need, therefore, to be viewed in the context of the conditions obtaining in each Region. Nevertheless it is the view of the Seminar that there is wide scope for inter-governmental co-ordination and co-operation at all levels of education.

I. *The Content and Scope of Education*

1. In any dynamic society, all areas of human activity undergo constant change; new ways of doing things are called for, new problems emerge as old ones are resolved, new skills, new tools and new knowledge open up new vistas and again create new problems and challenges. It is essential that new generations of Nigerians should be enabled to cope with these changes, by formal as well as by informal methods of education. In particular, it is recommended that the curriculum in primary education should be reviewed, where necessary, to meet the requirements of Nigerian society by giving greater emphasis, than has hitherto been the case, to elementary science, mathematical processes, practical skills including agriculture, civics, languages and physical education. A National Council should be set up for this purpose, under the aegis of the Federal and Regional Ministries of Education in collaboration with the institutes of education in Nigeria, and its terms of reference should include responsibility for promoting research into new teaching methods and the preparation of suitable textbooks.

2. If Nigeria's high-level manpower needs of various categories are

to be satisfied in all sectors of the economy it is essential to introduce and maintain a planned distribution of students among the various university faculties. This in turn involves the planned distribution of students and a review of the curricula structure at the secondary level. Only a proportion of the secondary school graduates, however, go on to university courses and the planned distribution must, therefore, also take into account the need to meet employment and training needs at the intermediate manpower level. It is therefore recommended that the distribution of students taking the various groups of subjects at the secondary level be planned with a view to ensuring an adequate and properly directed flow of the various kinds of intermediate and high-level manpower stemming from this source. This is a matter requiring further study which should be undertaken by the Manpower Board as quickly as possible.

3. Although sixth form work is expanding rapidly it does not yet meet the enrolment requirements of the universities, more particularly in the science options, a situation which is aggravated by the growing needs for science and technological disciplines. It is therefore recommended that in view of the great need for high-level manpower, particularly in the science and technological disciplines, in Nigeria, the universities should, for the time-being, continue to recruit students from both the school certificate and sixth form levels of the secondary schools.

4. It is recognized that mass illiteracy limits the efficient use of the nation's manpower resources and retards its cultural and socio-political advancement; in view, therefore, of the fact that a high proportion of the adult population in Nigeria is non-literate, it is recommended that the adult education programmes be intensified by the relevant Government Ministries in co-operation with the Universities, the objectives of the campaign being:

(a) to help illiterate adults attain literacy, that is, acquire the art of reading, writing and numeration;

(b) to help them appreciate their economic, cultural and political role in Nigerian society;

(c) to enable them to understand their physical and biological environment;

(d) to help them improve their skills as workers, thereby improving their own living standards and thus contributing to the economic development of Nigeria;

(e) to help them play their own role as good citizens of Nigeria and of the world.

5. Large numbers of primary school leavers are still unable to obtain places for full-time training in either Government trade centres, industrial training schemes, or in commercial schools. Literate adults who are in some form of employment and wish to either further their general education or acquire knowledge of a trade or skill, have only limited opportunities, and then, in the big urban centres only. It is therefore recommended, in the national interest, that evening class facilities be provided wherever staff and buildings can be made available to cater for this work and that local arrangements for itinerant teachers and mobile workshops or for correspondence courses be made to provide for those unable to attend the organized centres.

6. Whilst the value of certification is freely acknowledged there is a wide tendency among both students and employers to attach more value to certificates and diplomas than to the content of the candidates' training, to their aptitudes and ability and to subsequent experience. This attitude is unprogressive and it is recommended that ways and means of combating the problem should be explored by Government ministries and by the various advisory bodies, including employers' associations.

7. At its present stage of development, Nigeria is faced with having to produce large numbers of trained people as quickly as possible, very often using largely inexperienced teachers and, in many cases, new and untried methods. There is, therefore, an understandable tendency for academic and training standards to decline initially. It is however recommended that whilst this temporary lowering of standards can frequently not be avoided, deliberate effort should be made to ensure a development of the highest standards as a matter of priority; for this purpose the role of employers and professional associations is very important.

II. *The Economics of Education*

8. Education is one of Nigeria's biggest 'industries', over £23 million being allocated to recurrent expenditure each year. For the purposes of planning it is essential to ensure a proper allocation of the Nation's limited resources and the financial soundness of both existing and planned projects. This can best be accomplished by examining the education systems under the following heads.

(a) *Physical facilities*

9. There is need to pay greater attention to lowering the cost of buildings, to bulk purchasing procedures and to the use of inexpensive equipment. Classrooms and workshops are often not fully and economically used. The geographical location and distribution of schools is often defective and there is need to ensure maximum use of day and boarding accommodation. The latter is an expensive provision at the present stage of development in Nigeria and should be kept to the absolute minimum.

(b) *Human resources*

10. Staffing distribution and balances as between academic, administrative and other personnel are frequently unsuitable and costly, whilst in some higher institutions staff and teaching hours are too low and study tours are too frequent. Greater use of part-time teachers should be encouraged. Wastage of students is often high and this factor is not sufficiently accounted for in student/teacher ratios. More flexibility should be expected of staff in technical, scientific and related disciplines. It may well be that a longer academic year would be economically advantageous and this should receive early study. Junior staff are often not given any proper up-grading courses nor permitted to exercise any authority or responsibility against which to measure their suitability for higher work.

(c) *Student output*

11. Some of the school curricula are unsuitable for Nigerian requirements and in the case of vocational courses in particular, many courses could well be shortened. Choices are required as between quantity and quality and as to the most appropriate kind of terminal test or examination. There is some over-lapping of courses and of institutional programmes which can ill be afforded. Placement, follow-up and guidance are in a very early stage of development and need to be pursued vigorously.

(d) *Financial considerations*

12. Record keeping, cost and audit control systems are inadequate, particularly as regards grant-aided and private schools. Government follow-up of grants-in-aid expenditure appears to be weak. Excessive

fees are being charged by many private schools, whilst books and board-ing charges are too high for many students, at all levels of education. Current salaries appear to be insufficient for attracting qualified teach-ing staff, particularly in specialized technical and scientific fields. There is, therefore, a case for incentives to attract such teachers. More frugal use of recurrent expenditure should be possible, and the need for future expansion should be borne constantly in mind.

13. It is recommended that the Federal and Regional Ministries of Education and their advisory or other suitable committees should give urgent and earnest consideration to the problems outlined in the immediately foregoing paragraphs 8–12. It is further recommended that there should be a unit for evaluating existing and projected educa-tional schemes in each Ministry of Education.

III. *Training Within Industry*

14. Whilst the rapid and early training of additional manpower is a dire necessity for increasing productivity, a speedier and more often effective measure, and one which is equally necessary if optimum use is to be made of the nation's manpower, is the continuous training of the labour force already in industry and commerce. It is therefore recommended that a high priority should be given in private and public employment and training programmes to methods of in-service training.

15. In view of the need for each sector of the economy to play a full part in its own development and bearing in mind the normally accepted training role of industry and commerce in more advanced countries, it is recommended that Government should take positive steps, through mutual consultation with the interests involved, to induce the full participation of the private sector in national manpower training programmes, making provision for the assessment and regulation of such participation as will ensure its success.

16. In view of the acknowledged need for rapid and early Nigeriani-zation in the country as a whole, partly to satisfy national aspirations but equally in order to reduce the heavy cost of employing expatriate personnel, it is recommended that the private sector should be called upon, where necessary, to play its full part in Nigerianizing its man-power through the use of the public vocational system and its own training schemes; failure to do so, in a reasonable time, being met by the imposition of a sanction.

IV. *Planning, Organization and Administration*

17. In order to achieve effective planning of the education system in Nigeria it is necessary to set targets five, ten and fifteen years in advance of planning. Moreover, since the ratios of the various levels of manpower differ, often markedly, from industry to industry, a close approximation of planning to the sectoral needs can only be achieved if targets are identified with major industry groupings. It is therefore recommended that the Ministries responsible for economic and manpower planning should consider ways and means of making projections of growth and manpower needs, ten and fifteen years ahead on a global as well as on an industry by industry basis.

18. In view of the volume and variety of educational activity which Nigeria now has to face it is recommended that the Federal and Regional Ministries of Education be reorganized in order to enable them to handle or participate closely in such activities as planning, statistics, research, school building programmes and design, curricula modification, external aid, primary, secondary, technical and vocational education, higher and adult education, international education, school broadcasting, aptitude and other tests, guidance and placement, student scholarships and exchange.

19. The various Governments are currently faced with a multitude of problems and since this will be a recurring situation, it is necessary to institutionalize the machinery for handling these problems so that development can proceed smoothly and continuity maintained. In this regard the Seminar notes with satisfaction the establishment of the following instruments and Committees:

The National Manpower Board
The National Universities Commission
The National Scholarship Board
The Co-ordinating Committee for External Aid
The Joint Consultative Committee for Education
The National Advisory Council for Technical Education and Industrial Training
The Council for Science and Technology
The Committee for the Standardization of Educational Statistics
The Standing Committee for Teachers Certification
The National UNESCO Commission
The National Arts Council.

The Seminar believes this to be a step in the right direction and recommends that this procedure of institutionalizing the machinery of education should continue, bearing in mind the need to avoid duplication of functions.

Part Four

The Unemployment Problem

15

Employment and Economic Development in a Dual Economy

Ignacy Sachs

DIRECTOR, CENTRE OF RESEARCH IN UNDER-DEVELOPED ECONOMIES, WARSAW

I. The Characteristics and Problems of Dualism

The concept of *dual economy*, defined in terms of a traditional, precapitalistic sector and of a modern sector, does not allow itself to be easily translated in operational terms, as the border-line between the two sectors besides being a moving one, frequently cuts across the village or even the farm. In any case it cannot be assimilated to either of the following antinomies: town and country, industry and agriculture, export production and production for internal market. The only viable criterion is that of predominant relations of production, which cannot be grasped except through exhaustive field studies. In this paper we shall ignore this practical difficulty as we shall limit ourselves to evolve a local framework for the analysis of the problem of employment in a dual economy. We shall therefore assume that the relative size of the two sectors is approximate; i.e. that we can estimate the distribution between the two sectors of the following elements:

A (1) Population;
   (2) Population in working age;
   (3) Employment in agriculture, industries and services.
B (1) Subsistence production;
   (2) Market production in agriculture and industries;
   (3) Production for export;
C (1) Investment in kind (non-monetary);
   (2) Investment financed from private and public sources.

This static description of the relative size of the two sectors should be supplemented by the knowledge of the flows of people, goods and values between the sectors.

Even though conditions may vary from country to country, we are likely to find that in terms of population the traditional sector is much bigger than the modern one; the difference in total output of the two sectors will be much smaller, due to higher productivity in the modern sector; the gap will narrow still more if we take into account only the marketed production. As for effective investment, it may even run higher in the small modern sector than in the large traditional one,[1] thus contributing to the sharpening of contrasts between the two.

From the point of view of employment, we are likely to observe in the traditional sector a severe underemployment, not only in densely but, also, in scarcely populated countries. This underemployment can be ascertained by checking the average number of work days and the productivity per man—which does not even reach the low ceilings that are possible by the primitive equipment at hand and the prevailing techniques. Overt unemployment is rather exceptional in the villages, but the low standards of living in the countryside, coupled with the expectations of a better life in the town, originate the exodus of labourers.

Spontaneous migration of the labour force does not offer, as yet, the solution to the problem of underemployment in the traditional sector. The unemployment among the population of shanty towns is but a transformation of the underemployment of peasants. This unemployment in a less developed country differs basically from that in a developed capitalist one. It results from the shortage of capital equipment rather than from deficiency of effective demand.[2] Moreover, even the employment requiring little capital investment would meet the obstacle of insufficient food-supply. And, indeed, the processes of urbanization reach very quickly the danger-mark, if they are not harmonized with a rapid expansion of food supply, because of the inflationary pressures set in motion as a consequence of rising food prices.

Thus, the characteristic feature of a dual economy is the simultaneous existence of underemployment in the traditional sector, and of

[1] We abstract here from the problem: to what extent investment in the modern sector is being financed by the traditional one through taxes and profits, extracted from the traditional sector by local and foreign merchants and, if it is the case, through investment in the modern sector, of profits accumulated by landowners.
[2] See M. Kalecki, 'Unemployment in Underdeveloped Countries', The Indian Journal of Labour Economics, Vol. II, No. 2, July 1960, p. 59.

unemployment due to lack of productive equipment and food supply in the modern sector, both reflecting the essence of under-development. It follows from what we said that, a strategy of development, conceived in terms of mass migration from the traditional sector to the modern one, could not succeed, as it would clash against unsurmountable obstacles long before exhausting the backlog of the existing surplus labour in the traditional sector. The modern sector has but a limited capacity of absorption of labour from the traditional sector. While utilizing it to the utmost, and not forgetting that the decisive battle against backwardness is being fought on the industrialization front, we should at the same time take care of the traditional sector. In particular, it is necessary to improve the yields in agriculture, in order to increase the marketed surplus of food. The immediate aim being the maximization of output and not of productivity per man, labour-intensive techniques leading to higher outputs per acre should be commended. Higher marketed surpluses of food are a pre-condition of higher employment in town, that is why Professor M. Kalecki, in the paper already quoted, concludes that 'the basic prerequisite for a rapid industrialization of an under-developed country and in particular for the solution of the problem or unemployment and underemployment is a revolutionary upsurge in agricultural production'.[3]

Several other reasons necessitate the two-pronged approach, aimed not only at the expansion and/or multiplication of pockets of modern economy, but also at the raising of the standards and progressive modernization of the traditional sector. We shall point to a few. Firstly, when people migrate to towns in excessive numbers, too great a share of investment surplus is likely to go into housing and urban amenities, reducing thus still more the scarce availabilities of capital for industrial projects. Secondly, besides intensifying agriculture, it is possible to create seasonal or almost stable employment in the countryside by establishing there simple food-processing and building material industries; such a decentralization will decrease the volume of necessary investment for infrastructure and social overheads such as transport, housing, etc., while food-processing—even by primitive methods —will help to reduce the wastage of crops, particularly severe in tropical climates. Thirdly, excessive migration of men of working age is likely to endanger the agricultural work at peak seasons such as

[3] M. Kalecki, op cit., p. 61.

harvest[4] not to mention the fact that, in this way, the traditional sector pays a hidden subsidy to the modern one: it bears all the social cost of upbringing the young people up to the working age, but does not take benefit of their productive ability.

Fourthly, we should remember that in a market economy, and to a great extent also, in a mixed one with a dynamic public sector, all the market forces are set forth to attract more investment to the already existing modern pockets, thus tending to widen the gap between the sectors. To realize how inconvenient, not to say explosive, these disparities may be, both from economic and social points of view, it is enough to compare them to the abyss which today separates the 'have-nots' from the well-to-do countries.

II. *The Problems of Growth*

Though we have started our analysis with a two-sector model, we arrived, in the previous section, at the conclusion that the strategy of development in a dual economy should precisely aim at bridging the gap between the traditional and the modern sectors. The developmental process and the employment opportunities it creates, should be consequently treated as whole, at least at the level of general analysis.[5] We shall therefore continue our argument on the basis of a global picture of an under-developed economy.

In the long run employment opportunities are a function of the overall rate of growth of the economy, of the branch distribution of investment and of the chosen techniques.[6] We shall limit ourselves to the first, and the most general problem. What are the obstacles which prevent an under-developed country to speed up the overall rate of growth of its economy? Once more, the variety of situations and problems faced by different countries should be stressed at this stage.

---

[4] That is why it is wrong to equate the amount of 'surplus labour' with the ratio of the total number of idle days of the working population to the 'normal' average of work days per worker. In reality, the 'free labour surplus' is much less and a certain labour-reserve for harvest is necessary. The problem takes a new dimension: that of finding more work for these people in the slack season by introducing additional crops with different harvest times, adding animal husbandry to agriculture, stepping up largely non-monetary investment and creating industries.

[5] Of course, going back to the two-sector model is possible at a further and more detailed stage of analysis.

[6] The choice of techniques is, of course, subject to several limitations. See Z. Dobraka, *The Choice of Techniques in Developing Countries*, Research Papers of the Warsaw Center of Research of Underdeveloped Economies, Vol. 1, Warsaw, 1963.

But it would seem that the majority of cases can be interpreted with the following scheme of barriers to growth.[7]

An under-developed country on its way to speedier economic growth has to overcome a multiplicity of interlinked barriers to growth, producing a succession of bottlenecks, which have to be removed more or less simultaneously. Thus, as the arrows show in the diagram below, backward agriculture hampers the expansion of manufacturing industries by failing to deliver enough materials and food, which is the main wage-good; and, conversely, an incipient industry cannot deliver sufficient machines and inputs to raise the productivity in agriculture. Both agriculture and industry are hampered by lack of proper infrastructure and of skilled labour. The difficulties in agriculture and industry, as well as the lack of managerial and technical cadres, create additional pressures on foreign trade. Of course, the unsatisfactory situation described above arises from insufficient investment, which in turn can be explained in terms of low accumulation. Now, insufficient accumulation reflects the institutional set-up. In many countries investment could be stepped up by reforms aiming at a more rational distribution of the national income, just as institutional land reforms could free agriculture from the straitjacket of obsolete social and property conditions, and state intervention in foreign trade could lead to a more rational utilization of the capacity of import. Let us remark, to end this very summary description of the diagram, that difficulties in foreign trade—a common feature for almost all the developing countries—are bound to create a feedback and to reflect themselves in the level of investment. In drastic cases, the country may be unable to transform financial savings into physical investment because of lack of proper supply of foreign-made capital goods.

All the barriers mentioned above have to be carefully examined in the first stage of plan elaboration. In the context of this paper, concerned with employment, the more relevant are the following three:

(a) the barrier of low investment;
(b) the barrier of agriculture;
(c) the barrier of lack of skilled labour.

We shall discuss them briefly in the following sections.

[7] For a fuller treatment of this point see the author's paper on *Patterns of Economic Development and their Implication for Planning*; contributed to Professor D. P. Mukerji Commemoration Volume.

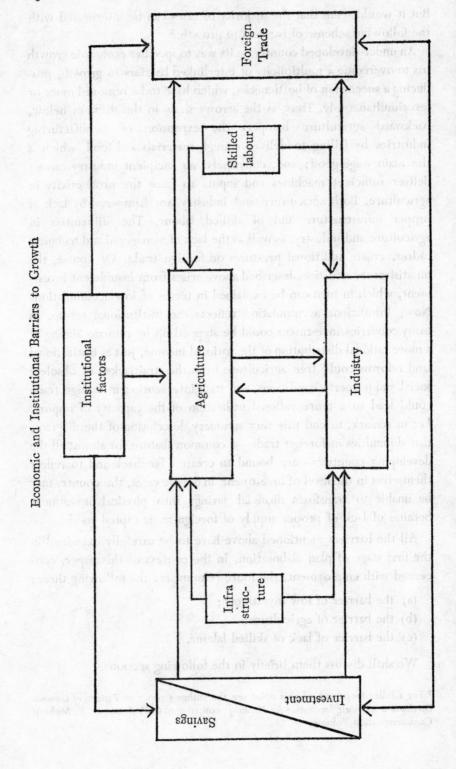

III. *The Barrier of Low Investment*

It is usually possible, as already mentioned, to step up the level of investment in a developing country by changing the distribution of income. Such a policy does not entail any reduction in the standards of living of the working population, as it should aim at shifting to investment, at least part of the funds spent on conspicuous consumption by the élites and also a portion, at least, of the income drained abroad by foreign companies. In his report, 'Towards a Dynamic Policy of Economic Development for Latin America', presented in May 1963 at the Mardel Plata Session of the United Nations Economic Commission for Latin America, Dr. Raul Prebisch, at present Secretary-General of the World Conference on Trade and Development, quoted the following data to support his strong plea for a policy of redistribution of national income: the consumption per head among the 5 per cent richest people in Latin America is, at present, 15 times higher than the consumption per head of the lower half of the population of that continent. If this disparity were reduced to the ratio of 11:1 through restriction of conspicuous consumption and the funds thus raised invested, the rate of growth of national income per head would go up from 1 per cent to 3 per cent per year. A ratio of 9:1 would permit the stepping up of internal accumulation up to a point, corresponding to a rate of growth of national income of 4 per cent per head per year, i.e. about 7 per cent in absolute terms, although the attainment of such a rate of expansion would be prevented by the barrier of foreign trade.

Mere stepping up of the overall volume of investment is a necessary, but not altogether sufficient, condition to achieve a higher rate of growth. It is necessary to look where the investments go to, in order to set a proper balance between productive and social investment, to prevent duplication and to harmonize the sectoral rates of growth in such a way as to avoid, as much as possible, under-utilization of installed capacities.[8] In this respect, the market often proves an ill adviser, as the priorities established by individual entrepreneurs—local or foreign —only exceptionally coincide with social priorities.

The answer obviously is planning and licensing of industries and of

---

[8] We know by experience, that idle capacities frequently exist in particular branches of manufacturing industry in less developed countries, in spite of the fact that, on the whole, they badly need to increase industrial output.

construction as a minimum requirement. In particular, it is imperative to prevent a 'perverse growth', that is, the excessive development of industries turning out luxury goods as well as of construction of luxury dwellings. At first sight, the development of such industries contributes to the process of growth, by increasing the employment roll and output. But luxury products do not participate either in the enlarged reproduction of the productive forces, nor do they contribute to the pool of wage-goods.[9] On the contrary, they utilize scarce capital goods, while the workers employed by them consume scarce wage-goods. In such circumstances, the development of luxury industries slows down in the long run the rate of growth of all the remaining branches of the economy, leading thus to an *impasse*.

Summing up, the barrier of low investment is a major obstacle on the way of increasing the number of jobs in the modern sector. It becomes all the more necessary, therefore, to plan investments carefully in order to achieve the best results from a given volume of investment.

IV. *Increasing Rural Employment Opportunities*

It is necessary, now, to see whether employment may be stepped up beyond the limit set by the investment barrier. We have in mind the pick and shovel variety of employment which requires very little capital equipment. Such possibilities certainly exist, as far as construction, road building, irrigation and similar activities, are concerned. But the limiting factor is the availability of staple food—the main wage-good. Additional employment of unskilled labourers out of the village where they reside, is bound to create pressure on the food market, as the income—elasticity for food runs in many cases as high as from $0 \cdot 8$ to $1 \cdot 0$ and the share of food in total expenditure of these workers may reach 80 per cent.[10] Thus each pound earned by them will increase the aggregate demand for food by 12 to 16 shillings. If supplies of food do not augment by the same proportion, the inflationary spiral will be set in motion, depressing the already low level of real wages. It is technically possible to increase employment in such a way, but it

[9] See P. Sraff, *Production of Commodities by Means of Commodities*, Cambridge, 1960, p. 7.
[10] For the relationships between the rate of growth of income and the rate of supply of the necessities, see M. Kalecki, *Financing Economic Development in a Mixed Economy*, in Research Papers of the Warsaw Centre on Underdeveloped Economies, Volume 11 (in press), and I. Sachs, *Levels of Satiety and Rates of Growth*, paper contributed to the Jubilee Volume in Honour of Professor M. Kalecki (in press).

comes to redistributing the total sum of real wages among a bigger number of wage-earners, the alternative being to tax low income groups or necessities. Either of these policies should be rejected on the ground of social justice.

It follows that the 'pick and shovel' variety of additional employment should be considered mainly in the context of largely non-monetary investment carried out at the village level, i.e. without dislocation of the labour force. The activities aimed at quickly increasing agricultural output per acre should be preferred, on two grounds; firstly, because they raise immediately the level of employment over the ceiling set by the agricultural barrier, and, secondly, because they help in the longer run to overcome this barrier. There is certainly considerable scope to try this latter approach both at the level of family farm and of collective effort of the whole village, although some economists[11] seem to overestimate this possibility. Collective 'human investment' at the village level on a somewhat bigger scale requires in general, as a prerequisite, far-reaching institutional reforms, which would create the proper climate for the efforts of the peasant in increasing his production.

V. *The Scarcity of Skill*

In practically all the developing countries overabundance of unskilled labour goes together with the most severe shortage of skills. Many years will elapse before the African countries will be able to get rid of this unhappy heritage from the colonial past. In many instances, the scarcity of skilled workers and technicians sets a limit to the rate of growth of particular industries and, of course, to the expansion of the employment of unskilled labour. While at the highest technical *échelon* it is possible to use for a while, and as a transitional measure, the services of foreign experts, at the intermediary levels this becomes much too expensive and inconvenient. That is why in the context of 'investment in human resources', education in general and vocational training in particular, must find, *per force*, a place of pride. But this indisputable directive should not be carried beyond a point where it defeats its very purpose, i.e. the speeding up of economic development. Excessive emphasis on investment in human resources may lead to an unnecessary slowing down of productive investment, which forms—let us not forget it—the core of the developmental process. It is not a mere coincidence that some of the most vocal advocates of massive

[11] See, for example, Rene Dumont: *L'Afrique Noire est ma partie*, Paris, 1961.

investment in human resources propose at the same time a policy of go-slow in industrialization, under the pretext that investment in human resources should precede, by a decade or so, the industrial drive. Actually this amounts then to a hidden attempt to freeze the existing international division of labour between the primary producers and a handful of industrial powers.

The right solution should be sought, as usual, between the extremes. Investment in human resources is necessary but it loses much of its meaning—in strictly economic terms, if not in humanistic—when it is dissociated from productive investment. In several under-developed countries, which, on the whole, desperately need skilled cadres, unemployment among educated people is wide-spread, because they lack the precise knowledge which is at the moment called for. This is due to lack of adjustment between the educational system and the perspective plans of economic development. Vocational training must be linked with the implantation of new industries. A developing economy is in a sense a 'war economy' and some emergency measures are called for, including some shortened programmes of vocational training, attuned to the pattern of industrial investment actually going on. At the same time, it is necessary to adjust the programmes of primary schools in the villages to the need of the rural economy. These schools should, first of all, train people who will undertake the crucial task of modernizing the traditional sector, rather than migrate to the town, enlarging the already bulky lot of candidates for junior white collar jobs.[12] Let us finally stress, that the volume of investment in education may be somewhat reduced if a policy of austerity is adopted with respect to building standards of schools, and if the campaign against illiteracy is backed to a great extent on social initiative, for which, however, an appropriate social climate is again a pre-condition.

[12] This point has been repeatedly stressed by such authorities as Professors Arthur W. Lewis and Rene Dumont.

16

Creating Employment for Africa's Youth

Archibald Callaway

RESEARCH ASSOCIATE, CENTRE FOR INTERNATIONAL STUDIES,
MASSACHUSETTS INSTITUTE OF TECHNOLOGY

I. *Youth Unemployment in a Setting of General Unemployment*

In recent years many countries in tropical Africa have seen the growth of an urgent problem: unemployment among young people. Although in some areas local unemployment has been a continuing difficulty, this new, more serious form has emerged as a result of accelerated social change, and demands complex policy decisions. The problem arises from the rapid expansion of basic education with limited facilities for further education and limited employment opportunities in the modern sector of the economy. Frequently the effect of primary schooling is to turn young people away from traditional means of making a living: those in villages reject farming and migrate to the cities to compete for the few wage-paid jobs. Each year the number of school leavers increases and the pool of unemployed grows.

Unemployment among school leavers is not, of course, the only form of unemployment in these countries. In most African cities today there are rising numbers of formerly wage-paid adult workers without jobs. Their condition is particularly poignant because after years in the cities they had adopted an urban pattern of living and, in many cases, have accumulated family responsibilities. Having lost intimate contact with the land, their return to rural areas where their costs of living would be lower, is not easy to accomplish. And in some areas (though usually of less importance) there are unschooled youths too who hope to find work in the cities. The setting to these forms of 'open unemployment' is provided by the widespread 'latent unemployment' represented by the multitude of those on farms and in other small enterprises whose labour potential is never fully used, or is relatively ineffective—either

237

at particular times of the year or all the time. These latter are the underemployed.

Such general underemployment is one aspect of low productivity which, in turn, is due to the lack of capital equipment, technical skills, and entrepreneurial ability. The problem then of reducing under-employment—or, to put it the other way, of creating employment opportunities for all at rising levels of real income—is to a large extent synonymous with the problem of development itself. By stepping up the rate of investment and by building capital at key points in the economy a growing number of people are absorbed into the productive system for longer periods of their labour year, and their contribution becomes more effective. But specific measures can also be taken. By using suitable incentives, for example, community projects can be encouraged both to provide higher local capital formation and to make better use of labour during the slack periods of the farm year.

The employment problem of school leavers—caused by the impact of education on a background of traditional society and an under-functioning economy—aggravates the existing unemployment and underemployment. Because of their rising numbers and the related social pressures, however, the unemployment of youth calls for the closest attention. About three-quarters of all unemployed in tropical African countries are under the age of 25; most of these have had some schooling. Their expectations have been awakened, but the develop-ment process lags behind.

What steps are being taken to create employment for these school leavers? Are these efforts seen as an integral part of national economic and social development? What further measures can be taken?

Policies should take into account not only the present situation but the dynamic nature of the problem. In these countries unemployment of school leavers is cumulative; the rate at which young people are leaving schools and seeking work continuously outpaces the capacity of the economies to provide employment outside farming. This type of unemployment, moreover, is not self-correcting, nor will any simple expedient solve it. For the individual—the young African hoping to place himself in the modern world—a long period of unemployment may undermine his self-confidence and turn his optimism to disillu-sionment. For the nation, unemployment of any kind represents a high waste of human resources. As increasingly large numbers of potential

workers do not contribute to the productive system, they become a
heavier burden on those who are working.

When urban areas become seriously overcrowded, with consequent
unhealthy conditions, governments are often pressured to provide
expensive amenities. And although these are certainly part of long-
term development, heavy expenditure on them at a critical period may
be diverted from the more fundamental aims of building productive
infrastructure, encouraging new industries, and improving agriculture.
And if policies are not achieved to balance rural and urban development, providing amenities in large cities becomes self-defeating: more
and more people from the countryside are attracted.

Politicians are becoming keenly sensitive to the threat of jobless
literate youth to stability, particularly at a time when many African
countries are going through a period of intense political re-alignments.
Existing income disparities become exaggerated when there is wide-
spread unemployment. Thousands of idle young men, dissatisfied with
their lot and prospects, aware of this widening gap in incomes between
the highly paid and the less fortunate, might well rally around a self-
appointed leader to press for a radical change in the established order.
And in an age of rapid communications, political agitation can erupt
quickly among young discontented literates.

Then there is the further danger that if long-term solutions in
harmony with the general pattern for economic advancement are not
designed now, some countries may be pushed during an emergency to
adopt stop-gap, or even coercive, measures that could turn out to be
very costly. Temporary set-ups organized under pressure have a way
of turning into permanent institutions—which may not be the ones
desired by the architects of national progress. In this way, priorities of
the economic plan get set aside.

II. *Rising Population and the Desire for Education*

The background to this problem of unemployed school leavers com-
bines two facts: the wide-spread popular demand for education together
with the rapidly rising populations in all these countries. These account
for the multiple expansion of facilities for basic education in both
rural and urban areas. But facilities for secondary and vocational education have by no means developed in the same proportion. At present,
out of every 1,000 primary school children, no country has more than
10 per cent going on for further formal education. This means, quite

simply, at least 900 young people looking for jobs or for training leading to jobs. And even with steady expansion of secondary, technical and university education, still a large number of primary school leavers will be seeking work. At the important Addis Ababa conference in May 1961 on the development of education in Africa,[1] the plan was presented to have universal primary education in all participating countries by 1980, with 23 out of every 100 advancing to second level education, and 2 out of every 100 reaching the higher education level. These are admirable objectives, yet the plan for attaining universal primary education might well be accompanied by a twin plan for achieving large-scale employment of its products.

The sharp rise in the rate of population growth is largely explained by the wider dissemination of health education and services. Most African countries today have an annual population increase of from 2 to 3 per cent. Recent estimates show: Uganda, $2\frac{1}{2}$ per cent; Kenya and Tanganyika, around 2 per cent; while Ghana and Nigeria both exceed 2 per cent. The 1960 population of the 34 countries represented at Addis Ababa was estimated at 172 million, with the figure of 281 million projected for 1980.

In contrast, European nations during similar stages of economic change seldom exceeded 1 per cent yearly increase in population and then only for short periods. As late as 1900, Great Britain had a yearly increase of slightly more than 1 per cent, while Germany, Austria, Italy and the Scandinavian countries were all less than 1 per cent.[2] Another perspective: capital accumulation in the economies of nineteenth-century Europe not only happened over many decades, with low population increases, but also well before public funds were spent in any great amount on health services or wide-spread primary education. African countries are attempting to speed up capital formation, with high population increases, and at the same time allocating heavy

---

[1] *Conference of African States on the Development of Education in Africa*, Addis Ababa, 15–25 May 1961. Final Report (U.N.E.C.A./U.N.E.S.C.O.).
Countries represented: Basutoland, Bechuanaland, Republic of Cameroon, Central African Republic, Chad, Congo (Brazzaville), Congo (Leopoldville), Dahomey, Ethiopia, Gabon, Gambia, Ghana, Guinea, Ivory Coast, Kenya, Liberia, Madagascar, Mali, Mauritania, Mauritius, Nigeria, Niger, Federation of Rhodesia and Nyasaland, Ruanda-Urundi, Senegal, Sierra Leone, Somalia, Sudan, Swaziland, Tanganyika, Togo, Uganda, Upper Volta, Zanzibar.
[2] *Report of the Royal Commission on Population 1949*, pp. 7–8; Marcel R. Reinhard, *Histoire de la Population Mondiale*, first edition, p. 164; H. Gille, 'The Demographic History of the Northern European Countries in the Eighteenth Century', *Population Studies*, Vol. III, No. 1, June 1949, pp. 20–1.

public expenditures to provide primary education for high proportions of school-age children. This comparison gives a hint of the immense task ahead.

Populations of the new African nations are thus becoming younger—with 35 to 40 per cent now under the age of 15. Of course there is nothing necessarily ill-advised about having such increases in population and sending such a large number of children to school. Increased investment in modern education, whether public or private, has certain economic benefits—such as higher productivity of educated workers and greater flexibility of the labour force—and can be thought of as yielding a social rate of return on the investment. The question is whether individual countries have the capacity to propel the higher rate of economic progress necessary to match the expectations people have for improvements in their living standards. Can economic development more than keep abreast of the rising population of, say, 2 per cent every year? And, related to this, can the administrative ability be developed—together with the techniques and the financial resource —to provide the opportunities for training and constructive work so eagerly sought by the younger generation?

Progress in basic education in Africa has three distinct stages. In the first stage only a relatively small proportion of school-age children attend school: perhaps no more than 10 to 30 per cent. The second stages comes when some 50 to 80 per cent or more receive this elementary schooling. The third stage is reached when nearly the entire population has passed through primary education and is literate; there is then acceptance by the whole community that all people, including farmers, need preparation for their economic tasks through exposure to the disciplines of formal school work.

In the first stage, those who pass through primary schools, even without attending secondary or vocational schools, are usually able to find work at a regular income outside farming. They find jobs as clerks in central and local governments and trading firms, as messengers, as assistants to produce buyers, and so on. In the second stage, the number of school leavers has been multiplied by three or four while the number of jobs has increased only slightly. Mass unemployment of school leavers then prevails and may last a long time. The advance towards universal primary education thus brings with it a new set of problems.

A few tropical African countries are still in the first stage. Most, however, have reached the second, and from all points of view—social, economic and political—this is the most difficult stage. Few will reach the third stage before the year 20,000.

Although the pace of educational change differs among and within countries, the elements of the school leavers' employment problems are much the same everywhere. Formal Western-derived education—because its disciplines, ideas and goals are alien to the traditional cultures of African peoples—everywhere disrupts the cohesion of tribal societies. For example, few parents (most of whom are farmers) want their school children to become farmers. Compared with the possibilities that education can lead to, farming—however necessary—is downgraded. The village school is more often thought of as a symbol of the means of freeing the younger generation from the drudgery of farming. These parents pay the modest school fees, often a considerable amount of the income that comes from local sales of surplus produce, with the hopes that their children later on will gain jobs that provide financial rewards and prestige.

III. *The Quest for Work*

The school leaver himself has become aware of the workings of the exchange economy. He has seen bicycles, transistor radios and gramophones, the fashionable clothes of those with steady incomes. But the material goods are not the greatest attraction. (In many cases, those school leavers who have found paid work show remarkable restraint and save a high proportion of their low incomes, often sending money back home for the education of younger brothers or sisters.) The main thing is that the school leaver cannot see any progressive future for himself in the village. And though he may have heard that jobs are difficult to find in the city, he is young and ambitious and fired with possibilities. With the blessings of his parents, he starts out on the long adventure.

Consider a school leaver who comes in search of work to the sprawling city of Ibadan, in Western Nigeria. He stays with his relatives, sometimes doing some domestic chores in return for his food and shelter. He becomes an 'applicant', first making contact with the wage-paid members from his home area, who form a kind of network for spotting potential openings. He fills out applications to the departments of government and to the few new industries. Most mornings he joins the crowds at the youth employment exchange. Then he roams the streets sauntering past the mechanic workshops and the small craft industries—the carpenters, tailors, sandal-makers. If his parents can afford the fees, he can compete to become an apprentice, perhaps to a motor mechanic. As an apprentice, his training might be negligible or it might be an excellent beginning to a career as a skilled craftsman. After he has worked faithfully for three to five years, he may then be given enough tools by his master and help by his parents and relatives to become a type of journeyman with the prospect later of becoming a master and starting business on his own. But there are examples of former school-leaver apprentices, too, who are not able to make the transition between training and gainful work—and who are now unemployed.

Or this school leaver may pay a few shillings a month to learn typing in one of the many establishments found in the city. Even if he learns to copy-type, he is still one of many, with similar rudimentary skills, meeting the ever-hardening employment market. If he is strongly built, he may be able to get occasional work as a daily-paid labourer. But this is often not enough to buy food, much less the new shirt he would like to have. After a year or so, the relatives with whom he is staying may treat him in a less friendly way. He may then even move on to another city to stay with other relatives. Recent sample surveys taken in Ibadan and in the nine other principal centres in the Federation of Nigeria show that many school leavers have been unemployed for two or three years, or even longer.

The decision to return to the home village comes hard. Those school leavers from areas where land is plentiful and where cash crops are grown can go back, however reluctantly, to the security of the farm. Others have strong negative feelings: 'I cannot go back. To confess failure would be a disgrace to myself and my family.' Still others come from areas where land is scarce and drained of fertility; there are no farms for them to return to. Empirical studies in Nigeria show no correlation between farm income and the migration of school leavers from the village, but a relationship does exist between the type of farming and the eventual return to the land.

Because of the unevenness of the spread of education within and among countries, there are consequent disparities in the patterns of migration. Centres of attraction are the principal administrative and industrial cities. By and large, school leavers follow those relatives and other village people who have gone before them. In this way, 'lines of migration' become established. Where, as in East Africa, there is considerable inter-country migration, school leavers cross national boundaries to stay with their wage- and salary-earning relatives. They go to Nairobi, Salisbury and the Copper Belt towns. Salisbury, for example, has some 50 per cent of all wage-paid workers in manufacturing industries originating outside Rhodesia.

The extent of the unemployment of school leavers can be measured by the number of applications that are made to employers in the few arge establishments, by the increasing time which individual school eavers spend without work and, ultimately also, by the statistics of deliquency and vagrancy. Particularly when relatives are no longer able to help and the school leaver is forced to live on his wits, then sometimes he crosses the line into deliquency. This marks the slow weakening of tribal disciplines and the rise of the individual on his own.

Who are these unemployed school leavers? They are mostly those who have completed, or nearly completed, their primary schooling. Because in many countries the average age of primary school leaving is falling (from 16 to 14 in some areas), most of these young people have very little qualification for many of the jobs they apply for—whatever may be their potentiality for improvement. In some areas standards have declined as a result of rapid expansion, and also the shortening of primary school courses.

In some countries those who have been forced to withdraw from secondary schools in the early years are finding difficulty in getting jobs, as are, for example in Western Nigeria, those who complete the course in the 600 secondary modern schools in the Region. Even those who complete secondary grammar school take much longer to find positions, which a few years ago they would have spurned.

IV. *Limits to Employment by Government and Modern Industry*

Since the problem of large-scale unemployment of primary school leavers is a new one, answers cannot easily be found by a scrutiny of the development patterns of other countries. Practical solutions can be arrived at only by closely examining structures of the individual African economies, by analysing points of growth in relation to potential employment absorption, and then by considering priorities of government expenditure and effort.

The reason for the relatively few wage-paid jobs, and apprentice places, lies within the nature and rate of expansion of the economies concerned. The pace of change is limited by available capital, managerial experience, agricultural and industrial skills, and all these are in critically short supply to meet the requirement of accelerated development. From the employment viewpoint, these African economies have certain significant characteristics in common: large agricultural sectors, accounting for over half of each country's total product and engaging 75 per cent or more of the working population: small industrial sectors, with, in most cases, only 2 to 5 per cent of the working population actually engaged in manufacturing or mining.

Creation of modern industries, so often thought of as a panacea for solving the employment problem, is a slow process. And since the trend in industry is for greater mechanization with proportionately few (and more highly skilled) workers, the capital investment needed to employ one worker often amounts to between £500 and £5,000. In the crucial decade that lies ahead, the flow of internal saving, together with foreign loans and investments, will create jobs in modern industry for only a small fraction of those demanding work. Even by 1980 it is unlikely that many countries will have more than 7 or 8 per cent gainfully employed people working in factories—the probable exceptions will be those countries which already have a headstart, such as Ivory Coast, Kenya and Southern Rhodesia. After some decades there will no doubt be instances of self-generating economic systems, but in the meantime the few large-scale industries with secondary effects arising from their establishment cannot come near to solving the problems of mass unemployment.

Setting up new factories depends not only on available capital and skills but also on the ability of the local market to buy the products. And the local market is where the bulk of the population is: in agriculture. One spur to development, then, is to invest money wisely in agriculture, thus raising income and achieving the conditions for encouraging new industries. Most of these countries have what might be described as 'export economies', with one or two commodities relied upon to provide well over half their total earnings from world trade. Improvements to agriculture can boost the quality and quantity of the existing main crops and bring a healthier diversification, thus increasing the export proceeds and lessening the risks of crop failures or fluctuating world prices. With the rise in national income, more funds—both public and private—come forth for investment in industries, perhaps in association with foreign capital and technology.

At the same time, the incomes of farmers rise and the individual family can now buy the plastic buckets, aluminium cooking utensils, locally made shoes—the products of the new industries. But this economic cycle takes time.

In the meantime, during the next few years, where can the jobs be found for young, literate Africans? Because of the huge areas covered by most of these countries, a comparatively large number of people are required for government administration, for public utilities, and for communications. But, while African university graduates and trained technicians are urgently needed for positions at the higher echelons, there is neither the expansion nor the turnover at the lower levels to allow employment for any great numbers. Public services in many countries, in fact, have too many employees and a push for efficiency often brings painful reductions in the need for lesser-skilled labour. Banks and the bigger commercial enterprises are not likely to need young recruits in any great quantity. Large plantations require many labourers at the beginning, during the planting period, but after that not many for maintenance. The large mines have, for the most part, stabilized their labour forces and are able each year to take only a few replacements; and these are usually selected from the miners' sons who have grown up on the mine compound. The modern building and construction industries hold greater prospects for wage-paid employment, but they are dependent on private and public funds as well as a continuing climate of political stability and business optimism.

V. *Encouragement to Indigenous Commerce and Industry*

Since there are no bright possibilities for providing employment on a sufficiently large scale in these more modern establishments, are there opportunities in the more traditional commerce and industry? Here the economies of these countries in tropical Africa show marked differences—in the variety and vitality of the 'transitions' between family subsistence farms and modern industrial units. And it is here that government policies are weakest.

These 'transitions' include the small businesses of traders, self-employed artisans and craftsmen, and the smaller firms of builders, transporters, and processors of agricultural products. This whole array of indigenous enterprises represents the only really competitive element in these economies as they vie with each other for customers and strive to provide the most attractive price and quality of goods or service. What is the capacity of these 'transitions' to absorb more African young people into profitable work? They take far more workers in proportion to each unit of capital than do the large modern factories; they also often provide low-cost training within the traditional apprenticeship patterns. And they are of fundamental importance to the progress of any country both in conveying a flow of incentive goods to farmers and in creating the atmosphere for entrepreneurial talent to develop.

But there are wide differences among countries in the strength of these small enterprises. In Eastern and Western Nigeria, for example, colourful markets thrive with the vigorous exchange of goods, and in every city and town small entrepreneurs energetically advertise their goods and services on a myriad of signboards. These traders and craftsmen and artisans struggle against obstacles and use brave initiatives in the attempt to move ahead. And there are cases of those who have made the breakthrough from small beginnings to large-scale operations —in transport, building and road contracting, and in modern furniture making. The women traders—with shrewd intelligence and aggressive business sense—add an extra vitality to the West African scene. Not only do they train and employ girls in their activities, but they often accumulate large sums of capital for further investment.

In Zambia, on the other hand, where school leavers set out from their villages and trek, as their adult relatives before them, to the 'line of rail', these small enterprises do not flourish with such strength or variety. Because of the low order of exchange in local markets and the lack of transport facilities, the local economy in farming is less advanced. In many parts of the country the task is to create an agricultural economy—to encourage bringing surpluses to local and export markets.

The scene changes again in East Africa. Here the Asian members of the community have for several generations carried out the activities of produce buying, selling imported articles, and fabricating in small industries such as tailoring. Against this accumulated experience, it is difficult for Africans to start in competition, or to win their way forward once having started. And most parts of East Africa show restrictions on trading in urban areas, especially as to location, that are unknown in West Africa.

It is true, of course, that the impetus for these small enterprises to emerge and develop derives from the general strength of the economy of which they become a part. They are especially sensitive to movements in export trade and to the often related rise or fall in government spending on general development. But governments might now begin to think of industrial policy on a gradation stretching all the way from the modern large enterprises to these backstreet small industries. The aim of policy should be to help improve the techniques and management of these small concerns, to blur the edges of this 'technological dualism'. After all, careful examination will reveal that in some instances, this is occurring naturally. For example, a mechanic working in a small workshop in the backstreets finds employment with a modern motor works; after some years of service and of saving, he returns to set up his own improved workshop. The old takes from the new and narrows the differences that exist.

Depending on local variations, governments can, at low cost, design policies to improve the functioning of these smaller enterprises which will in turn provide training and employment for some of the school leavers coming forth. There are the familiar arguments that in the long run raising productivity in these small industries will lower employment needs. But certainly, in the meantime, employment opportunities will rise. As the cost of production falls and the design and quality of products improve, the smaller industries are better able to compete against the cheaper range of imported goods. This would mean a saving on foreign exchange, making more capital imports possible.

An industrial extension service might be formed to give advice to selected small industries—on designing more attractive products, improving techniques of workmanship, marketing more successfully, and organizing the business more efficiently. Another scheme might be to recruit some of these masters and apprentices on a highly selective basis for short-term courses on the pattern set by the French-speaking West African countries. Efforts might also be made to interest some of the larger trading establishments as well as the biggest consumers—the various departments of central and local governments—in purchasing those products and services that meet specified standards. And finally, governments should not impede the emergence and growth of these small enterprises by too hastily adopting imported notions about the need for strict apprentice laws.

One aspect of development, then, is to find out what already exists and learn to work with it. Improving what is already functioning is often a much less costly operation, both in money and in human effort, than starting something completely new. Even if there is a healthy growth of the 'transitions'—the smaller units of commerce and industry within the traditional structure—the chances of training and work for the rising number of school leavers will still be limited.

VI. *Educated Youth as Innovators in an Agricultural Revolution*

The greatest number of employment opportunities must therefore be found within agriculture (and to some extent fishing and forestry). Arguments against attracting these school leavers back into agriculture are made by those who interpret the economic history of advanced countries as the movement of labour from farms to the cities, from agriculture into industries. This movement has occurred, of course, but only as agriculture becomes efficient enough to create a steady surplus of food and raw materials. 'An agricultural revolution—a marked rise in productivity per worker in agriculture—is a precondition of the industrial revolution in any part of the world.'[3] Economic growth comes not as a result of labour surplus moving to cities but because of farm output surplus which serves to finance industrial development.

And such rises in agricultural productivity are most likely to come about through youth whose education has conditioned them to ideas of change and innovation. But it is no use telling school leavers to go back to farming without any plans for them; they will need some practical help at the beginning, some on-the-job training, even if only by regular visits, to ensure continuous improvement which in turn gives them greater rewards and makes farming worthwhile from their viewpoint. In farming, after all, there is an essential difference between one year's experience and another.

There are many who believe that the most fundamental approach to creating modern farmers is through curriculum reform in the thousands of primary schools. By making the schools more farm-centred, it is said, the employment problem will solve itself. The arguments are that schools should be made more 'environmental', should foster the idea of dignity of labour, and should encourage greater realism and resourcefulness among pupils in their home surroundings. The school farm plot should serve as a training ground for improved farming while the school workshop should develop skills in such general crafts as carpentry and bicycle repair and in the local crafts which might be

[3] Simon Kuznets, *Six Lectures on Economic Growth* (Free Press, 1959).

pottery-making and weaving. Academic subjects should be related to the local scene: mathematics to include simple account-keeping using local farm and market examples; language lessons to be developed from African life and literature; geography and history to begin with reference to the local and national scene; science studies to start by analysing the world around them. Certainly the trend for African education is in this direction. But curriculum reform *alone* will not solve the employment problem.

The fact is that school leavers' views of their vocation in life are determined largely by what happens outside the school, in the society and economy. As long as they see in farming a poor and stunted life, they will seek for what seem to them the better opportunities of the cities. What is wanted, first of all, is a really effective *general* policy towards agriculture which would demonstrate that improved farming can bring as much money and as rewarding a life as other occupations.

Yet, at the outset, countries are faced with what seem to be intractable problems in achieving low-cost changes within traditional farming patterns. Africans farm mainly for subsistence food, with some surpluses going to local and export markets. These export crops are valuable providers of foreign exchange: cocoa, cotton, groundnuts, for example. But most farming puts family needs first; specialization among farms is very small. Human power and the use of 'the blade system' are everywhere; animal power is seldom used, and mechanical power rare. And the pattern of shifting cultivation is universal. While suited to a low density of population, such a system is subject to strains when population rises at present rates. Then the cycle of fallow and cultivation gets shorter and shorter, which means eventual deterioration of soil by over-cropping. Fragmentation of holdings is also wide-spread. Much African farming thus demands very hard work; and, when measured against the handicaps, it is often efficient. But productivity per person and per acre is low everywhere.

In the present context, what specific policies can be worked out that have meaning both for improving this system of farming while at the same time providing a future for young school leavers? Experiments already under way in tropical Africa show some possibilities: first, establishing large farm settlements on unused tracts of land which might draw young farmers from a radius of, say, forty miles; second, encouraging smaller farm settlements on unused land close to their present villages; third, helping individuals to introduce improved methods while engaged on family holdings.

Zambia and Western Nigeria, for example, took a courageous and imaginative approach to the problem in establishing large farm settlements. Congo (Brazzaville) also plans to create new village settlements. The Zambian scheme at Mungwi (which accepts illiterate farmers as well as school leavers) and the Western Nigerian settlements were financed on a long-term loan basis. They have new model villages with such modern facilities as tap water. The thirteen farm settlements spaced throughout Western Nigeria began in 1959 with large sections of donated land—from 4,000 to 6,000 acres for each settlement, allowing some 200 school leavers (after two years' instruction in farm institutes) to be settled on individual holdings of from 20 to 30 acres. All-out efforts have been made to use modern technology (tractor pool, for example) and tested scientific approaches in deciding on a combination of arable and tree crops, techniques of planting, possibilities of raising livestock, and co-operative marketing. These settlements are expensive: from £1,000 to £3,000 per settler, repayable over a period of fifteen years beginning from the time the tree crops come into production. On grounds of finance, the concentration of scarce administrative talent, and the many human problems that emerge—when youths are striking out for themselves away from their familiar environment—the direct employment possibilities of schemes of this size are necessarily limited. Their demonstration effect, however, can be considerable; by showing what modern farming in the tropics can be, they make more modest follow-up schemes easier to execute.

Although these large farm settlements are too expensive to be widely imitated, some of their features can be retained in a greatly modified version. Experiments have begun in which villages provide land to their own school leavers and the government gives initial support with subsistence payments to the settlers, subsidized seedlings, and advances for buying tools. Settlers then pay their own way as they go along. Agricultural extension advises on blocking out the land into individual units of economic size which allow for expansion over a series of years and which combine suitable crops for the area in a judicious selection between income now and income later. Co-operative buying of requisites and selling of products are introduced. Since in the early stages the young farmers live with their own families in the villages, the costs are kept to a minimum. Yet these young farmers do make a distinct break with traditional farming. And when the farm unit reaches its full size and the cash crops come into full bearing, they will have an income equal to, if not above, the lower wage-earners in the cities. They will also have the greater security of growing their own food, ultimately living in their own houses, and not worrying about losing their jobs.

For those school leavers who start on their family land, agricultural extension personnel can make regular visits to encourage them, individually or in groups, in overcoming the obstacles they meet in trying to put into practice the improved methods learned in school. Small amounts of credit may be given and advice on techniques of production and marketing. Such an approach to specialized training and settlement in existing villages has been tried out, for example, in Dahomey and Ivory Coast. These examples show that much can be accomplished under existing land tenure arrangements—without waiting for big change-overs in these patterns.

As sufficient farm extension staff becomes available—we could call them *les animateurs*, to use a descriptive expression from French-speaking West Africa—a start can be made in using visual aids and perhaps introducing local and national merit awards for high performances. Such awards can have immense incentive value during intense periods of innovation in farming. Finally, young farmers' clubs can be expanded everywhere to extend instruction, encouragement, and group feeling through the period after the youth leaves school and before he is ready to start farming on his own—and, of course, after beginning on his own as well.

Any realistic programmes for helping to create young modern farmers based on arrangements of low cost and community self-help will be steps in the right direction. The aim is twofold: to initiate expanding economic farm units and to furnish a local exhibition of what improved farming could look like. Where new nutritional crops, higher-yielding strains of existing crops, better poultry, and more skilful methods of management are introduced by these young settlers, they represent an effective demonstration to local villagers. Adult farmers will take greater notice of the accomplishments of their own sons than of the work of government demonstration farms. They will then be more willing to meet farm extension officers and try out some of their suggested improvements.

VII. *Priorities in Educational Financing*

Most economic plans in tropical Africa (and in other continents, for that matter) treat the objective of creating more employment as peripheral to the main theme of economic advance. To some extent this is justified—at least it is understandable—because development normally does create some employment now, with the prospect of more later. Government policies derived from the economic plan are those which have to do with the general conditioning of the economy (for example, by tariffs, regulation of money supply, trade agreements) and those related to spending on capital projects. Since most African governments account for over half of the total capital formation in their countries, government spending is a major stimulus to the working of the economy. The more immediate results can be measured: the lift in output, income and number of wage jobs. But the less immediate results arising from the response of private enterprise to government participation in the economy are much more difficult to assess. These responses may be illustrated by countless examples from African countries. A new feeder road brings multiple results: transporters and traders move into the villages; more consumer supplies flow in; higher surpluses move out; a co-operative for marketing farm produce is started; farm extension work becomes more effective. And as incomes rise, more money is spent locally: the tailor has more orders; the carpenter has more business; more apprentices are required; more jobs are available. Or take another example. Government initiates a highly selective programme for technical and other aid to small industries. After a time several firms meet success; others emulate; output and employment rise. By taking sufficient examples, gradually a record can be built that would be valuable in helping to determine future public spendings or to adjust present ones for maximum results in both productivity and employment. In achieving economic growth, the objectives of higher output and higher employment can coexist much more harmoniously than is commonly supposed.

When weighing the priorities of public spending, however, African countries have a difficult choice to make. The more money that is spent on education (and other social expenditure including health measures), the less there is left to spend on promoting economic development, which could provide more employment for school leavers. This conflict lies at the centre of all planning throughout tropical Africa.

In these countries at present the most compelling reason for education is to provide the high-level skilled people to take over responsibilities in the expanding public services, in firms, in the professions and in politics. All concerned with education in Africa today agree that many more young Africans must go through the universities and higher technical institutions; and in order to provide a broad enough base for selection, many children will need primary schooling. But the large percentage of those who cannot go beyond the primary stage must not be considered merely 'discards' in the process of educating a few to the highest level. The paradox, now and for some years ahead, is the shortage of university graduates and the over-supply of primary school leavers. And governments must discover the means for doing something about both problems simultaneously.

In an attempt to solve this quandary, a few countries have already made the difficult decision to reduce the rate of expansion of primary school opportunities for the time being, thus allowing more resources to go into the establishment of secondary and technical schools and universities. Even so, as mentioned before, all countries subscribing to the May 1961 conference at Addis Ababa endorsed the ideal of universal primary education by the year 1980. Carrying this out will require vast expenditures. Already some countries have between 20 and 30 per cent of their national budgets devoted to education. Having accepted the goal of a widely based educational pyramid, governments must now find the means to pay for it, without compromising the chances of raising employment opportunities for the primary school leavers.

Thus the question is: How can rising education costs, both capital and recurrent, be met in the years ahead? It is clear that because of unequal endowments in natural resources among African countries the probable course and pace of economic progress will vary: and the ability to press on with expanding education will be a greater or lesser burden. Capital and recurrent costs per pupil also vary by country. But there are certain common elements in the problem. In every country there is a need to achieve the extra revenue required without at the same time destroying incentives to work and earn. To accomplish this, more responsibility for paying education costs must be devolved to the local areas—both for capital and recurrent costs. People are much more willing to contribute towards something they value highly which is close at hand. On the capital side, many thousands of schools could be built by voluntary contributions in money and labour (with government standards observed and survey services provided by local governments). For recurrent expenses, special education rates or fees could be introduced, or present systems strengthened. Where some farm areas are devoid of money circulation—depressed areas—governments can obtain a higher contribution through labour donations in building, compensated for by grants-in-aid for recurrent costs.

When this has been done, not only will central governments be in a better position financially to afford programmes to increase employment opportunities for the ever-increasing numbers of primary school leavers, but the case of African countries for international aid for higher education will be all the more valid.

VIII. *The Illusion of Stop-Gap Measures*

Difficulty sometimes arises at policy level because unemployed school leavers are thought of as *surplus labour*. 'Make-work' schemes may then be hastily designed, often with little attention to their economic value to the community or their training value to the individual. Part of the confusion on this basic principle comes from the fact that individual school leavers may often be surplus to their home farms as at present organized. To the nation as a whole, however, unemployed school leavers cannot be surplus. The problem requires a different perspective: the task is not how to absorb surplus labour but rather how to make the best use of scarce resources. The desired solutions, therefore, are those which make the fullest use of limited resources—financial and other— for the economy as a whole; in this way productivity reaches towards its maximum and many more school leavers are employed to greatest advantage.

Another fallacy sometimes occurs: it is thought that short-term solutions can alleviate present pressures and the problem will later solve itself. But solutions worked on this premise usually will be quite costly and will serve only to aggravate the problem in a few years' time. These projects tend to band young people together as if they were homogeneous units possessing equal abilities and gaining equal rewards. From the point of view of the nation and of the individual, policies towards raising employment for school leavers must be regarded as *long-term*. There are no short-term solutions. The youths want an outlet for their ambitions, opportunities for self-government, recognition of the diversity of their talents. Clearly, policies that do not purposefully relate special short-term experience to the expected employment scene later run counter to these individual goals. Even those projects that admittedly are experimental (and the right to experiment should be guarded jealously in any African country) are better conceived with reference to their likely employment outcome.

Again, there are the despairing cries, 'School leavers only want white-collar jobs.' Naturally enough, youths want the highest-paying jobs they can get, and as long as the returns of a clerk or a messenger are considerably higher and steadier than those of a subsistence farmer, they will seek these jobs first. But this is an indication of their economic alertness, certainly not a sign of character defect or laziness. In fact, close inquiries show that African school leavers are most realistic and quickly revise their expectations when they find that these jobs are not available. But it is no use expecting them to go 'back to the land' unless there are positive policy measures to improve agriculture.

In the same way, control of the influx of school leavers into cities, perhaps with forced repatriation, is ultimately futile. Such controls not only create dissension but also are usually inefficient in their operation; moreover, they merely pass the problem back to the rural areas. They are no substitute for real incentives: in particular, a detailed agricultural policy encouraging self-improvement on the job.

If such a policy does exist, then the need is to pass on the information to school leavers. In more general terms, vocational education and counselling about employment and training opportunities can be conducted in schools and in the labour exchanges, both in rural and urban areas. This flow of information, in fact, is an integral part of any country's bid for awakening and harnessing its people in national drives towards economic improvement.

IX. *Experiments in Training and Employing Africa's Youth*

In recent years the gathering concern for idle urban and rural youth has given rise to a variety of schemes in almost all countries of tropical Africa.[4] Kenya, for example, began in 1957 and now has over 160

---

[4] An excellent—though incomplete—survey is given in, 'Youth Employment and Vocational Training Schemes in the Developing Countries,' in *International Labour Review* (Geneva), LXXXVI, No. 3, September 1962.

Youth Centres throughout the countryside and main cities, training some 14,000 young people up to the age of 19. The name is appropriate: the Youth Centre provides a place for unoccupied youths to come together to improve themselves. In a school-like atmosphere they do some general academic work, learn improved farming, and work at a variety of trades. They also take part in sports and in recreation, such as playing in a band. For girls, there is special emphasis on the home sciences. The ideal of community service is upheld; individual pupils are encouraged to give care to old people and the sick in their villages. In Nairobi, the Youth Centre has pioneered in providing a home for orphans and in helping to rehabilitate vagrant and delinquent youngsters. The unique feature of Kenya's movement is the remarkable response from local communities; they donate the land, construct the buildings, and—through local authorities—pay staff salaries. Further funds have been contributed by commercial firms in Kenya and, recently, by overseas foundations. The central government contributes a minimum of direct aid.

A quite different plan has developed in Mali. In 1960 the Civic Service began with 1,500 young men in some 37 camps, mostly situated in rural areas. Here the minimum age is 20, and the service period of two years begins with three months' training conducted by military officers. The main object is to perform work of national importance— such as building roads, dams and bridges—as specified in Mali's five-year development plan. At the same time, the youths are trained in modern agricultural methods and in trades, so that they can settle back in their villages with increased skills. This Civic Service has been worked out at modest cost. Youths are housed in simple buildings and huts, and they sleep on mats. They receive free clothing, small monthly allowances, and a bonus at the end of their service in the form of tools. This plan was designed in the hope that the value of the public works accomplished by these youths will match the cost of their training period.

These are only two of the many projects designed to meet the pressures of the 1960's. What lessons can be drawn from the variety of experience in all these African countries? By and large, the projects are too recent for any clear prototype to have emerged that could have wide validity as a guide for the future. Some are markedly experimental in design; there is a groping for correct procedures. This is a field, however, in which even the exchange of facts and events could be most valuable.[5] And the schemes that failed are as instructive as those for which some success is claimed. But in testing the validity of any scheme there is always one ultimate question: What is the best use of the nation's scarce resources, particularly of capital and organization?

Although the range of these projects in tropical Africa is very wide, they fall roughly into two categories: (a) works schemes, usually of a temporary nature, in which vocational training is sometimes provided, and, (b) specialized training schemes, which may include practical work. Some schemes emphasize social objectives such as the discipline and dignity of work; they stress the idea of national service for its own sake, at the same time as building new skills. The great diversity in characteristics is revealed in the manner of recruitment (age of entry, whether selective, whether voluntary or with some degree of coercion); in the manner of operation (the proportions of training and work involved, money or other allowances, the means to enforce discipline, the length of time school leavers are associated with the scheme); and in the provision, if any, made for helping these school leavers later in their attempts to find suitable work.

Among the large works schemes are: national construction, human investment, workers' brigades, compulsory national service, civic service, labour volunteers. Most of these are found in French-speaking West African countries; a notable exception is Ghana's Workers' Brigade. Some of these include unschooled youths and adults. Some involve military-type discipline. A general recognition is growing, however, that when dealing with youth the less coercive the methods the more effective the responses; in particular, almost all tropical African countries have agreed to the important Conventions 29 (1930) and 105 (1957) of the International Labour Organization on compulsory labour.

On economic grounds, these schemes may lend themselves to criticism because of their high public cost and because they often divert scarce capital and administrative talent from more urgent development tasks. And often such labour-intensive works can be accomplished more cheaply by the use of machinery and perhaps with more experienced labour. Another difficulty frequently occurs in introducing specialization and differential reward for work done; without these, youths

---

[5] Under the auspices of the Commission for Technical Co-operation in Africa (C.C.T.A.), an African inter-governmental symposium was held at Dar-es-Salaam, 25–29 September 1962.

have less spur to self-improvement. Then, also, there are problems in finding continuous work that has meaning within the general development of the area and for which recurrent costs can be borne once the capital works have been completed. If a scheme keeps school leavers for a very long period, or has no definite time limit, the best answer may well be simply to recruit them into central and local government service for public works—as apprentices of various kinds—and thus give them the benefit of training on the job and participation in specialized work, with reward changing as they gain ability and experience. But against these economic appraisals should be weighed the less measurable social gains of improved personal discipline and attitudes towards society.

Specialized training schemes, on the other hand, include youth centres, youth clubs, civic centres, trade centre, and trade schools. They are usually on non-military lines, and are voluntary, with selective recruitment. Some give attention to furthering general education; some are 'correctional'; all provide training in skills—usually farming or trades, or both. These schemes vary in the extent of local self-help, the contribution of voluntary workers (by missionaries and others), and the amount of finance and organization provided by the local or central government. A few of these institutions aim to be self-supporting by charging fees to trainees or making products for sale.

Experience all over Africa suggests one big problem related to both kinds of youth schemes: What happens to the school leavers once their courses of training and work have finished? Have the conditions of these camps and special schools made them better or less able to meet the competitive job market? Are those with farm training more or less willing to undertake farming in rural areas? How many later rejoin the ranks of the unemployed? Almost universally there is lacking an effective follow-through system which could both guide these youths and evaluate their experience.

X. *A Youth Employment Plan*

In order to provide a focal point for the multiple policies having to do with the employment of school leavers, a Youth Employment Plan might be worked out and kept continuously under revision. With manpower and education assessments, it would form an integral part of the nation's general economic planning. The Youth Employment Plan would bring together all the aspects of the problem into a meaningful pattern so that, instead of fragmentary solutions based on limited perspectives, the solutions will be viewed as reinforcing each other within the whole process of development. Thus, the difficult balance between rural and urban advancement will be more correctly appraised. Curriculum reform will be seen in its relation to agricultural extension; vocational guidance and a flow of information can take place in relation to government schemes for helping young farmers and aiding small businesses; the respective roles of central and local governments can be worked out to mesh with the contributions of local self-help and voluntary organizations. The Youth Employment Plan would sponsor continuous research to determine the relative costs of various training and work schemes, to review pilot projects in terms of costs and results, and to exchange information with other countries.

Unemployment among school leavers is perhaps the most serious long-run socio-political problem facing African countries. Governments obviously have a decisive role in determining the many dimensional policies to meet these employment demands. Meaningful solutions can be achieved, consistent both with national goals and with the aspirations of individuals.

17

An Approach to the Problem of Creation of Opportunities for Gainful Employment in Nigeria

Sudhakar J. Bhatt

FORD FOUNDATION ECONOMIST, NATIONAL MANPOWER BOARD, LAGOS

Nigeria's Six-Year Development Plan has as one of its general objectives, 'the creation of more jobs and opportunities in non-agricultural occupations'. No separate specific machinery was provided for working out detailed employment objectives to fulfil this consideration within the frame-work of the Plan. The Governments of the Federation, however, are cognizant of this need and are endeavouring to supplement the Plan by developing specific objectives and programmes for the creation of gainful employment opportunities through the National Manpower Board and the respective Regional Manpower and Unemployment Committees. This writer has been intimately connected with the development of these programmes and the practical difficulties envisaged in their implementation. This paper presents the writer's initial appraisal of the problems and some of the basic approaches to meet them.

The nature of the problem

According to the 1952–3 census, 44 per cent of the total population was 14 years old or younger. In view of the estimated phenomenal growth of the population during the past decade, it seems probable that this proportion would have increased. Therefore, the present pressures generated by young job seekers in the labour market may well be the signs of things to come. The Six-Year Development Plan, with an investment programme of 767 million pounds, including direct investment of 90·3 million pounds in trade and industry, may possibly create about 500,000 new opportunities in commerce, industry and service industries. As this would make little impact on the demand for more employment, it means that the task of creating jobs for several million job seekers entering the labour market during the Plan period would of necessity fall on agriculture. The direct investment programme of 91·8 million pounds in primary production, however, is unlikely to meet these requirements over the six-year period. Besides, even if enough employment were so created the resultant expansion of the *proportion* of the gainfully occupied population in agriculture would tend to raise the farm output to the extent that prices of food crops would fall precipitously and would tend to lower the income of farmers. This would have the effect of generating further pressures on the rural population to move to urban areas. Of course, this situation need not arise if the expanded production is largely concentrated in commercial and other exportable crops. But in view of the relatively high invest-ment requirements for cash crops, and the associated marketing and price problems, it seems unlikely that this sector of agriculture could absorb a sufficiently high proportion of the new job seekers during the next decade or so, to make a significant contribution to the creation of employment opportunities. The fact that many job seekers are leaving the farms in great numbers and swelling the ranks of the unemployed persons in urban areas, without seriously affecting the output of agriculture, indicates that they were probably surplus to manpower requirements in agriculture. In any case the situation suggests that creating employment opportunities in these circumstances would call for the establishment of more farm units rather than im-proving the production of existing acreage.

In many quarters the primary blame for the urban unemployment is laid at the door of universal primary education. I, for one, believe that this flow from the country to the city would have occurred any way. Universal primary education might have somewhat accelerated the process of transforming rural underemployment into urban unemploy-ment. To insist on keeping people on the farms whose absence is unlikely to have any influence on the agricultural output, would, at all events, amount to a transcendent mismanagement of manpower. On the above views, therefore, I believe that agriculture will not be the key that would open up opportunities for gainful employment for the rising army of young job seekers in Nigeria. On the other hand, it is felt that the creation and stimulation of rural industries would significantly assist in the diversification of the rural economy and reduce the latter's dependence on one or two crops. This development of rural industries, together with the existing farm programme would help slow down the flow of young job seekers from the country to the city.

A practical approach

The above approach is based on the consideration that Nigeria is a free market economy and the purpose of economic planning is mainly to provide basic infrastructure and such props as are necessary for economic growth. As in all countries, Nigeria needs to approach its unemployment problem from both the short-term and long-term points of view. It has to develop a series of co-ordinated programmes which would result in gainful employment in the immediate future. These short-term programmes also must have long-term growth potential; i.e. they must have ingredients of becoming permanently profitable within a reasonably short time. Unless businesses are profitable and expanding, it would be hard for labour to remain employed.

The key pin in these programmes is the entrepreneur. It may sometimes be possible to recruit potentially good entrepreneurs from schools, colleges and agricultural institutions. But the surest way to find and develop the entrepreneural timber in Nigeria is in the backroom shops where the small-time operator with his one apprentice (sometimes more) is making trunks and boxes, shoes and leather goods, furniture and so forth. This man is already servicing a market. He buys his raw material, designs his products, finds buyers and sells his wares. If he is convinced that he can be assisted to do all these things better, he is ready to listen and to learn. Once he tastes the results of even modest improvements he would want more of it. In this way he is drawn into the vortex of economic dynamism. This applies to both industry and agriculture. It is easier to upgrade an existing farmer or small entrepreneur, than to train a brand new recruit and then establish him as a farmer or as an entrepreneur.

The following outline embodies some programmes aimed at the most economic utilization of two of the scarcest ingredients available for economic growth in Nigeria—first, the entrepreneural talent and, second, capital for the task of creating employment opportunities. The scarcity of the first ingredient would be overcome by providing extensive consultative services to supplement the existing entrepreneural talents; the dearth of the second factor would be overcome by emphasizing small industries which would generate maximum possible jobs for every pound invested. The underlying objectives of the programmes are the following:

(a) The fullest utilization of existing production capacities in large- and medium-scale enterprises employing 10 or more people, through the establishment of consultative services.

(b) Expansion of the base of operation of these enterprises by introducing new lines of products which, with their present know-how, they could conveniently manufacture and market.

(c) The fullest utilization of existing skills of very small entre-preneurs in urban and rural areas by providing them with extensive consultative and operational extension services.

(d) Development and expansion of cash crops and the processing and manufacturing industries based on them.

(e) Canalization of the existing demand, which is now met by imports, towards the acceptance of indigenous products. This would be primarily accomplished by the creation of compre-hensive indigenous marketing institutions trading in products manufactured or assembled in Nigeria, and harnessing of these institutions to the task of economic development.

In short, the whole approach emphasizes the more effective use of what already exists; for it is much easier to expand and improve on the existing structures than to create something quite new, in the circumstances prevailing in Nigeria, where capital is short and formal training facilities are meagre and expensive.

Expanding production capacities

In a developing country a great emphasis is often put on creating new industries and enterprises for the development of human and material resources. This is perhaps inevitable. In pursuing this endeavour, however, an obvious consideration is often omitted or does not receive the attention it deserves. This consideration—the possibilities of expansion of the existing large- and medium-scale enterprises which might be already operating below their existing capacity or market potential—should have even a greater role when the prime entre-preneural and managerial skills, so essential for the starting and operating of new industries, are scarce or unavailable.

This objective could be largely achieved through the establishment of Business Expansion Service under the relevant Ministries of Commerce, Trade and Industries. These services should be sufficiently extensive to cover the entire Federation and should be responsible for:

(a) Checking the production and employment potential of each establishment as against its present performance.
(b) Developing marketing programmes for the fullest promotion of existing products.
(c) Developing programmes for addition of new products to the existing lines which would boost the company's sales.
(d) Recommending possibilities of entering into new lines of products consistent with their present know-how and for which there is effective demand which, at present, is met by imports.

In this programme the existing firms would have a vital role to play, and the co-operation and participation of trade associations and chambers of commerce should be sought so that enterprises in a given line and related products could be serviced by one group of experts.

Further utilization of the skills of small entrepreneurs

As mentioned earlier, the crux of this whole endeavour would be to get the small entrepreneur interested in the improvement of his business and to draw him into the dynamics of business expansion. What is envisaged here is to set up a semi-autonomous Small Industry Development Board on a national basis, with a series of strategically located Small Industry Development Centres functioning under it. The relevant Regional Ministries would co-operate with the Board in order effectively to tackle the task of up-grading the small existing entrepreneurs. The example of what is now happening at Owerri in Eastern Nigeria, what is intended to be accomplished through the Small Industries Development Centre in Zaria in Northern Nigeria, and what is already under way in the Ministry of Trade and Industry, Industrial Division, in Ibadan, Western Nigeria, should be multiplied several times through the establishment of the Small Industry Development Board.

Under the umbrella of the Board, specific extension services, mobile operational and demonstration services with respect to tools and machines, designs and styling, technical matters, layout of shops and equipment, raw material and marketing problems, accounting and cost problems and related matters, would be made available to each Centre.

The Small Industry Development Centres will be provided with training workshops and facilities for conducting two to four weeks practical courses for shoemakers, leather workers, furniture makers, artisans and craftsmen. After this training the small business operators will return to their shops and apply the new methods they have learnt. After a few weeks, this would be followed by a visit of an extension worker from the Centre who would provide further operational help.

In short, these efforts would make local businessmen with self-developed skills more adaptable to improve methods of production and more responsive to new ideas. Once they taste the fruits of improvement, they would be inexorably drawn into the dynamics of growth. The success of this endeavour is the key to the success of the entire programme of employment creation in rural and urban industries. The success of these entrepreneurs would provide vast employment opportunities for young job seekers at both urban and rural levels.

Development of cash crops and related industries

Creation of a sugar refining mill would normally create employment for not only 200 to 300 workers on the plant but, possibly, also for several thousand farmers in the field. The same would be true in the case of cotton, groundnuts, cocoa, cashew-nuts and so forth. Programmes to this effect are already under way under the aegis of various ministries in the Governments of the Federation. However, what is required is a sense of urgency and priority in the expansion of these programmes with a view to diversifying the rural economy, and creating more employment opportunities.

Creation of comprehensive marketing organizations

Today in Nigeria there are virtually no indigenous marketing institutions. The main marketing and distribution channels (i.e. processes through which a manufactured product travels from the factory or assembly to the ultimate selling unit, store or local market) are in the hands of foreigners. Thus, trading channels—a sizeable generator of profits and capital, are in Nigeria, not indigenous. Therefore, they cannot be harnessed to the objectives of economic development as effectively as if they were indigenously owned and operated. The main objective here is, accordingly, to create indigenous marketing institutions which would, in course of time, develop sufficient hold over the retailing of products and thus encourage economic development through the promotion of local products. When accounting for a significant proportion of retail and wholesale distribution of products, these marketing organizations would generate demand for local products in domestic and foreign markets. This would in effect create full employment for existing producers so that they can take on new trainees in sufficient numbers to keep their supply line flowing and expanding. This would also stimulate the formation of new local industries.

If small-scale industries are created prior to the organization of effective marketing of their products, these industries would tend to dry up and most of the producers would continue to be marginal suppliers. However, the successful undertaking of the creation of indigenous and effective marketing institutions could not be undertaken by the Regional Governments alone. Participation of all the Governments of the Federation would be necessary in these endeavours. Two such organizations to fulfil the above objectives recommended here are:

(a) A National Emporium of Nigerian Arts and Handicrafts, and
(b) National Co-operative Markets.

It would not be necessary to go into details regarding the short-term and long-term objectives, framework, organization and operations of these institutions in this paper. It would suffice to state here that if successfully implemented, these two marketing organizations would generate demand not only for products of Nigerian arts and crafts, here and abroad, but also for local household and food products in the country. They would help foster indigenous industries by providing them effective marketing facilities and guidance regarding the quality, pricing and styling of products. In short, there appears to be immense possibilities of growth of industries and employment through successful development of these marketing organizations.

Conclusion

It is considered that the successful implementation of the foregoing basic programmes would create conditions for the fuller utilization of existing industrial capacities and capabilities, would stimulate the growth of the entrepreneurial class so essential for accelerated or any type of long-range economic growth, and would provide for indigenous marketing institutions. To be really effective, these programmes would have to be powerfully supported by Government efforts such as 'Buy Nigerian Campaign', Government purchase policies in favour of local products of reasonable quality at all levels, tariff protection, and general and administrative measures to promote local industries.

18

Summary of Discussion and Conclusions (IV)

I. *The Nature and Scope of the Problem*

1. Underemployment and unemployment of labour (and to some extent of land and capital) resources are familiar features of most economies. They are specially prominent elements of developing economies at the stage that Nigeria has now reached. In the process of economic development in Nigeria it is essential that a high and rising level of employment should be maintained in the various sectors of the economy: in production, distribution and exchange of goods and services. For such a heightened level of work opportunities to be generated, certain preconditions must be met. Several of these have particular meaning in present-day Nigeria.

2. First of all there must be a thorough and continuing documentation of relevant facts. Also, understanding of local cultures must be sufficiently well informed that incentive patterns can be designed which can go a long way towards encouraging economic activities in village, town and city. Again, there must be adequate and continuing supply of technical ability, and complete dedication to the extension of such programmes as will enable the most effective use of the labour force and the provision of increasing opportunities for those without work. Such programmes for raising output and employment simultaneously will need to be imaginative and well planned.

3. Underemployment of labour resources can be found in most sectors of the Nigerian economy—in farming and in small industrial enterprises, for example—and should be regarded as one aspect of low productivity which, in turn, is due to inadequacy or ineffectiveness of co-operating factors: of capital equipment, technical skills and entrepreneurial ability. Therefore, the problem of reducing underemployment—or, to put it in another way, of creating employment opportunities for all at rising levels of real income—is to a large extent synonymous with the problem of development itself. By stepping up the rate

of investment and by building capital and abilities at key points in the economy, a growing number of people are absorbed into the productive system for longer periods of their labour year and their contribution becomes more effective.

4. The recent sample survey of unemployment in the major cities of Nigeria by the Manpower Office, shows that the number of unemployed persons is large and is growing rapidly. Available evidence suggests that within a few years the total unemployed persons in Nigeria could approach half a million. Of the unemployed persons covered in the survey about 90 per cent were males, 10 per cent were females. And of the total, some 85 per cent were less than 30 years of age (45 per cent being less than 20 years of age, and 40 per cent between 20 and 30 years of age). Of the total recorded as without work, some 60 per cent have not worked before, while about 50 per cent claim to have done nothing productive for more than 12 months.

5. Thus it is apparent that unemployment of labour comprises mainly male youths. Most are school leavers. They are to be found not only in the cities and minor towns but also in the rural areas where many spend time in their villages hesitating about fully committing themselves to traditional life and work. The number of these unemployed youths grows each year; it is cumulative. It is estimated that during the current Plan period, 1962–68, about 400,000 school-leavers will join the labour market each year, whereas only a small proportion are likely to find wage employment in the modern sector of the economy. In addition there are formerly wage-paid, adult workers in the cities, some of whom are semi-skilled, and others unskilled. Their contest is to match the competition of the rising number of applicants. Especially in cases where these adult unemployed have accumulated immediate family responsibilities their return to the rural areas is not easy; they have adjusted to an urban pattern of living and they hold on tenuously. These forms of unemployment can be explained within the context of the expectations that people have about the kinds of jobs they can get and the hard facts of the process of economic development. Although their expectations are for personal and family gain, and perhaps for status, nevertheless they are consistent with the much-needed driving force required to reconstruct and develop the Nigerian economy.

6. Creation of suitable work for school leavers needs to be given particular emphasis by Governments for several reasons. Firstly, their

numbers are rising. Secondly, heavy expenditure of scarce public resources has had to be devoted to their education. Thirdly, the great social pressure resulting from the manner in which parents and relatives have denied themselves other forms of expenditure in order to promote children's education and thereby prepare them for beginning tasks with a future in the improving economy cannot be ignored; their own hopes are implicit in the expectations of the younger, educated generation. Fourthly, elementary education infuses the basic notion of self-improvement and, in the minds of most school leavers, this is incompatible with the technologically static environment that often surrounds them in their home area. Fifthly, unemployment of any kind —and youths form the preponderant part of the total—has a high social and economic cost: these unemployed reduce the disposable money income of those who are working and distort the expenditure and saving patterns of the immediate families with whom they are staying; and their lack of useful work represents a high waste of human resources.

7. Jobless youths today include those with primary school passes, those with full secondary modern schooling, and withdrawals from secondary grammar schools (withdrawn usually for reasons of finance). There may be a certain number of those who have completed their courses at secondary grammar schools—some with passes in school certificate, some without: for some of those who have passed, there remains the awkward gap between school leaving and gaining, perhaps through correspondence, sufficient higher level passes to qualify for entrance to universities. On account of the growing desire and opportunities for education, the rate at which new, educated recruits enter the employment market will continue to rise. General indications from recent trends are that, in the years ahead, unless the rate of growth of the economy improves significantly, university graduates will be required to accept employment at a lesser starting salary, and in most cases with promotions coming less frequently; that school certificate holders will require to take jobs of a lesser order; that secondary modern and primary school leavers will have little chance for wage-paid work.

8. The systematic elimination of underemployment and unemployment in a developing economy like Nigeria is, by its nature, a rather long-term problem which calls for steady and persistent effort. The larger the increase in national output striven for, the larger must be the

demand for labour of all kinds. Especially is this the case if care is taken to adopt labour-intensive processes wherever technically and economically feasible. Thus, expansion of employment opportunities at rising levels of real income will proceed side by side with the development of the economy and, like the development process itself, will become cumulative as soon as there is a marked improvement in the capital equipment of the economy.

9. But in the short run there will certainly be difficulties of adjustment. There may appear to be a conflict, for example, between the need to reduce the social cost of maintaining unemployed labour and the need to raise the productivity of labour. In the nature of things there will not always be clear-cut answers to these difficulties. Unemployment is, however, not merely an economic problem, it is a social problem as well (replete with human values) and needs to be viewed broadly. In framing employment policy in relation to development, several criteria need to be borne in mind: unused manpower should be drawn on to the maximum; capital formation must be speeded up and technical efficiency improved and thereby increase the productivity of labour; the distribution of capital in new lines should be planned, keeping in view the need to increase employment in the short run, as well as the larger pattern of development necessary for an expanding economy. With at least 10 per cent of the present labour force unemployed, such imperatives as these must be continuously scrutinized in relation to employment creation. Decisive action must follow in moving as rapidly as possible towards the ultimate objective of full employment. Indeed the Seminar is emphatic in the view that with unemployment at its current level, employment objectives must receive the utmost priority in development planning and programmes.

II. *Underlying Assumptions*

10. The discussions of the Seminar have been influenced by certain assumptions which reflect the existing policies of the governments of Nigeria and the political framework of the country. Others appear to flow from certain stated economic objectives. The recommendations which follow can accordingly only be fully meaningful in the light of such assumptions. It seems necessary, therefore, to summarize them at this stage.

11. There will be no resort to forced labour. This assumption is

based on the fact that Nigeria has ratified the relevant Conventions, No. 29 of 1930 and No. 105 of 1957, of the International Labour Organization. This fact does not, however, rule out a certain high degree of persuasion, including advanced forms of propaganda, relating to the choice of vocation and of the opportunities and method of individual employment creation.

12. The Governments will endeavour to work within the present system of mixed economy and to improve its functioning. Towards this end it is necessary that Governments should foster such policies as will help to remove obstacles to the free flow of labour, capital and goods among Regions within Nigeria.

13. The Governments will intensify their efforts to help increase employment opportunities of economically productive nature.

14. In providing formal training facilities of whatever kind for youths, the most strenuous efforts will be made to relate these forms of vocational training to expected employment opportunities.

15. Nigeria is characterized by unevenness in the distribution of natural, human and capital resources; in particular, capital and population density and the spread of education facilities vary widely in relation to local resources. Public expenditures on specific programmes for output and employment creation will thus not necessarily follow an even geographical spread. Rather the economic principle of the best use of scarce resources will be adhered to. (For example, in the establishment of training facilities and small industries in villages, and in the location of farm schools.)

16. When special public policies are designed to encourage a higher level of output and employment, these will be balanced between rural and urban areas—and among the various sectors of the economy—in accordance with the broad objectives and priorities of the National Economic Plan.

17. The National Manpower Board will continue its efforts to evolve an overall national policy for the effective elimination of unemployment. In doing so the Manpower Secretariat will continue to co-ordinate regional programmes.

III. Recommendations

(1) There is need for a nation-wide quantitative population sample survey to determine the levels of employment, underemployment and unemployment by type of activity, and related questions such as migra-

tion. The survey would include information on adults and youths, both male and female, literate and non-literate. The internationally accepted definitions of the International Labour Office should be used for this purpose, with necessary modifications to reflect Nigerian conditions. In particular, the possibility of using a broad concept of female labour force should be examined.

(2) There is need to ensure a thorough analysis of the 1963 census data to provide maximum information on the above lines.

(3) A detailed qualitative sample survey should be undertaken in chosen areas of Nigeria in order to determine the yearly family and hired labour commitment on farms.

(4) There is need for research into the general problems of rural development with particular reference to the use, in areas of high unemployment or depressed agricultural conditions, of a combination of community development, stimulation of co-operatives, improvement of village amenities, intensified agricultural extension work, etc., with a view to evolving a strategy of rural development.

(5) Research is needed into the effects of existing land tenure arrangements on the efficiency and productivity of agriculture.

(6) Research should begin in order to assess the relative importance of the values, interests, attitudes and other socio-psychological factors, which influence willingness to undertake and perform various kinds of work.

(7) Studies should be made to discover the suitability of different courses of formal study, testing and certification, for various occupations. Systematic inquiries should also be made to find out not only employers' requirements, but also their experiences in employing people with varying educational attainments.

(8) Work opportunities for the physically handicapped need to be regularly assessed.

(9) A combined project, involving both engineers and social scientists, should be launched to discover the relative merits of labour-intensive and capital-intensive methods in executing various development projects, including public works.

(10) Government measures to combat underemployment and unemployment should be continuously under review with the object of making firm suggestions on how these could be improved upon.

(11) In developing proposals for manpower research, full use should be made of the facilities in Nigeria's employment exchanges. The

development of the facilities for this purpose should be undertaken by specialist officers on lines agreed by the National Manpower Board.

(12) In carrying out these research exercises the fullest advantage should be taken of the experience of other countries, especially in Africa (for example, the Institute of National Planning, Cairo). By this means field procedures and processing can be co-ordinated and results made comparable.

(13) Along with output targets the national and regional economic plans should establish employment targets, broken down into their component parts. A special effort is required to analyse and discover the expected employment potential of the present Plan and of its revised editions. The aim should be to promote a higher job content not only in the present Plan but in its successors.

(14) It is recommended that the Federal Government should take a special interest in the financial capacity of the Regional Governments to meet the cost of well-planned policy proposals for increasing employment opportunities for Nigeria's youth. Since the Federal Government cannot, without the co-operation of the Regions, make much headway in reducing the extent of youth unemployment in Lagos, such special financial interest is not only logical but also imperative.

(15) In order to help break through the cordon of restraints that retard the progress of many of Nigeria's indigenous small industries, it is recommended that an Industrial Extension Service manned by technical experts, technical help—and, in special cases, credit provision—to small entrepreneurs, could be most valuable in enabling their firms to compete with some of the imported consumer products. Such help would illustrate the better use of existing resources, or assist the expansion of existing facilities. The Industrial Extension Service would also,

(a) assist in developing upgrading on-the-job training programmes of apprentices by master craftsmen;
(b) development and use of simple accounting procedures;
(c) advise on better work processes, improved product design, and introduction of new products;
(d) help by exploring the means for widening the markets, for instance, by evolving quality standards as a necessary prerequisite to a co-ordinated 'Buy Nigerian' campaign (led in the demand for these products and services by Governments,

statutory corporations, and the school system); a specially designed marketing institution might well supplement existing trade channels in moving locally-produced goods to wider markets.

Raising production in this manner—spread by the small industrialists' capacity to emulate—can raise the level of employment.

(16) It is recommended that Regional Governments explore more closely the means by which school leavers of sufficient maturity can begin their careers as improved farmers, at lower costs than as in existing farm centres, especially in circumstances where land is available close to their home villages or where this can be made available through proper changes of land tenure, etc. Such a programme would be based largely on self-help. The objective of such low-cost farm settlements would be twofold; first, the youths would settle on expanding economic farm units, and second, they would represent an effective demonstration to adult village farmers of the advantages of improved farming. As a consequence they would make the work of farm extension more effective in the village. Markets need to be explored to discover the prospects of various combinations of local food and of other cash crops. Such settlements would be based on private enterprise but would be assisted to develop co-operatives to facilitate purchasing farm requisites and marketing products.

(17) Continuity should be preserved from the period of teaching of farm subjects in schools, by the setting up of Young Farmers' Clubs and by eventual assistance in farm settlement for deserving school leavers.

Part Five

Productivity

19

Concepts and Measurement of Productivity

S. K. Wolf*

I. *Introduction*

Two hundred years ago industrial labour was considered merely a production factor. The industrial communities and nations showed no personal or social responsibilities, creating an artificial separation between industrial labour and industrial management. This led to severe political and social stress and to wars among nations competing for world markets and raw materials. Against this background, the development of industrial production underwent three phases:

(a) Technical improvement and invention based upon the findings of the natural sciences and of research.
(b) The development of new techniques of production and distribution, mass sales, division of work and division of duties.
(c) The discovery of man as the centre of all economic life.

Today we have arrived at a stage when we have developed a philosophy that emphasizes the importance of high wages as a prerequisite to high industrial labour productivity. High wages are a means of increased purchasing power of the majority of the people, thus constituting a primary requirement for mass production and mass marketing.

High labour productivity is not necessarily a panacea nor an index of social progress or economic welfare. Professor Tinbergen has concluded on the basis of several theoretical models which involve the effects of changes in industrial productivity upon the terms of trade, that: 'The old thesis that an increase in productivity leads to an increase in welfare should not be misunderstood. Not under all cases does

* Dean of the Faculty of Business Administration and Social Studies, University of Lagos, at the time of writing.

it lead to consequences that are in all respects attractive. In a number of cases the consequences are definitely mixed, some of them favourable, others unfavourable. It does not always entail an increase in total expenditure; nor does it always yield an increase in real worker's income. Often it reduces the volume of employment'.

A country with a high ratio of labour to capital such as Nigeria or India may well prefer to employ a relatively large admixture of industrial labour in the productive process. This is not only true in Nigeria and India. President Roosevelt in 1932 made efforts to get the United States economy out of the throes of depression by putting unemployed workers to work at low capital-using tasks, with resulting lower national industrial labour productivity. Unless comparable levels of employment, industrialization and economic activity are at the basis of industrial labour productivity comparisons, erroneous conclusions may be drawn from unqualified statistics on industrial productivity. Productivity measurements *per se* provide little guidance for either public or private economic policy and such measures only take significance when the factors associated with the change or difference shown have been analysed. It is true nevertheless that the crude measurements of productivity, if joined with an analysis of the factors responsible for the changes discovered, can be useful tools of economic appraisal.

II. *Concept and Scope of Productivity Measurement*

Every economy, developed or underdeveloped, is faced with the problem of industrial productivity. An attempt is made here to examine and evaluate some of the difficulties of defining and measuring industrial productivity. The nature, importance and complexity of industrial productivity has led it to be examined from various angles resulting in a large variety of conceptions. It has been viewed in a broad sense, as the barometer of the economy as a whole: more often its reference has been limited to specific industries. A narrower definition is reflected in the remarks of businessmen who relate its complexity to the degree of efforts to be applied by the workers to their job.

A definition which claims to cover the explicit or implicit definitions presented in various studies by various authors from various countries is, 'the ratio of output to the corresponding input of labour'. Such a sweeping statement, however, does not solve any problem, for it is too broad and leaves the terms 'output and input' open to interpretation, and, at the same time, closes the door for quantitative analysis. Industrial productivity is a **multivariable** function. An indefinite number of factors may affect an individual employee's ability to do his job.[1]

Thus

$$P\ (x_1, x_2, x_3, x_4, \ldots x_x)$$

Where, $P =$ Productivity of Labour, and

$x =$ Each factor affecting Productivity in the form of Multiple Regression Equation

$$x_1 = a + b_2 x_2 + b_3 x_3 \ldots$$

Where $x_1 =$ Productivity

$x_2, x_3 \ldots =$ Various factors affecting productivity

The net regression coefficient accompanying the variable indicative of labour's efforts would be a criterion of how productivity is influenced by labour's efforts alone and ratios between the coefficients obtained at different times would constitute a significant index of changes in productivity of labour. Thus, the application of multiple correlation analysis would make the error component so large as to render the results untenable. Bela Gold thinks that this is full of shortcomings.[2] First, the terms used may be interpreted as reinforcing the common tendency to stress the relation between physical conceptions of output and input, instead of explicitly calling attention to the applicability of broader conceptions as well. Second, the definition omits mention of the necessary role of purpose in giving concrete meaning to the concept of productivity. Third, its failure to mention that input and output are essentially different from one another tends to encourage misuse of productivity concepts. Fourth, its specific differentiation of technical change from factor price adjustments may represent so serious an underestimation of the extent of interaction between these categories of change as to limit the general applicability of the definition. Finally, its separation of the effects of changes in the scale of production from other changes in input-output relations would seem to be theoretically questionable as well as practically unattainable, at least in the present state of economic theory and research techniques.

[1] For example, see S. P. Zobel, 'On the measurement of Productivity of Labour', in Journal of American Statistical Association, Vol. XLV, June 1950.
[2] Bela Gold, Foundation of Productivity Analysis (University of Pittsburgh, 1955).

In a report prepared for the Seventh International Conference of Labour Statisticians, the International Labour Office, Geneva, sorted the various definitions of productivity into two large groups:

'The first concept, that is, an average productivity which will remain unchanged when each individual productivity is unchanged will normally be used when variations in the productive efficiency of an industry or the combined effect of such variation in a group of industries is studied. The second concept is an average productivity which may vary owing to the changing composition of productivity if each individual productivity is unchanged. The first concept will answer such questions as the following, taken from the report of the United States Works Progress Administration:

"What relative volumes of labour time are required to produce a given composite of products at different times?
What relative volumes of production of a given composite or products are obtainable at different times of a given amount of labour time?
Answers to these questions are of use in estimating:
(1) employment requirements for different levels of production, and
(2) future employment under various conditions of future availability and utilization of labour."

(*Production, Employment and Productivity in 59 Manufacturing Industries 1919–36*, May 1939, Part I, P–3, National Research Project.)

The second concept is of much wider scope; it takes into account that average productivity increases when products, undertakings, or industries corresponding to a high level of productivity increase their importance in comparison with those corresponding to a low level. The second concept will be used when comparing overall changes in the ratio of manufacturing output to total manufacturing employment or national output to total employment or total labour force'.[3]

Thus the choice between these two concepts will depend on the information sought, although it will always be preferable, whenever possible, to compute data on both bases in order to ascertain, for instance, the influence on the observed changes of the modification in the composition of the production. However, most of the considera-

[3] International Labour Office: *Higher Productivity in Manufacturing Industry*, I.L.O., Geneva, 1954.

tions on the measurement of production and labour apply to both conceptions and can be examined independently of these two concepts.

A concept introducing relationship between product and factors was put forward by the French National Committee for Productivity. It is as follows: 'Productivity is the measurement of the economic soundness of means.' It may be said that all authors agree on matters of substance. However, such a relationship does not solve our problem of measurement, it does not produce a procedure that can combine heterogeneous factors into one form and does not clear the confusion in interpretation of this kind of calculation. Dr. Rostas[4] thinks that the measurement of productivity involves the following difficulties: **The measurement of the past labour incorporated, say in capital equipment, raises serious new problems.** Should it be measured by the original labour input or by current input relevant to the past technique known at that time or by current input relevant to technique?

Evans and Siegel[5] present an approach which they assert is more commonly and widely used today and which they define as: 'For a single uniform product, unit labour requirements for any particular time is the labour consumed per unit of output of the specified product or (which amounts to the same thing), the ratio of the total labour required for the production of a given volume of a homogeneous product to the given volume of that product.' One of the important advantages of the concept of the ratio of output is that the data concerning man-hours per unit of product can be added and substracted whereas the data concerning ratio and output to input cannot be treated quantitatively. Thus in comparing the productivity of labour of two undertakings, only one of which is integrated, man-hours expended per unit of output can be shown for each stage of the production and hence corresponding stages be compared.

Let us take the example of two cotton textile plants. In one only weaving is done. The other performs two functions: spinning and weaving. Our new concept will give us completely separate data for

[4] L. Rostas, *Comparative Productivity in British and American Industry*. National Institute of Economic and Social Research, Occasional Paper, No. 13 (Cambridge University Press, 1948).
[5] For fuller accounts of their views, see H. Seigal, *Concept and Measurement of Productivity* (U.S. Bureau of Labour Statistics, 1952); and D. Evans, 'Recent Productivity Trends and Their Implications', in *Journal of American Statistical Association*, Vol. XLII, June 1947.

spinning as well as weaving functions of the second plant. We will now be able to compare the productivity of weaving plants. (U.S. Works Progress Administration consistently utilized this approach in developing formulae for productivity indices.) This formula, too, neglects the influence of factors other than that of labour.

Dr. Walstedt in his efforts to make his formula all-comprehensive proposed that only those measurements be regarded worthwhile that introduce all factors, separately measure the ratios of capital to output and raw materials input to output or present some combined measurement of all elements of input in relation to output. So sound a theoretical proposal is, however, difficult to put into practice. The most usual and, in many ways, the most important meaning of productivity is that of productivity of labour. ('. . . as a measurement of general efficiency in the use of labour and not of the effort of the labour which latter is obviously too narrow a concept to be of much value'—Dr. Rostas.)

There are manifold reasons for choosing labour productivity as the primary subject of measurement. Its importance is derived from the central position of labour and is particularly appropriate for a society in which, in Marshall's words, man is both 'the end and agent of production'. The other reasons are:

(a) The most important cost factor in all types, branches and sectors of productive activity is labour.
(b) It facilitates quantitative analysis and measurement.
(c) Labour provides general measurement of the economy and efficiency in the use of labour.
(d) It reflects and is influenced by the combined effect of a large number of separate, though interrelated production factors.
(e) The relevance of labour, whether actual or assumed, to wages and costs, to wages and price flexibility and to projections of employment and output.

However, labour productivity cannot be a substitute for all factors and, therefore, no causal relationships could be established. Labour productivity reflects at best the average productivity of labour in a sequence of static equilibrium situations. The information on productivity levels does not give any information on the factors determining these levels.

Extending our analysis of labour productivity measurement and the role of labour as a causal factor in industrial productivity, we find that emphasis on labour as a measurement factor has introduced a confusion about what could be done by workers to increase productivity and has tended to minimize the role of other factors of production. For example, in industries whose cost structure comprise more of material and capital costs and less of direct labour, attention should normally be directed toward economizing materials, fuel, improved production methods, and making better use of the machines. Efforts should also be made to increase the productivity of the capital.

To summarize from the foregoing, it may be concluded that firstly, it is difficult to define, let alone measure, an absolute level of productivity; so we define and measure relative productivity levels; e.g. in comparison with a level achieved in the past or in comparison with a level achieved in another unit in the same industry or in comparison with a level achieved by another nation. Secondly, output per unit of labour is a universal concept for comparing all types of productivity. Alternative concepts are many but their applicability is limited. Thirdly as Dr. Eric Ruist of Sweden and Dr. Walstedt make quite clear, such measurements will not give a manufacturer the most important information he can use—what can lead to the variations in the structure of production costs. Indeed, higher production is not the manufacturer's goal. What interests him most is whether new methods are likely to bring down the costs. Industrial efficiency is the ability to produce at the lowest possible cost, given (a) the product (b) the prices of all available factors—of production, and (c) the quality of all factors other than the single factor of management. Fourthly, despite the apparent conceptual similarity between the concept of man-hours per unit of output and the concept of output per man-hour, the former offers considerable advantages over the latter. The main difference and an apparent advantage of the first concept is that the unit of measurement in the former concept always remains the same whereas the unit in the latter concept is different for every industry, e.g. shoes, automobiles, petroleum, etc. This difference, statistically interpreted, gives an additive character to the first computations which the second can never have. This helps to isolate, interpret and compare the same phases of production processes.

The comparative utilization of manpower by basic organizational function, done by the American Management Association with the co-operation of American industry may, perhaps, be mentioned at this stage as being worthy of further study in the developed as well as the under-developed economies.

III. *Problem in the Measurement of Input and Output*

Input measurement

Labour may be defined broadly as the mental and physical efforts applied during a given period of time. Physical effort could be measured but the quality of effort, particularly the mental effort, is scarcely measurable. The productivity of labour is measured by comparing the labour input and the quantity produced during a given period of time. But we meet here with the difficulty: how can the labour input be measured if not by the quantity produced? The work of the labourer or his effort is not merely mechanical; the choice of the point of application of his effort is of fundamental importance. So even if it were possible to measure physiologically the mechanical effort, how could the corresponding cerebral effort be measured? One has, therefore, to admit that labour input is, in practice, difficult to measure. The obviously measurable factor is the time during which the effort is made. Hence labour is usually measured by the number of man-hours spent. Introduction of time factor in the measurement of unit labour requirements produces unrepresentative indices when technological changes introduced in a production factor do not reduce time for a particular operation, but make it easier to do for the worker and thus increase productivity. Such an increase in productivity would establish wrong causal relations.

Problems again arise in the measurement of labour input when supervising labour, management and even the labour entering into the manufacture of tools used, or the sale of the goods produced have to be taken into account for certain productivity measurements. The following distinctions of labour output are usually made. Operating labour is that required directly in a particular process such as the operation of a brick-moulding machine. Auxiliary labour is that required in the plant for such operations as oiling, inspecting, adjusting and repairing the machine, in short, all plant labour that is necessitated by the use of the equipment but not considered as engaged in its direct operation. Embodied labour is the labour applied to the production of the machine itself and the materials of which it is made, the materials used in machine repairs, the power, oil, grease and other materials consumed in the operation of the machine. Indirectly required labour is the labour required beyond the manufacturing stage, for transportation and marketing. While studies in productivity and labour displacement ordinarily stop short of the point of allowing for all these indirect factors, we should recognize that until they are included we have not ascertained the real change in productivity or the real amount of labour saved or displaced.

The concept of 'hours worked' is very brilliantly defined by Dr. Rostas. In estimating output per worker, we may have in mind either the workers employed in producing the particular product, who are on the books, or the workers on the payroll or the workers actually at work. Workers on the books may include persons who have left the industry altogether; workers on the payroll will perhaps include persons who are absent for part of the week, those who left during the week, or were taken on during the week, or those who went on holidays during the week all of whom worked only part of the week. Workers on the payroll may or may not include those on holiday for the whole week. Workers actually at work would exclude both the absentees and those on holiday and would make allowances for those working only for part of the week. On the other hand, in estimating 'output per man-hour' there will be differences between productive hours and hours paid, and the latter, at least for time workers, includes payment for time spent in meal-breaks and other non-productive occupations. The widest concept is 'output per man-year' inclusive of absentees and those on holidays. This is the most useful concept when estimating national incomes or labour requirements. In measuring productivity technically, output per worker actually at work or output per productive man-hour (the latter is a narrow concept) are relevant. When mastering costs of production 'output per man-hour' is probably an adequate concept.

Thus when measuring productivity with the object of determining the changing value of output in relation to the time actually worked, the productive capacity of labour, or the cost of production in labour units, it is better to use the man-hour concept. When measuring productivity with the purpose of estimating man-power requirements, employment possibilities, future national incomes, etc., the concept of output per man is more appropriate.

A limitation common to all studies of labour productivity is that the labour is treated as a homogeneous entity without any differentiation of age, sex, aptitude, or application of skill. So the concept 'hour of work' is not homogeneous. In this respect, it is well to remember that the 'worker' and the 'man-hour' are statistical abstractions. There is no precise measurement of a unit of labour.

Data on total man-hours worked are collected regularly and comprehensively in very few countries. In most cases only indirect data are available, obtained through various methods which are often not comparable. Dr. Rostas proposes the following alternative input concepts and their measurement.

Monetary Measurements:
  1. Price per unit of output
  2. Total costs per unit of output
  3. Profits per unit of output
  4. Prime costs per unit of output
  5. Wages costs per units of output

Physical Measurements:
  1. Capital per unit of output
  2. Horse power per unit of output
  3. Labour requirement per unit of output
  4. Man-hours unweighted
  5. Man-years unweighted
  6. Man-hours weighted
  7. Man-years weighted.

Analysis of monetary measurements

Costs and prices are affected by many factors (allocation of resources, forms of competition, etc.) among which productive efficiency is only one element. The question also arises of how to eliminate the causes and factors which bear no relation to the phenomenon under review. Since the changes in the resources utilization is profoundly affected by changes in the prices of raw materials or changes in wages or other purely monetary factors, effectiveness of monetary measures for inter-temporal comparisons is seriously curtailed. Similarly, it would not be an ideal instrument for inter-firm comparisons as competitive firms would quote broadly the same price (subject, of course, to minor deviations due to quality differences). It is also inadequate for international comparisons due to the problems in the selection of rate of exchange in terms of the related products and the effect of differences such as wages, raw materials and prices.

Analysis of physical measurements

Two different approaches are widely presented. One suggests that the elements entering input be measured individually and the other prescribes that some aggregate measures of such elements be formulated. It has been argued that various input elements are not supplementary but complementary, that the importance and effectiveness of each varies with the functioning of other elements. Measuring them individually is in many cases more complicated than those involved in the measurement of the productivity of labour.

Aggregations could be effected in two ways: monetary unit, and labour unit. According to Dr. Hiram Davis, for labour time to be taken as fully representative of total resources expended in a productive undertaking, one of two conditions must prevail; either labour time expended must be so large in relation to the other resources that the total is changed appreciably only by changes in the labour item, or changes in other resource inputs must move in the same direction and at the same rate as labour. However, either of the conditions is rarely fulfilled.

Some problems make their appearance in practice. Should labour incorporated in capital equipment be measured by original labour input or by current input relevant to the past technique or by current input relevant to the current technique? Interpretation of such composite measurement of both constant price and man-hour data of all input elements is extremely difficult. It is impossible without the knowledge of the productivity of various elements of input. Also, the labour is treated as a homogeneous entity; differences in skill and knowledge and their application are not considered and, therefore, we cannot measure the degree or quantity of effort expended by the labour force in the production process.

The concept of 'man-hours' is statistically interpreted in more than one way making any data hard to compare. Besides, few countries regularly collect the data necessary for comparison and interpretation.

Output

One important problem is this field is the choice of unit where there are differences arising out of quality of different outputs. Also, while the quality of goods does change in time, it is but one of the several changes which may take place. It seems much more important, when studying production and productivity to emphasize over-all changes in the make-up without limiting the concept of change to the qualitative characteristics to the exclusion of others. Such over-all changes are best described as changes in the product specifications. Such a concept encompasses, at least theoretically, the sum total of all possible variations in the product make-up which may occur over a period of time.

The definition of a product is often predetermined by the classification used by the agency which collected the productivity statistics. The criteria probably used in distinguishing production are physical characteristics, composition, function or use, process of manufacture, unit and aggregate values as compared with those of other recognized primary products of the same industry. Whatever the criterion used, each reported product really represents a number of more or less heterogeneous items or a 'range' within which the gradations may be imperceptible or marked.

'First, to what extent does the given industry make only products described by the name of the industry? That is, what percentage of the total value of products of the industry is represented by its primary (normal) product? Second, of the total production of the commodities described by the name of the industry, what percentage is made within the industry itself? . . . The two questions are inter-related. . . . It should be remembered that the statistics under-state considerably the true amount of overlapping, because many of the units relate to group of industries. Indeed, the combination into particular groups is probably attributable to the large degree of overlapping among these industries.'[6]

When productivity reflects a difference in the degree of integration, industries undertaking the production of semi-manufactures previously obtained from outside sources, the productivity ratio will decline and thus would not give an accurate index of productivity. The suggestion that production be measured in terms of net output instead of physical output overlooks the fact that the value of net output is influenced by many factors other than the actual work done within the plant. Further, an actual change in physical output per man-hour may be partly cancelled when measuring production by the value of net output, by a corresponding change in the selling price. Such may be the case if, in order to sell more goods, the selling price is reduced when the prime cost is reduced, the profit per unit remaining the same. Therefore, the

[6] Solomon Fabricant, as quoted by I.L.O., op. cit., p. 47.

value of net output appears to be a very unsatisfactory measure of output for the purpose of measuring absolute productivity. The above applies more to an industry or a group of industries than to plant-level productivity.

The numerous difficulties raised by the difference from plant to plant of product specifications, degree of integration, and differences in lay-out can be avoided to some extent by the measurement of process rather than the volume of production. Taper defines 'process' as a 'specialized activity which may be used by companies making various products'. A variety of processes are almost always necessary to produce any product and by switching attention from production to process a greater range of comparison becomes possible. Many processes are common to firms making totally different products so that dissimilar companies can compare their efficiency. By the relation of many processes necessary to produce a particular product to a common standard, it is practical to arrive at conclusions regarding the productivity of a firm or the industry as a whole.

Another important problem is the selection of a composite measure for a group of heterogeneous products or a product with different qualities. For example, should the production of a shoe factory be established on the number of pairs of shoes produced whatever their price, or should the low-cost shoes be counted separately? Should the production be divided according to the price of the shoes, considered as representative of their quality? Here, the use of certain weights is called for. The questions involved in weighting are more or less the same encountered in the weighting of the measurement of production *per se*.

The theory of input-output analysis

A relatively new way of looking at an economy is through its national income accounts. The emphasis is on the value added in each of the productive sectors of the economy. Care is taken to eliminate from these accounts all intermediate transactions. Value added analysis look at basic inputs such as labour, land and capital and their contribution to the national income.

The procedure is to take each industry and list all its outputs and their destinations. This is done for all the industries in the economy, and these figures are arranged in a table; the result is an input-output matrix.

The input-output table must divide the economy into a number of 'sectors'. Ideally, the table would have as many sectors as there are different types of activities. In a developed economy the number would be quite large and the calculation prohibitive without computed techniques.

Uses of input-output analysis

The most common use is in the case of an individual industry, to determine its part in the economy.

One important use of input-output analysis is in development planning. The effect of price changes in basic industries can be studied, the effect of increased demand or, inversely, a decline, in demand.

The following table indicates a preliminary analysis of the Nigerian economy containing eleven sectors, prepared by D. N. G. Carter.[7]

TABLE 19(i)   *Preliminary Input-Output Data: Nigeria Fiscal Year 1959–60*
(in million of pounds)

Purchasers

Producers	1	2	3	4	5	6	7	8	9	10	11
1	—	24·1	2·5	2·9	+	0	0	+	0	496·0	10·4
2	·8	—	0	+	0	+	0	7·9	0	36·7	23·4
3	0	0	—	0	0	0	0	0	•0	23·5	+
4	0	0	0	—	0	0	0	0	0	25·9	0
5	0	+	+	+	—	+	1·6	·2	+	3·5	9·4
6	+	·3	·1	·1	·3	—	0	·2	·1	3·7	0
7	0	·2	·2	+	·1	·6	—	·1	·3	91·6	8·9
8	0	0	·1	0	0	0	·7	—	+	30·0	·2
9	·1	·3	·1	+	+	·3	7·7	·2	—	7·4	0
10	3·9	21·8	2·5	10·5	2·3	·1	4·9	5·0	6·2	—	103·8
11	5·6	·9	6·2	·5	2·9	·9	17·2	2·2	3·0	147·3	—

1. Agriculture
2. Agricultural Manufacturing
3. Food, drink, tobacco
4. Textiles and apparel
5. Mining and Oil
6. Utilities
7. Transport
8. Nonmetallic manufacturing
9. Metallic manufacturing
10. Unallocated (including domestic consumption, trade, government)
11. Export-import

+ Small transaction (less than £50,000)
o = No transaction

[7] cf. D. N. G. Carter in, *Managing Economic Development in Africa* (edited by W. H. Hausman), M.I.T. Press.

The author says it is not a true input-output table; and it has been modified to illustrate better the composition of the economy, and further, in its present form, it violates some of the requirements of input-output analysis. Nevertheless it illustrates the application of input-output techniques to the Nigerian economy and also gives some idea of the magnitude of the transfers involved.

IV. *The Measurement of Labour Productivity*

In discussing the subject the following points need to be noted at the outset. The measurement of industrial labour is not possible in all branches of activity due primarily to the fact that complete data cannot be collected. Thus, for the most part industrial productivity indices are ratios of production indices computed for a *limited* number of industries, to labour indices computed also for a limited number of industries. This invites misuse by those who may interpret such a combined index as one representative of industry as a whole. In such industries as bread bakery products, newspapers and periodicals, production index should be regarded as rough approximations because output is measured, not by production figures but by relating it to a basic material that is found to vary, more or less, as the product does. Classification used for production statistics often differs from the one used in labour statistics.[8] Differences in the size of the industries on which the production and labour statistics are based may introduce bias in the conclusion. Many of the deficiencies of this data disappear when use is made of production and labour employment indices specially computed for the purpose of obtaining labour productivity data.

The International Labour Office has offered four general approaches to the solution of measurement problems. 'Firstly, a common approach is to consider the two periods under consideration, the total volume of labour required to produce the same complex of goods, under the conditions prevailing in each period as regard unit labour requirement.'[9] 'A second approach is to consider that the variations of the unit labour requirement for a certain production composite should be an average of individual indices of unit labour requirement.

[8] For example, if in production statistics the classification is based on the criteria of goods produced and in labour statistics classification is based on the main raw material used (e.g. in manufacturing toys and musical instruments from the same raw material—wood or metal) the data will not be comparable.
[9] International Labour Office, *Higher Productivity in Manufacturing Industry*, I.L.O. Geneva, 1954.

In this case the index of each current unit labour requirement as compared to the base period unit labour requirements is computed for each industry, the results are then grouped in an average which may be an arithmetical mean or a weighted average. The weights can be chosen to represent the relative importance of each industry in the total production composite chosen, on the basis of total labour expended, gross or net value of production, or any other factor.'[10] A third approach is to compare the average unit labour requirements needed in the current period in order to produce the current period complex of goods with the average unit labour requirements needed in the base period to produce base period complex, the averages of each period being computed as ratios of the total labour expended to the total production. This will involve a measure of total production for hetero-geneous outputs and thus use of weights for the computation of these total productions. The weights used to measure the current and base period production should be identical; if it were not the case, the individual unit labour requirements for the output of various goods remains unchanged, and the unit labour requirements index would not be equal to one. 'Finally a very common approach to labour production or unit labour requirements measure is to relate variations of the total labour expended in each period to the variation in the total output of each period; or in other words, to compute the ratio of an index of labour to an index of production.'[11] Let us analyse these four basic approaches. In the first case, importance is centred on the complex chosen, for results will directly depend upon such a choice. The choice should be made in relation to and after complete consideration of the specific problem at hand. If computations are made on the basis of the base period production composite, the unit labour requirement index will measure the ratio of the labour that would have been spent in the current period to produce the base period complex of goods to the total labour actually expended in the base period. This is called Formula 1.

If the computations are based on the current period production composite, the unit labour requirement index will indicate the ratio of the labour actually spent to produce the current complex of goods to the labour that would have been spent in the base period to produce the same complex. This is called Formula II.

Notwithstanding the apparent differences, each approach differs

<hr />

[10] Ibid., p. 56.   [11] Ibid., p. 57.

very little from the other. Thus, since the result depends upon the choice of weights, if the weights chosen in Formula II correspond to the amount of labour expended in the base period of the productivity of each industry, the result will be equal to the Formula I. If the weights chosen correspond to the labour that would have been expended to produce the current output of each industry with the individual unit labour requirements of the base period, the result obtained would be similar to the results obtained with Formula II.

Different results are obtained by using Formula I (A—indices with base year man-year weights) and Formula II (B—indices with changing man-hour weights). This illustrates the necessity of computing labour productivity of a group of industries in such a manner that the shifts in the relative importance of each component in the total output will not influence the results of the computation if labour productivity is being considered as a characteristic specific of each industry. And if it is considered that shifts in the relative importance of each component in the total output are inherent variations in labour productivity, the measurements should be made to allow for the influence of such variations.

The specific advantage of each formula is given in the United States Work Progress Administration's Research Project:

'The use of a base year composite has greater significance under relatively stable conditions of production and is usually more appropriate in dealing with relatively short periods of time, it has the advantage of permitting comparisons between any two years, since the changes in the required volume of labour in each year are measured relatively to the same base year composite. The use of a changing composite does not theoretically permit year to year comparisons and can only be used to measure the change between the base year and any other year. Such an index has analytical value particularly in periods of major shifts in the composition of production, and is usually more suitable for studying relative periods'.[12]

The computation of data on the basis of Formula I or II involves two types of measurements. First, the total labour expended to produce the complex of one of the periods with the unit labour requirement of that period; second, the total labour required to produce the complex of the periods with unit labour requirements of the other period. Usually data for the latter measurements, even for few products are difficult to obtain.

[12] *Production Employment and Productivity in 59 Manufacturing Industries 1919–1936.* op. cit. 1939. Part I, p. 13.

In general, although fairly detailed production data can be obtained, the available employment statistics refer to workers engaged in the manufacturing of aggregates of more or less related products. Consequently, the productivity index can, in almost every instance, be constructed only as the quotient of a production index for a group of products and the corresponding labour index. Substitute weights such as value added per unit price are therefore used.

Thus the two general concepts outlined above are different. However, neither is essentially better than the other. Careful attention should be paid to the choice and wherever the data is made public the choice should be made known. The theoretical advantage of an index computed on a fixed weight base, lies in the fact that it measures but a single element of change to the exclusion of others. Yet the use of such a formula does not prevent the confusion of many factors, each of which changes in time, and several of them may possess peculiar patterns of their own. So long as such influences are not eliminated, and the index reflects more than one element of the dynamic changes which take place in the economy (including those which are responsible for the growth in the production of some goods and the decline in others) it would be of great significance for economic analysis. Such an index would reflect changes in the relative importance of the different products as they make their appearance. An index number so constructed then could be described, in terms of its significance, as the index of manpower utilization (measured in units of time input) needed at different times to produce a unit of physical output in accordance with specifications, efficiency and the nature of economic organization at each of the periods under consideration.

'Thus labour productivity data obtained by the division of production figures (or indices) measured *per se* (i.e. weighted by net value, price, etc.) by employment of labour figures or indices, corresponds to the second (and larger) concept of productivity of labour in which all factors of variation have their influence including those due to the changes in the composition of production. In particular, when the total output of the nation as compared to total employment or total man-hours expended, is implicitly or explicitly considered; since gross national product, for instance, is a production complex weighted by value added.'[13]

Depending on the problem at hand many formulae may be developed

[13] I.L.O., op. cit., p. 68.

for the measurement of industrial productivity. This has been true for all economic or statistical measurements. 'Even with ideal data a number of plausible productivity indices may be constructed. Our choice is reduced to one of those many alternatives only when the question asked about productivity changes is so specific as to be equivalent to a verbalization of only one of the many possible indices'.[14]

V. Economy and Nation-wide Estimates of Productivity

The total input as an aggregate of undifferentiated work time expended in production is measured by determining the total number of man-hours or man-years of effort entering the national product for a given period. This is computed by relating the total number of employed members of the labour force (including all degrees of skill and all kinds of persons engaged in productive operations) with the average length of the work-week or work-year. The estimates of the total volume of employment are based upon monthly surveys, which are blown up to cover the whole economy.

Real national product is measured by estimating total output in terms of current monetary unit value and then 'deflating' the elements of this total to correct for the effect of price changes. Changes in total real national production as ratios to changes in total labour input gives indices of production.

Since the basic data are often prone to different interpretations, and complete accuracy of the data available being questionable, they are subject to wide margins of variability and almost impossible to standardize. Neither is any precise measurement of errors available. Data collected in the earlier years is frequently more untenable. The accuracy of estimates of national product as indices of *change* from year to year, or decade to decade, is greater than their accuracy in absolute terms. However, as in correcting for fluctuations in prices, we can be reasonably accurate in data for some economic processes. The deflation procedure is far more accurate in peacetime than in abnormal economic upheavals of war-time. Usually, the margin of error for war-time is far wider. Thus, our measurements are always rough approximations. However, indications of major changes may be accepted with more confidence than the indications of minor changes and short-period movements.

[14] Evans, D., *Recent Productivity Trends and Their Implications*. Journal of American Statistical Association. Vol. XLII, June 1947.

The product of many governmental services (e.g. armed forces) cannot be measured in any satisfactory way, except by equating them to corresponding labour input. This assumes no change over time in production. The same is true with some of the service industries in the private sector of the economy. Continuous change in the composition and quality of many of the goods entering into national product also introduces difficulties in the formulation of production indices. Since the importance of intermediate goods sector for one country differs from the importance in other countries and since, even in one country it changes in different periods of time, such goods shall have to be excluded from the output. Some of the other problems are:

(a) the lack of comparable price series for some industries;
(b) the problem involving the purchase of materials by one segment from another; and
(c) when the increase of production of labour in a plant is due to a technical improvement which results in the dismissal of a number of workers, it might be considered that the nation's production has actually increased only if those dismissed workers have been re-employed. Otherwise their 'productivity' is nil: and when combined with the increased production of the plant, may show no improvements in the nation's production.

It follows, therefore, that firstly, only in long-term trends and in indicating the magnitude of major changes, will actual changes in production reasonably exceed the margins of error. Therefore, short period movements or year to year changes may not be measurable. Secondly, for war periods or periods marked by great changes in the structure of a nation's economy, the margins of error in global production measures will be substantially greater than for periods during which structural changes are modest. Thirdly, in the construction of productivity measures for a national economy few of the many variables that may affect the ratio of output to effort input can be held constant. There is little opportunity, therefore, to disentangle the diverse factors that affect industrial productivity, or to attribute causal roles to specific factors. And fourthly, in the study of economic development, measures of changes in the ratio of output to effort input are tools of great value. They can illuminate the past; projected, they help to define expected resources needs in normal growth or in contemplated changes. The industrial productivity of a nation is generally based on gross national product per worker or man-hour, or real national income per head. Gathering of such data is involved and complex, and is often subject to differing interpretations. Gross National Product is computed in 'real' terms by deflating it in current monetary unit for each expenditure segment by approximate price series.[15] In addition to the difficulties already noted, it should be observed that estimates for long periods are very inaccurate and that the deflation of the price element may be hindered by the absence of accurate deflators.

[15] 'GNP per worker or per man-hour is not a measure of production efficiency, primarily because the measure is affected by changing patterns of production from year to year.' Evan, D., *Recent Productivity Trends and Their Implication*. Journal of American Statistical Association. Vol. XLII. June 1947.

20

Developments in the Search for Higher Productivity in Africa

P. A. L. Chukwumah

DIRECTOR, INTER-AFRICAN LABOUR INTITUTE, BRAZZAVILLE
(COMMISSION FOR TECHNICAL CO-OPERATION IN AFRICA)

I. *Historical Background*

The recommendations adopted by the Third Session of the Inter-African Labour Conference in 1953 constituted perhaps the first concerted attempt by a group of countries[1] then having authority in Africa to search for means of improving productivity on the continent, South of the Sahara. The item then reviewed by this conference was the 'Preliminary Consideration of Methods of initiating the study of productivity'. Taking the view that specific factors affecting productivity and labour relations in Africa were mainly to be found on the 'human side', this third conference drew attention to particular factors, viz:

'certain objective influences: nutrition, disease, climate;
psychological and social factors: motives in life, attitude to work and wealth, tradition, customs, tribal security, sense of 'belonging', prestige, sense of responsibility, education;
economic factors: discipline of industrial life, concept of time, supervision.'

and expressed the view that certain items were of immediate and urgent importance. These were:

'Incentives, motives, workers' status, attitudes to work;
Attitudes to working with, or for, members of other racial or tribal groups;
Diet and efficiency;
Effects of climate (e.g. high temperature) on sustained work;

[1] Belgium, France, Portugal, Southern Rhodesia, Republic of South Africa and the United Kingdom.

Labour instability, particularly among migrant labour;

Status and influence of women in African society, particularly on attitudes to work and standards of living.'

In these first attempts to define areas of general and immediate action, it stands out that in the production triangle, the points of which are the employers, the worker and the environment, attention was focused on the second element and on those aspects of the third, with the exception of 'supervision', which attach to the worker. The employer himself was left out as well as those aspects of the environment for which he is alone or mainly responsible.

II. *Survey of Human Factors of Productivity*

As a practical investigational approach, a special Working Party was later established to draw up the questionnaire which was circulated to African territories of Member Governments of C.C.T.A. Their replies which were summarized by the governments formed the basis of a working paper presented by the Inter-African Labour Institute to the Fourth Session of the Inter-African Labour Conference (Beira, 1955). A fuller synthesis of the information then gathered was published by the Institute under the title, 'The Human Factors of Productivity in Africa —A Preliminary Survey'. The publication, however, included not only the reports supplied by Member Governments, but 'much of the original material furnished by some of the territories on which those reports were based, supplemented by other contributions to the subjects'. A broad summary of the conclusions which could be drawn from the comments of the then competent countries on the items on which the survey was conducted is as tabulated on page 302[2].

The broad conclusions constituted no more than a 'mere stock-taking' of existing knowledge flowing out of the practical experience of government officials, their advisers and employers. On the basis of this survey, the fourth Inter-African Labour Conference, among other things,[3]

recommended that while campaigns against endemic diseases should be concentrated in areas of growing economic development, preventive aspects of medical work should be stressed in areas from which workers originate;

[2] Taken from *The Human Factors of Productivity*.
[3] *Human Factors of Productivity*, op. cit., Appendix B.

TABLE 20 (i) *Summary of Conclusions on Productivity in Africa: Inter-African Labour Conference, 1955.*

Subjectory Comment	Broad Conclusions
Health-effect of a balanced cooked meal on productivity	There was a unanimous view that balanced diet was of vital importance and that weak physique arising from malnutrition adversely affected the productivity of the African worker.
Climate	Although extreme high or low temperature affected output adversely cold had greater adverse effect on the African worker than heat. Manual work was adversely affected by excessive humidity in summer or at high temperature.
Cultural and mental factors conditioning attitude to work	Tribal economy and existing cultural and traditional life failed to provide the mental attitude for higher productivity achieved in industrial societies.
Human relations	Joint consultation was almost invariably found very difficult at the initial phase, first because the African did not understand its purpose and limitations, secondly owing to the scepticism and lack of sympathy of employers. In general, better results were obtained from homogeneous than mixed racial or tribal groups. Satisfactory management-worker relations depended on the personality, capacity and example of the supervisor. Too often the supervisor was ill-selected, ill-equipped and untrained for his responsibilities.
Management, Organizations and Public Policy	Selection of labour was normally based on alleged 'previous experience'. For entry into trade schools educational qualification was demanded. Belgian and French rapid trade training centres applied psychotechnical tests and these proved effective. Proficiency tests and certificates were not widely in vogue. Neither the adaptation of worker to tools nor vice-versa was widely studied.
Accidents, Industrial Diseases and Preventive Measures	Africans were in general no more and no less prone than other races to industrial accidents, but their relative unfamiliarity with tools and machines in movement made them more vulnerable in their early days of employment. Industrial diseases had scarcely begun to appear. Various methods of accident prevention which were practised were 'successful on condition of treating their themes simply and in an *African* context'.

drew attention to the importance of medical services for workers and considered periodic medical examination of workers desirable; recommended that all possible means be employed to educate workers in the use of proper diets and that appropriate commodities for such diets are readily obtainable;

considering that abnormally low wages result in the persistence of low productivity, recommended that guaranteed minimum wages, where established, should take account of the vital needs of the workers;

recommended that all appropriate means be used to facilitate the technical advancement of the worker;

recommended that in the selection of managers and supervisors, attention be paid not only to technical qualification but to appropriate qualities of character and, where necessary, selected managers and supervisors be instructed on the social and economic conditions of the area in which they would be employed;

recommended that in the case of African supervisors appropriate remuneration and other conditions of employment be offered them such as would help them to maintain their authority;

recommended that the Advisory Committee of I.L.I., assisted by experienced experts, should define areas and patterns of further investigation, also direct and supervise such studies which should be synthesized by the Director of I.L.I. for the fifth Inter-African Labour Conference.

III. *Absenteeism and Labour Turnover*

Taking note of the recommendations of the Fourth Inter-African Labour Conference, the Fourth Advisory Committee of the Inter-African Labour Institute (1956) authorized that a general investigation be undertaken defined as a 'Study of human factors capable of minimizing Absenteeism and Labour Turnover and of providing the maximum incentive to greater efficiency in output'. The project, expected to include research in the territories of all member-Governments was to cover the following industries:

building and works of construction
factories
mines
plantations

It is to be noticed that the nature of the terms of reference implicitly assumed that the existing rates of absenteeism and labour turnover in Africa were more than normal and that the phenomena constituted a drag on the achievement of higher levels of productivity.

The next I.L.I. Advisory Committee recommended the setting up of a committee of six experts, commissioned by Member Governments, to draw up a technical plan to work on the subject of absenteeism and labour turnover. The Committee of Experts began its work in Salisbury in 1956. As a preamble to its agreed technical plan it adopted the following statement:

> 'This Committee considers in the light of its own discussions and the published findings of the Fourth Inter-African Labour Conference that the Human Factors influencing the productivity of African Labour are mainly the following:
>
> (a) skill—deriving from aptitude, training and experience;
> (b) will to work—deriving from individual, physical, environmental and social factors. The latter relate both to the social environment of the working groups and to the large community in which the group functions;
> (c) managerial interests and practices—these are mainly factors that determine good human relations and effectiveness of supervision.

The Committee considers that two of the most important symptoms of poor work motivations are absenteeism and labour turnover. On common sense grounds, the Committee believes these to have a very appreciable effect on productivity. The Committee therefore decided to concentrate on the formulation of research projects on absenteeism and labour turnover in the belief that by gaining an understanding of their causation, it will ultimately be possible to recommend adequate remedies.

> 'The Committee considers further that in addition to projects concerning absenteeism and labour turnover the importance of the following should not be overlooked:
>
> (a) investigations into the practicability of applying aptitude tests to African labour,
> (b) the usefulness of applying various methods of training off and on the job,
> (c) studies on the effects and desirability of wage and other incentives,

(d) techniques of personnel management, particularly those of supervision as a means of improving productivity and maintaining work morale.

The Committee has so framed its plan of research on absenteeism and labour turnover, that the preliminary conclusions concerning the other topics it has mentioned and useful points for the formulation of further research concerning them are likely to emerge.'

The Committee ran into an early difficulty because some of its members signified that they would not be prepared to recommend research into Government Departments in the territories of their governments. A Government also wished to exclude mining in her territory on the ground that research was already in progress there. Although these reservations ran counter to the intentions of the Fourth Advisory Committee of I.L.I., they did not, as would be observed later, prevent the achievement of conclusions of satisfactory general applicability.

Following its several meetings the Committee of Experts reached agreement on a standard presentation of reports to be transmitted by Research Directors to the I.L.I. for synthesis and submission to the Sixth Inter-African Labour Conference. Discussions were held on various elements of research including such matters as method of calculating absenteeism and labour turnover, definition of labour categories, in terms of skill, wages or any other criteria and problems of group relations. With the outlines agreed on, each Research Director took charge of investigations in the area controlled by his government. His final report and conclusions were then forwarded to the I.L.I. In practice, research covered a wider field of industries than those specifically named by the Fourth Advisory Committee of I.L.I.

In the paper[4] presented to the Sixth Inter-African Labour Conference on the research, it was reported that in the course of investigations it had become evident that:

'absenteeism and labour turnover were proving to be quantitatively less important, at any rate in urban areas, than had generally been supposed. This emerged not only from the five research programmes based on the "Salisbury Plan, but also from the empirical investiga-

[4] CCTA document *Labour VI (61) 35* of 8.3.61.

tion carried out at two centres in Nigeria without the use of the formulae and methods adopted at Salisbury''.

'The Rates of Absenteeism and Labour Turnover, particularly absenteeism, have been shown to be much less than was commonly supposed before this investigation began. With some exceptions[5] the verified rates prove to be not dissimilar to those experienced in technologically-advanced countries and amongst industrially-sophisticated populations, in other countries. This clears away many misconceptions and is the most important single result of the research.'

The misconception was very deep indeed, as could be observed both in the direction for research charted by the Fourth Advisory Committee (research was to show means of 'minimizing' absenteeism and labour turn-over) and in the preamble to the technical plan of research adopted by the Committee of Experts. It was, however, to the credit of this Committee that whatever their own misconception might have been it did not prevent them from drawing objective conclusions from their empirical investigations.[6]

IV. Level of Productivity of the African Worker

Having considered and noted the above conclusions of the absenteeism and labour turnover team of experts, the Sixth Inter-African Labour Conference considered that opinions also widely held about levels of productivity of the African worker might likewise prove incorrect on examination. In response to further wishes of this conference, the Advisory Committee of I.L.I. decided that meetings of employers should be convened in early 1963 at national levels in Congo (Leopoldville), Lagos (Nigeria) and Kampala (Uganda). Although Government representatives were to participate, the purpose of these meetings would be for employers to compare their experience on the level of productivity, providing as much information as possible on whether the level of productivity of the African worker was low. The Committee rejected the organization of a research as an immediate point of take-off. In its view the organization of such research would depend on whether the national level pilot meetings did, indeed, establish the need for such a venture.

[5] Ibid.
[6] See CCTA Publication No. 69, *Absenteeism and Labour Turnover*, for a comprehensive report on the research and the Sixth Inter-African Labour Conference.

The wisdom of the cautious approach of the Committee is obvious, not only in view of the results of research on absenteeism and labour turnover, but from the fact that the observations and comments of employers as active agents in the field were vital for starting a research. If, for example, meetings of employers in different parts of Africa independently arrived at conclusions suggesting that research in the field was unlikely to be of significant value, then the energies of government might better be directed to other elements of the productive scene.

It was unfortunate that the Leopoldville national meeting could not be held owing to environmental factors. The employers' organization has said that 'the whole problem of labour in the Congo and notably productivity finds itself actually dominated by factors strange to labour itself, corollaries to continued political and economic situation which was becoming more and more alarming. At this time these factors camouflage those very real problems which merit our attention and occupy all the energies of employers who try to minimize their effects. Thus their attention is turned away in a very decisive manner from problems such as productivity.'

The Nigeria and Uganda meetings were guided by the concept of 'Productivity' defined in an I.L.O. publication 'African Labour Survey', viz:

'Productivity in the widest sense can be defined as the ratio between output and all the resources used in production, i.e. capital, labour, raw material, etc. The problem of raising output is one of making the most efficient use of all the resources available.'

The managers of industries who attended the meetings considered technical, organizational as well as individual worker factors, e.g. health, intelligence, sensory motor activity, response to training, absenteeism. Discussions covered the following points:

Broad outline of firm's background including general information on products.

Extent to which machines and equipment used are similar to those used elsewhere, e.g. in kind and degree of demand for manual or non-manual operation.

Whether production targets are set; if so, whether this is done solely on the basis of knowledge of performance of local workers, or on experience elsewhere or on both.

Whether existing machines are used to full production capacity;

M.P.D.N.—11*

or, if not, the extent to which this situation is due to the low performance of workers, and to the capacity of the existing market to absorb products.

Suitability of skill of local labour on engagement, availability of training schemes and response of learners to such training.

If Africans are employed in managerial or supervisory positions, whether significant differences were observed between their effectiveness and that of their expatriate colleagues.

Whether trade unionism or consultative schemes operate in the organization.

Any special features noticed as inhibiting performance of workers and items to which it is thought attention should be given in any move to improve the existing level of productivity.

The tables on pages 309 and 310 show a condensed picture of the two meetings.

In addition to the conclusions on factors affecting the level of productivity (see pp. 309-10), an independent research carried out in Nigeria in 1960 by Mr. P. Kilby had challenged certain popular statements on African labour productivity and arrived at the following conclusions:

the African does not possess any inherent incapacities or attitudes which are detrimental to efficient production;
the African's willingness to work is not lower than observations in developed economies;
while because of his environmental background there are certain facets of machine operation and maintenance which the African does not 'naturally adapt to', training will rectify such shortcomings;
careful selection, monetary incentive and surveillance from higher management will reduce supervisory weaknesses to negligible proportions;
the empirically relevant determinants of labour productivity are various management functions, e.g. organization of work process, supervision and production control, planning and co-ordination of work process, provision of incentive and maintenance of plant and equipment.

Another independent fieldwork carried out by Mr. Poupart in Elizabethville, Congo (Leopoldville), came to much the same conclusions as Mr. Kilby. Finally the report of the Committee of Experts

TABLE 20(ii) *Summary of Lagos Seminar on Productivity, 1963*[7]

The meeting was attended by seven representatives of Ministries of Federal and Regional Governments, six employers representatives of private industries and the Director of the Inter-African Labour Institute.

Industries represented	Main factors selected as affecting level of productivity in Africa	Conclusions and Recommendations
	General Facts	*Conclusions*
Asbestos	Relative skill of workers. Facilities for improving skill.	Nigerians are able to achieve high
Cement	Facilities for acquiring experience.	levels of productivity.
Vehicle Assembly	System of wage payment and incentive schemes. Demand for industry's product. Security of employment.	In similar systems of production the Nigerian's achievements are
Pepsi-Cola	Layout of factory, heat control and ventilation. Adequate supervision.	not inferior to those of his counterpart in Europe.
Portland Cement	Management-Worker relations. Health and nutrition of workers. Provision of transport and factors	*Recommendations* That the research planned by the
Brewery	which reduce incidence of fatigue. Co-operative attitude towards trade unions	Nigerian National Manpower Board for the purpose of
Timber and Plywood	Fullest national support for Local industries.	advising Government and employers on improving general level of productivity in the
	Local Factors	country's key industries should
	Increased family commitments associated with rise in income. Lack of skill and industrial experience. Health, nutrition and fatigue.	bear in mind factors such as lack of skill, effect of health, nutrition, fatigue, systems of wage payment and incentives.

[7] For full report, cf. *Report on Nigerian National Seminar on Productivity in Selected Industries* (12–14 February 1963), Federal Ministry of Information, Lagos, 1964.

TABLE 20(iii) *Summary of Kampala Conference on Productivity, 1963*[8]

This meeting was attended by three representatives of Government Ministries, eight private employers, the Chairman of the East African Institute of Social Research, University College of Makerere, and the Director of the Inter-African Labour Institute.

Industries represented	Main conclusions of factors influencing level of productivity	Other Conclusions and Recommendations
	General	*Conclusions*
Textiles	Standard of equipment and material. Factory lay-out, lighting, heat control.	The Ugandan has been found capable of achieving the same levels of productivity as achieved elsewhere.
Tobacco	Experience of supervisors. Quality of supervision. Proper work study including time and motion assessments.	In processes similar to those used elsewhere, the African with sufficient training and experience achieves similar
Sugar	Effective selection methods.	results.
Cement	Proper training in depth and breadth. Degree of worker's experience. Industrial relations including communication.	The pressing need is thus to attend to general and local factors in the second column rather than organization of research on the level of productivity of the African
Tea	Demand for product.	worker.
	Particular Local Factors	*Recommendations*
Mining	Tribal conflict among workers. Kinship duties and obligations. Lack of mechanical environment in local setting. Lack of industrial consciousness. Health, nutrition, fatigue.	Wide circulation by Government of these conclusions to workers and employers. Periodic organization of meeting of workers and employers by Government on identified general and local factors. Expansion of Labour Department's middle-grade training to include supervisory skills. Employers to pay careful attention to identified general and local factors. Co-operation of Government and East African Institute of Social Research in the examination of identified local factors.

[8] c.f. C.C.T.A. document L(63) 49 of 6 June 1963 for full report.

on Absenteeism and Labour Turnover placed before the Sixth Inter-African Labour Conference said that it became evident in the course of research that 'the role of management and supervision, in providing working conditions, wage structures, etc., likely to attract a stable labour force, merited closer attention.'

V. *Conclusions*

In so far as there has been a departure from the broad hypothetical worker-oriented elements identified as most important and needing urgent attention by the Third Inter-African Labour Conference, empirical investigations strongly point to the fact that management functions on the productive scene and public policies are much more important. Given favourable conditions there is really nothing to choose between the achievements of the African and those of his counterparts elsewhere. In addition to such evidences as appear in these papers, both the Anglo-American teams on Levels of Productivity and the Ghana National Productivity Conference, 1963, emphasized elements which are almost entirely management functions.[9]

A breakdown of the productivity field in Africa would show three main areas. First, there is the area of technical and organizational factors. These include physical conditions of work, selection, induction and training arrangements, supervision, fatigue-defeating and morale-boosting practices and worker-management relations. These are predominantly areas of action for management. However, governments can obviously influence the readiness of employers to take appropriate action on some of these factors through the enactment of basic laws (e.g. factory laws) which are sufficiently wide and deep.

Secondly, there is the area of national action. Among these are health measures in factories, as well as in urban and rural areas. Of course, action would include effective campaign at right points in the rural and urban settings to minimize chances of failure of any government programmes. Another field for government action is workers' education, not merely on trade unionism but on carefully selected themes on the industrial scene. Also government services could provide information on training methods and establish centres for supervisor courses either as separate institutions or encourage such courses as are attached to established institutions of higher learning. Finally, government policy could do a lot in effecting a re-orientation in school curricula with a

[9] See *III Information Sheet*, Vol. V, No. 2 for April 1963, pp. 8 and 9.

view to encouraging technical mindedness and industrial consciousness.

Thirdly, there is the area which one might broadly call the social
milieu. This includes industrial consciousness, traditional elements,
effects of extended family system on income and propensity to work,
inter-tribal relations and their effect on the work scene. While some
of these elements are bound to be affected by actions taken on the two
areas already broadly defined as those for employers' and government
attention, they are on the whole elements which will tend to alter with
the changing pattern of society. Already the emergence of industrial
society in Africa, as could be seen in urban areas, is creating a population of Africans whose mental disposition has shifted from the rural
level pattern. Explanations for this are fairly obvious.

The message in the various activities dealt with in this paper is that
both Government and employers should take measures such as those
broadly analysed above to equip the African worker for the work which
industrial society calls on him to perform.

21

Summary of Discussion and Conclusions (V)

1. On the basis of the papers presented, the Seminar considered a number of specific questions as follows:

   (i) What should be the concept of productivity for the Nigerian economy?

   (ii) Is the National Manpower Board the appropriate place for the location of work relating to productivity movement?

   (iii) When a suitable set-up is established for improving productivity, what should be the priority of work?

   (iv) What should be the role of large-scale industry in productivity improvement? What should be the relationship between such industries and the productivity organization to be set up?

   (v) What are the implications of the productivity movement on manpower problems?

2. Some related questions were also discussed. In these discussions, the Seminar was of the view that the concept of productivity was of universal application and that the stage of development had no special relevance in this respect. It was thus agreed that the concept of productivity in Nigeria is the same as anywhere else, in which the manpower element was of overriding importance. Essentially, however, the aim of a productivity movement should be to provide more and better quality goods and services at a lower price to the people of Nigeria.

3. The Seminar emphasized that productivity is partly a problem of attitudes of mind, and any movement to improve productivity should be based on a preparation of the people to accept change. In this context the role of proper incentives, mainly through adequate wage levels, was recognized. In particular, it was suggested that offer of incentives to persons to translate ideas—innovations, etc.—into specific work programmes is a necessity, particularly in the early stages of promoting a

313

productivity movement. Any agency which is set up for this purpose should see to it that public opinion is geared to accepting its recommendations to employers and workers, and that innovations are encouraged through suitable incentives. The Seminar recognized that in a developing economy it should be possible, as has been possible in many countries, to improve productivity without an undue increase in the use of capital per worker. Much improvement in productivity can be achieved even without advanced high-level specialized knowledge. The application of relatively simple techniques of investigation and analysis combined with normal common sense, is often sufficient to achieve very substantial results. It is only for the higher stage of improvement that the highly specialized experts would be necessary. Case studies based on such successful productivity experiments should be sought and publicized.

4. The Seminar endorsed the view that while the workers have an important role in improving productivity, a far greater responsibility lies with the management. The primary urge for improvement has to come from the management and this should express itself in seeking co-operation from workers to improve productive effort in the larger interest of the firm as well as for himself, and in the overall interest of the economy. For this purpose, programmes for workers' education and, more importantly, management education, require to be suitably developed. In fact, in many countries, this has been the manner in which productivity improvement has been initially made possible. A stage is then reached when workers' demand for improving their living conditions have made managements productivity conscious and have compelled them to seek trade union co-operation in this field. This co-operation appears not to have developed sufficiently in Nigeria, and it will be prudent to give attention to this aspect right now in view of the need for accelerating the rate of economic development.

5. Apart from the general consciousness about productivity which the relevant programme should generate in all members of the community, more specific action is required, sectorwise, because each sector of the economy has its own peculiarities of manpower development, its own ratios of capital/employment, and capital/output, etc. Generalization in this area will, therefore, often lead to an over-simplification of the problems. In terms of sectors the Seminar indicated (a) agriculture, (b) industries, (c) Government work, (d) teaching profession, as suitable for initial attention. In each case the importance

of training at all levels was emphasized, for those who work as well as for those who have to plan and supervise the work done.

6. In regard to the methods to be used, the Seminar recognized that the general approach must be multi-dimensional, through

(a) organization;
(b) production planning;
(c) plant layout;
(d) work studies;
(e) material handling;
(f) maintenance;
(g) production control;
(h) quality control;
(i) safety measures;
(j) human relations;
(k) incentive systems, etc.

But within this general framework of ways for improving productivity a combination of one or more factors, with changes for different sectors in terms of application, would be necessary.

7. The Seminar took note of the Nigerian experience summarized in the conclusions of the Productivity Seminar in 1963.[1] The importance of agriculture to the Nigerian economy made it necessary that early emphasis be given to programmes for improving efficiency in agriculture. The question of improvement and standardization of tools, and adequate distribution of fertilizers and insecticides was mentioned. Different types of problems were usually encountered, however, between plantations, on the one hand, and small farms, on the other; and similarly in respect of large industries as against small-scale enterprises.

8. Essentially, the problem of plantations and large industries were somewhat similar and those of handicrafts, village industries and small-scale agriculture as undertaken by farmers' families fall in a different category. The tertiary sector of trade, commerce, transport and allied services could be similarly differentiated.

9. In the initial stages of work in the field of productivity, considerable emphasis will need to be given to the promotional aspect, i.e. popularizing the movement. This should receive the early attention of the appropriate agency. The need for diffusion and devolution of this work up to the Regional level should be borne in mind. Experience of

---

[1] *Report on Nigerian National Seminar on Productivity in Selected Industries*, op. cit.

other countries has shown that with an active Central agency, it is possible to energize the smaller constituents at the regional and unit levels for improving efficiency.

10. In agriculture, small or large scale, the Seminar recognized the need for improving hand-tools in various processes; the possibility of improvising small tractors was also mentioned. Some participants felt, however, that this was a secondary problem and that the main goal at present should be the maximization of output from agriculture by increasing the output per acre, rather than displacing labour by introducing tractors. It was further suggested that there might have been certain factors in the traditional methods of agriculture which probably made it more attractive in the past than it is today. These require exploration. The Farm Institutes set up in Nigeria should be harnessed for studying the possibilities in this direction and a general plan of action should be drawn up by the central productivity organization with the help of productivity experts. Along with agriculture, productivity consciousness should also be aroused in respect of those engaged in forestry, fisheries and other primary production.

11. The large-scale industries recently established in Nigeria appeared to be highly productivity conscious. It was felt, nevertheless, that it would be in their own interests also to assist in stimulating improvements in the general level of productivity by imparting such of their experiences as would be useful to others. Large-scale employers should, therefore, invite persons interested in productivity problems to study their experience for wider dissemination. The productivity teams organized by the central agency usually benefit immensely from the experience of the more efficient plants.

12. Two points were specifically mentioned with regard to small industries: (a) the need for improved tools, and (b) the need for improved accounting techniques among small entrepreneurs. Apart from these, the usual application of job analysis, time and motion studies, job methods and job relations which are in use in larger units, require to be adapted for small scale producers. Work on these lines has been done with some success in India, in the Productivity Centre and in the Small-Scale Service Institutes. The Seminar considered that it would be useful for Nigeria to seek to benefit from this experience of India, as well as of other countries.

13. Apart from these specific considerations, massive training programmes at all levels—through seminars, study groups, short-term

courses for selected personnel—will require to be organized. For this purpose, technical experts will be needed in different areas of the productivity movement. It will be equally necessary to constitute well chosen teams from within the country to visit selected countries where productivity techniques have sufficiently advanced.

14. The Seminar felt that the maximization of productivity in those Government departments responsible for the general administration and development of the country must be actively sought—for a variety of reasons, of which the following are particularly compelling:

(a) Inefficient administration can severely hamper the work of all industrial enterprises, whether public or private; for example, excessive time and effort spent on unnecessarily protracted processing of properly authenticated accounts and claims, of approving plans, licences and other permits, of bases of taxation, etc., is time and effort diverted from the main national task of accelerated economic development.

(b) Wasteful internal procedures, whether resulting from outdated techniques, or from the workings of Parkinson's law, or from excessive counterchecking, etc., tie up a significant body of manpower which may be desperately needed elsewhere.

(c) Evident efficiency of Government administration sets, by example, the pace of much of the national life. A poor example can only lead to frustration and stagnation.

15. Similar considerations apply to industries under Government control, whether existing as statutory corporations or integrated in a Ministry as in the case of Posts and Telegraphs. Most of these nationalized industries exist to provide vital services—electric power, airways, railways, communications, harbour facilities, etc.—and anything short of maximum productivity and efficiency will prejudice any efforts made elsewhere in industry and agriculture.

16. The Seminar discussed at length the agency which should normally undertake productivity work at the national level in Nigeria. Irrespective of where this agency is located, the Seminar felt that it is essential that it should include respresentatives of Governments— Federal and Regional; employers, workers, technical institutions, and public men interested in the movement, etc. The National Manpower Board which is at present expected to undertake these functions has a somewhat similar composition. A view was therefore expressed that

it would be useful to recommend to Government to consider whether, and in what manner, the National Manpower Board could more effectively promote the productivity movement. The Seminar also saw, however, that there may be difficulties in associating the Productivity agency too closely and directly with a Government department, especially in view of the necessity to ensure the continuous co-operation and participation of private employers.

17. It is recognized that in the early stages of the productivity movement, public funds will be required for the purpose. A productivity agency, however, has a self-sustaining potential if it is adequately organized and permitted to charge fees for its services. This reinforces the argument for a semi-independent productivity agency. The Government should examine how such an arrangement can be effected. It has been possible in some countries to provide public funds for the running of such productivity organizations on an independent basis but with some form of Government control.

18. The Seminar discussed at some length the implications of the productivity movement on planning for manpower. In the very nature of things, it was recognized that improved efficiency would mean the raising of workers to a higher level of skill. Apart from the better personnel developed for different productive occupations for reaching a higher level of efficiency, the productivity centre itself would require high-level manpower in various subject categories for the purposes mentioned in paragraph 6 above. Though in the long-run improved productivity will help in raising levels of employment, at the very early stages of the movement, it will be necessary to have some stand-by arrangements for re-deploying persons likely to be rendered surplus as a result of the productivity drive in specific areas.

19. The Seminar also considered certain related points like health, nutrition, working and living conditions of workers, wage incentives, association of workers in job analysis, trade union recognition and the effect of working hours on productivity. In the light of this discussion, the Seminar recommended that greater attention should be paid to better wages as well as to the working and living conditions of the workers.

20. In the light of the foregoing considerations, the Seminar made the following recommendations:

(a) Considering that the aim of the productivity movement is to bring about better living conditions for all, an important objective of policy should be a reduction in the relative costs of output and an increase in the wages of labour. In order to achieve this it is necessary that an atmosphere should be built up within the community for improved efficiency. Suitable literature should be developed for this purpose along with other publicity avenues like newspapers, films, public discussions, etc.

(b) There should be a simultaneous drive for improved productivity in different sectors of the economy. The components in each may be different, but the ultimate aim will be the same.

(c) National experience about improvement in productivity should be publicized through case studies and by organizing national productivity teams.

(d) International agencies should be utilized to provide facilities for well-selected Nigerian productivity teams to visit different countries to study various aspects of productivity movement.

(e) Promising young men should be recruited for individual training in specified aspects of the productivity movement, first within the country, and ultimately sponsoring them to advanced countries for training in productivity techniques currently in use.

(f) To arouse productivity consciousness among those who work in a managerial capacity, Seminars should be organized regularly at top management, middle management and supervisory levels. Workers representatives of the appropriate level should be associated in all such Seminars. In addition programmes of workers' education will also have to be set up.

(g) For improving efficiency, it is necessary to operate on various fronts at once such as organization, layout of work, materials handling, utilization of tools, adequate remuneration, better human relations and intelligent co-operation between management and workers at all levels.

(h) Large industrial units should help the productivity movement by making their experience available to others less favourably placed. Their productivity efforts should be integrated with the productivity movement.

(i) For small industries, arrangements should be made for proper technical assistance through experts attached to the productivity organization, or through specialized organizations like Small-Scale Industries Service Institutes. Other impediments to the development of small industries, such as efficient accounting should be removed by organizing suitable training programmes.

(j) Every Government unit, of say more than one hundred persons, should have a sufficiently senior officer in charge of basic productivity improvement techniques within his unit. In smaller units the responsibility should be specifically devolved upon an appropriate officer, e.g. an establishment officer, a training officer, etc. The training of these Government officers in productivity techniques should preferably be carried out by the agency charged with responsibility for promoting productivity, not only to inculcate the spirit of mutual co-operation and understanding throughout the Government service, but also to enable the Government productivity officers to get to know and exchange ideas with their counterparts in private enterprise. While it is noted that some productivity work is already being carried out by the existing Government 'Organization and Methods' units, this work should be greatly developed and integrated with the general duties of the central productivity agency.

(k) In the agricultural sector, the productivity programme should fall into two parts; firstly, that concerned with small agricultural units, worked on the basis of family labour, and secondly, that which should cover larger farms and plantations. With regard to the first, the considerations in recommendation (a) above will specifically apply; but, apart from this, there is scope for analysing the present hand tools in agriculture and improving their efficiency and/or introducing simple machines. Expert investigations in this area should be undertaken. In the case of plantations additional considerations applicable to industry will be relevant. Along with agriculture, the productivity movement should be adapted to reach animal husbandry, fishery and forestry. The specific problems in these areas should be studied separately.

(l) To achieve the above aims, it is necessary to establish a separate semi-autonomous National Productivity Council. It should consist of representatives of Federal and Regional Governments, employers and workers organizations, professional associations, technical institutions and other prominent persons interested in the productivity movement, and equivalent bodies should be set at regional and unit levels. The productivity agency should receive grants from Governments and employers' organizations and should collect fees for expert services rendered by it. If the productivity agency established is separated from the National Manpower Board, it should work in close collaboration with relevant Government Ministries especially, and with the National Manpower Board. But in view of the imperative need for initiating work on productivity, immediately, a formal productivity unit should now be set up within the National Manpower Board.

(m) An assessment of trained personnel required for productivity work should be made and this requirement should be integrated with the overall requirements for high-level manpower. In the initial stages of the development of the personnel required for this programme, technical assistance from the advanced countries under the technical aid programmes of national and international organizations or foundations should be secured.

Appendix
International Seminar on Manpower Problems in Economic Development
March 2–11, 1964

I. List of Participants

Name		Country
Chief Ayo Adeleke	United Labour Congress Enugu	Nigeria
Mr. D. B. Adekoya	Employment Commissioner, Federal Ministry of Labour, Lagos	Nigeria
Mr. G. E. Aihie	Statistician, Benin City	Nigeria
Mr. B. Arnold	Ministry of Education, Kaduna	Nigeria
Chief S. O. Awokoya	Permanent Secretary and Chief Federal Adviser on Education, Lagos	Nigeria
Mr. S. O. Babalola	Senior Economist, Ministry of Economic Planning and Community Development, Ibadan	Nigeria
Prof. M. S. Daratz	Professor of Economics, University of Ibadan, Ibadan	Nigeria
Alhaji H. Bawa	Ministry of Economic Planning, Kaduna	Nigeria
Mr. W. Bispham	Nigerian Institute for Social and Economic Research, Ibadan	Nigeria
Mr. S. P. Brown	Assistant Secretary, Ministry of Development, Freetown	Sierra Leone
Dr. A. Callaway	Ford Foundation, Research Associate, University of Ibadan	Nigeria

Name		Country
Mr. Wade Cooper	Lecturer in Economics, Institute of Administration, Ahmadu Bello University, Zaria	Nigeria
Mr. James L. Cox	Head of the Bureau of Labour, Monrovia	Liberia
Shri B. N. Datar	Chief, Labour and Employment Division, Planning Commission and Adviser, Ministry of Labour and Employment	India
Dr. K. O. Dike	Vice-Chancellor, University of Ibadan, Ibadan	Nigeria
Mr. E. A. Fabiyi	Ministry of Trade and Industry, Kaduna	Nigeria
Dr. Babs Fafunwa	Head of Department of Education, University of Nigeria, Nsukka	Nigeria
Chief Fagbenro-Beyioku	United Labour Congress, Lagos	Nigeria
Mr. A. M. Fagbulu	Ministry of Education, Ibadan	Nigeria
Mr. G. Foggon	Labour Adviser, Dept. of Technical Co-operation, London	United Kingdom
Mr. J. W. Gailer	Adviser on Technical Education, Lagos	Nigeria
Mr. W. Hamza	Professor of Social Planning and Labour Power and Secretary General of the U.A.R. Institute of National Planning, Cairo	U.A.R.
Prof. F. H. Harbison	Director, Industrial Relations Section, Princeton University	U.S.A.
Prof. J. Henderson	Visiting Professor of Economics, University of Nigeria, Nsukka	Nigeria

Name		*Country*
Mr. J. Hilliard	Deputy Assistant Administrator, Agency for International Development, Washington	U.S.A.
Dr. M. O. Ijere	Lecturer in Economics, University of Nigeria, Nsukka.	Nigeria
Mr. B. L. Kasse	Special Assistant to the Secretary-General, C.C.T.A., Lagos	Nigeria
Dr. D. Kingsley	Ford Foundation, New York	U.S.A.
Mr. O. A. Lewis	Lecturer in Economics, University of Ife, Ibadan	Nigeria
Mr. A. P. Nwaipyana		Tanganyika
Mr. Odelola	C.C.T.A., Lagos	Nigeria
Mr. P. T. Odumosu	Permanent Secretary, Ministry of Economic Planning and Community Development, Ibadan	Nigeria
Mr. B. H. Ogola		Kenya
Mr. Ayo Ogunsheye	Director of Extra-Mural Studies, University of Ibadan	Nigeria
Mr. Onitiri Oradubanya		Nigeria
Mr. I. O. Osemeka	Senior Statistician, Enugu	Nigeria
Mr. N. F. Pepple	United Labour Congress, Lagos	Nigeria
Dr. B. Ramamurti	Chief Statistician, Federal Office of Statistics, Lagos	Nigeria
Dr. Ignacy Sachs	Director, Centre of Research on Underdeveloped Economies, Warsaw	Poland
Mr. V. G. Sanda	Ministry of Agriculture, Kaduna	Nigeria
Prof. C. L. Shaffer	Vice Dean of Business, University of Lagos	Nigeria
Mr. H. M. B. Somade	Permanent Secretary, Ministry of Education, Ibadan	Nigeria

Name		*Country*
Mr. G. Tobias	c/o World Bank, New York	U.S.A.
Mr. C. S. Umeadi	Economic Commission for Africa, Addis Ababa	Ethiopia
Mr. T. Wilson	Chief of Mission, UNESCO, Lagos	Nigeria
Prof. S. K. Wolf	Dean of Business, University of Lagos	Nigeria
Mr. Zabeline	Gosplan, Moscow	U.S.S.R.
Dr. O. Arikpo	Secretary, National Universities Commission, Lagos	Nigeria
Mr. M. Omolayole	Lever Brothers (Nig.) Limited, Apapa	Nigeria
Mr. G. H. Reeve		Nigeria
Mr. W. Shaughnessy	Ford Foundation, New York	U.S.A.
Mr. I. A. Adebanjo	N.E.C.A. Lagos.	Nigeria
Mr. J. R. W. Parker	U.K. High Commission Lagos	Nigeria
Mrs. L. Rice	Ford Foundation	U.S.A.
Mrs. M. P. Rowe	c/o U.S. Embassy, Lagos	Nigeria
Dr. R. A. Rowe	American Institute for Research, Lagos	Nigeria
Dr. P. A. Schwarz	Director, American Institute for Research, Lagos	Nigeria
Mr. A. Sokolski	Assistant Programme Officer U.S.A.I.D., Lagos	Nigeria
Mr. R. Thomas	Ford Foundation, Nairobi	Kenya
Mr. C. Eicher	Economic Adviser, University of Nigeria, Enugu Campus	Nigeria
Mr. R. Loken	Ford Foundation, Accra	Ghana
Mr. E. C. Martinson	First Secretary and Labour Attaché, U.S. Embassy, Lagos	Nigeria
Mr. E. U. Oton	Ministry of Information, Lagos.	Nigeria

II. *Officers of the Seminar*

Chairman:	Chief S. O. Awokoya Permanent Secretary and Federal Chief Adviser on Education, Federal Republic of Nigeria.
Vice-Chairman:	Dr. Donald Kingsley Director, Middle East and Africa Programme Ford Foundation, New York, U.S.A.
Adviser:	Professor Frederick H. Harbison Director, Industrial Relations Section, Princeton University, New Jersey, U.S.A.
Secretary-General:	Dr. T. M. Yesufu Secretary, National Manpower Board, Nigeria
Steering Committee:	Professor F. H. Harbison Chief S. O. Awokoya Dr. Donald Kingsley Professor S. K. Wolf Dr. T. M. Yesufu

III. *Conference Committees*

Committee	Chairman	Reporters
1. Machinery and Methodology of Manpower Forecasting	Mr. G. Foggon, C.M.G.	Dr. B. Ramamurti Mr. I. O. Osemeka
2. Education and Training Problems in Economic Development	Mr. Wade Cooper	Mr. J. W. Gailer
3. Unemployment and Under-Employment	Dr. M. Hamza	Dr. A. Callaway
4. Economic Planning	Dr. I. Sachs	Mr. Tobias
5. Productivity	Shri B. N. Datar	Dr. M. O. Ijere Mr. K. Hansen

IV. List of Papers Submitted

1. *Economic Development and Planning in Nigeria, 1945–68*. N. A. A. Okuboyejo.
2. *Manpower Problems in the Context of Economic Planning*. Ayo Ogunsheye.
3. *Toward an Integrated Manpower Policy for Accelerated National Development*. John Hilliad.
4. *New Markets for Manpower Planning*. George Tobias.
5. *The Objectives, Machinery and Methodology of Manpower Planning*. Fredrick H. Harbison.
6. *Organization for Manpower Planning in Nigeria*. T. M. Yesufu.
7. *Forecasting Nigeria's Manpower Needs 1963–8. A Note on Methodology*. T. M. Yesufu.
8. *Educational Philosophy and Structure for Economic Development*. A. Babs Fafunwa.
9. *The Structure and Development of Nigerian Education*. Stephen O. Awokoya.
10. *Educational Problems in Economic Development. (Professional and Managerial Staff*. K. Onwuka Dike.
11. *Employment and Economic Development in a Dual Economy*. Ignacy Sachs.
12. *Creating Employment for Africa's Youth*. Archibald Callaway.
13. *An Approach to the Problem of Creation of Employment Opportunities in Nigeria*. S. J. Bhatt.
14. *Concepts and Measurements of Productivity in Developing Economies*. S. K. Wolf.
15. *Developments in the Search for Higher Productivity in Africa*. P. A. L. Chukwumah.
16. *Educational Problems in Economic Development*. Charles L. Shaffer.
17. *The Role and Organization of the Employment Service in a Developing Economy*. ILO, Geneva.
18. *Manpower Problems (General)*. G. Foggon.
19. *The Role and Organization of the Placement Service in a Rapidly Developing Economy*. Federal Ministry of Labour, Lagos.
20. *Urban Unemployment Survey, 1963*. National Manpower Board, Lagos.
21. *A National Plan for the Development of Technical Education in the*

Federal Republic of Nigeria. J. W. Gailer, Federal Ministry of Education, Lagos.

22. *Crafts and Industries in a Nigerian City.* Archibald Callaway.

23. *Report on Nigerian National Seminar on Productivity (12–14 February 1963).* National Manpower Board, Lagos.

24. *Problems of Planning of Full Employment for Labour Force and Supply of the Qualified Labour Force for Country's National Economy (According to the experience of the U.S.S.R.).* N. Zabelin, U.S.S.R.

25. *Nigeria's High-Level and Skilled Manpower 1963–8.* National Manpower Board, Lagos.